# A Handbook for the K–12 Reading Resource Specialist

**Marguerite C. Radencich**
Dade County Public Schools, Miami, Florida
**Penny G. Beers**
School Board of Palm Beach County, Florida
**Jeanne Shay Schumm**
University of Miami

**Allyn and Bacon**
Boston   London   Toronto   Sydney   Tokyo   Singapore

Copyright © 1993 by Allyn and Bacon
A Division of Simon & Schuster, Inc.
160 Gould Street
Needham Heights, Massachusetts 02194

**Library of Congress Cataloging-in-Publication Data**

Radencich, Marguerite C., (date–     )
    A handbook for the K–12 reading resource specialist  /  Marguerite
C. Radencich, Penny G. Beers, Jeanne Shay Schumm.
       p.    cm.
    Includes bibliographical references (p.   ) and index.
    ISBN 0-205-14081-5
      1.  Reading teachers--Training of--United States--Handbooks,
manuals, etc.  2.  Reading--United States--Handbooks, manuals, etc.
3. Classroom management--United States.  I. Beers, Penny G.
II. Schumm, Jeanne Shay, (date–     )   .  III. Title.
LB2844.1.R4R33      1993                                              93-2920
428.4'07--dc20                                                          CIP

Printed in the United States of America
10  9  8  7      06  05  04  03

*To John, Jerry, Jamie, Mitch, and Megan*
*—and to all our coaches: our teachers, families,*
*friends, and colleagues who have challenged,*
*inspired, and supported us in all our endeavors*

# About the Authors

**Marguerite C. Radencich** is the K–adult reading supervisor for Dade County (Miami) Public Schools. Among her experiences are elementary and secondary teaching, serving as an elementary assistant principal, and university teaching, including a graduate course on Methods for the Reading Resource Specialist.

Dr. Radencich envisioned and chaired the Florida Reading Association's First Annual Reading Resource Specialist Conference in 1990. She has co-authored with Dr. Schumm two books, *How to Help Your Child with Homework* and *School Power: Strategies for Succeeding in School,* and has also co-authored two software programs, *The Semantic Mapper* and *The Literary Mapper.* Dr. Radencich frequently writes for refereed journals and regularly serves on national editorial review boards, currently the board for *Journal of Reading.*

**Jeanne Shay Schumm** is an assistant professor at the University of Miami, where she teaches graduate and undergraduate courses in literacy education, supervises federally funded classroom-based research projects, and directs the university's Student Literacy Corps.

Dr. Schumm has extensive experience in elementary and secondary classes. She has taught in public and private schools in general education and clinical settings. While teaching at Louisiana State University, she served as a Reading Resource Specialist at the university's laboratory school.

In addition to authoring textbooks and numerous professional articles, Dr. Schumm writes a regular column for the *Journal of Reading.* She collaborated with Dr. Radencich on two books, *How to Help Your Child with Homework* and *School Power: Strategies for Succeeding in School.*

**Penny G. Beers** is the K–12 English and reading curriculum specialist for the School Board of Palm Beach County (Florida). She has established and conducted secondary reading labs, taught secondary English, and served as a secondary reading resource specialist.

Dr. Beers regularly presents reading workshops at state conferences and conducts inservice sessions for school administrators, teachers, and parents. She has developed workshops on using content area reading strategies, marketing reading programs, establishing staff development programs, writing and producing reading handbooks, creating reading newsletters, and enhancing teacher image. She serves on the editorial board of the *PDK News of Palm Beach* (Phi Delta Kappa) and has published articles in the *Journal of Reading* and *The Florida Reading Quarterly.*

# Contents

# CONTENTS

## CONTENTS

**CONTENTS**

# Foreword

*Donna Ogle, National-Louis University, Evanston, Illinois*

**T**HIS HANDBOOK COMES at an auspicious time. Schools are restructuring. The roles of teachers are changing. Reading specialists, too, are transforming themselves from remedial reading tutors into schoolwide resource specialists. This new role gives the knowledgeable reading specialist an opportunity to help shape the whole school literacy program, provide staff development, and help meet the needs of all children.

Several important educational issues provide the momentum for this opportunity. The societal need for even higher levels of literacy and critical reading has been well publicized. New ways of utilizing teachers' professional talents and of configuring schools are being tried. Recognition is growing that having trained reading specialists devote all their energies to pull-out remediation with disabled readers may not be the most effective way of using their talents. The need for focused and sustained staff development at the school level is well documented. Each of these issues supports expanded responsibilities for reading specialists.

In our own field, too, there have been many important changes that support an expanded role for reading specialists. Our understanding of how literacy develops in children has changed considerably over the last twenty years. We know, for example, that children need regular opportunities to construct meanings, not just receive information that is already organized for them. Teachers need opportunities to learn about the significant advances in our knowledge and their implications for teaching. This knowledge then needs to be translated into new teaching practices if higher levels of literacy are to be attained.

Impetus to reconfigure the role of the reading specialist also comes from school restructuring efforts. These major initiatives often include expanded professional roles and responsibilities for teachers. Many critics argue that reading specialists can be more effective working in classrooms with teachers than focusing on pull-out programs with individuals or small groups of remedial readers. Using data on student achievement, they add that children, too, are often better served in the classroom setting where the additional adult support can be provided without stigmatizing children.

In addition, dramatic changes in staff development are occurring. The single-day institutes school districts have held for years are being replaced with long-term, more focused efforts. Many districts build in major components at the building level—the place where real instructional change must be implemented. Reading specialists are in an ideal position to provide leadership in such school-based initiatives.

The new opportunities available to reading specialists are rich with potential. They are also challenging because they represent a dramatic change in role from working with children to providing leadership in the loosely structured context of schools. In the resource role, specialists must work closely with new constituencies—especially teachers, administrators, and parents.

This shift is all the more dramatic because this resource role is often new for both the specialist and the rest of the school staff. For too long teaching has been conceived of as an isolated, independent activity. Neither classroom teachers nor reading specialists have generally had experience working closely together on instructional issues. For teachers, opening their doors to someone else can be threatening. For the reading specialist, serving as a "leader" or mentor to teachers can also be very challenging.

There is, however, a growing realization that schools function optimally when teachers coordinate efforts, share a common philosophy, and implement instructional strategies across the grades. When the reading specialist is asked to facilitate this goal, the challenge is clear. Establishing a new community identity requires risk taking and vision. The process is important and stimulating, but not easy.

We are experiencing major changes in schools. For the emerging reading resource specialist, they provide real challenges and exciting opportunities. Therefore, professional materials that provide concrete and pertinent information are vitally important. Radencich, Beers, and Schumm must be thanked for compiling this guide. Their recognition of the need to deal with both process and content within this challenging role will be very useful to all readers, whatever their positions. The issues facing reading resource specialists are highlighted here, and a treasure chest of information and practical guidelines is included. No new reading resource specialist should feel lost after reading this rich guide; specific suggestions and real examples make the role and the responsibilities clear. The appendixes are replete with just the kinds of ideas and resources the RRS needs. Clearly these authors have turned challenges into opportunities for themselves and their schools. I hope each reader will do the same with this supportive guide.

# Preface

THE ROLES OF READING teachers are evolving from pull-out or classroom remedial models to models that include resource specialists who serve the school as a whole or who may serve a number of schools. Indeed, the International Reading Association's new Guidelines for the Specialized Preparation of Reading Professionals (in press) include closer attention to the reading resource specialist (RRS) role, one that requires a wealth of both procedural and content knowledge. Not only should the RRS have a wide array of ideas, strategies, and creative solutions readily available upon request, but the RRS should also have the skills to offer such information to teachers in a collaborative, nonthreatening manner. The research base supporting this role is provided throughout this handbook.

Those teachers now working in RRS roles have had to learn their responsibilities on the job. Although reading specialists may have taken courses in content area reading and in the administration of reading programs, neither of these has fully addressed their needs as reading resource specialists. This handbook is a reference tool that can help address unmet needs of elementary or secondary RRSs and of their supervisors and administrators.

No handbook can be all-inclusive. Even though many specialists do work directly with students, we have chosen not to focus on this role but, instead, on the role of the RRS as support to a whole school or to more than one school. The book was written primarily for an audience of school-based specialists, whatever their title might be. It will, of course, be of value also to persons in any number of related positions, such as grade chairperson, department head, and district specialist.

Note that we often refer to other parts of the book when discussing certain topics. This is done because of the necessary overlap that exists in many areas.

In our professional experience as RRS, building administrator, reading supervisor, and university professor, we have spoken with reading resource specialists from across the country. We have noted elements that are common to most RRS programs as well as factors that differ. In this book, we will explore both the common and the unique facets of RRS programs.

# Acknowledgments

**W**E WOULD LIKE to gratefully acknowledge Francis Golden, Anne McKinney, Gloria Albanese, Priscilla Nelson, and Marcia Modlo for their reviews of the manuscript. Thank you also to Margaret Bettendorf, Carol Francia, Dawna Lubell, Stephanie McCamley, Rose Meltzer, Lois Meyer, Edith Norniella, Gloria Plaza, Jo Tanner, Dade County Public Schools, and the School Board of Palm Beach County, Florida, for the tools they allowed us to include; Lyn McKay, Pat Nelms, and Pam Moore for allowing us to include their Pinellas County flexible grouping model; and all the reading resource specialists who have inspired us.

Marguerite C. Radencich
Penny G. Beers
Jeanne S. Schumm

# PART ONE

# The Resource Role: The Process

This first half of the handbook focuses on the process involved in the role of the reading resource specialist (RRS). It is our concern about this process that led us to write this handbook. We have had teachers with spanking new advanced degrees in reading from good universities come to us for jobs with no idea of what the role of the resource specialist might be or of how to go about preparing for such a role. In this section, then, we discuss the competencies required for this role; the job interview; school cultures; ways the RRS can ensure acceptance and market him- or herself to enhance that acceptance; and ways of organizing a year-long program, of effecting change, and of evaluating the program's success. The graphic organizer on the next page shows key areas in the process of becoming a good RRS.

1

# THE RESOURCE ROLE: THE PROCESS

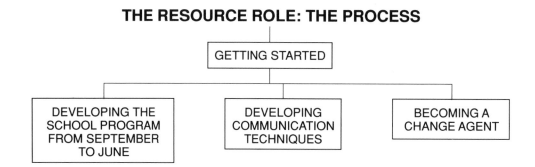

# 1

# Getting Started

| Recommended Competencies | The Job Interview | Learning about the School Culture |

**T**HE READING RESOURCE SPECIALIST (RRS) is required to have a variety of competencies as well as a familiarity with the school and its philosophies. Your competencies and your willingness to understand the school culture should be established during the job interview. Once you begin working as an RRS, your competence and your knowledge about the school culture should continue to increase.

## Recommended Competencies

A variety of competencies are necessary to be a successful RRS. Reading resource specialists provide a myriad of services within their schools. These services, assigned at the discretion of the principal and other administrators, require that the RRS be competent in the areas of educational leadership, psychology, sociology, assessment, evaluation, correction, research, content area study, and—last but not least—reading.

Reading teachers must take the initiative to become instructional leaders in their schools. Resource teachers can have an impact on almost every student in the school, rather than just a few, by leaving the traditional "clinical closet" and working in conjunction with other teachers (Readence, Baldwin, & Dishner, 1980). As a result of the increasing interest in the RRS position, reading teachers must be fully prepared to undertake the demanding reading resource role.

In 1986 the Professional Standards and Ethics Committee of the International Reading Association (IRA) delineated the recommended course work and minimum number of credit hours that all reading specialists should complete. In addition to academic preparation, the IRA committee outlined the following major competencies:

1. Linguistic and cognitive bases for reading
2. Comprehension
3. Word identification and vocabulary
4. Appreciation and enjoyment
5. Diagnostic teaching
6. Continuing program maintenance planning and improvement

Fucello (in Wepner, Feeley, & Strickland, 1989) found that many states are beginning to require reading specialists to devote 50 percent of their time to the resource role. To facilitate the coordination of reading programs in the public schools, the Florida legislature authorized the employment of reading resource specialists in the high schools (Woods & Topping, 1986) and established the following criteria:

1.  Attain certification in reading as provided by the state board of education.

2.  Have a minimum of three years' teaching experience.

3.  Possess the qualifications and necessary experience, in the judgment of the district school board, to serve as an RRS.

These criteria would be reasonable for resource specialists at all grade levels. "Qualifications and necessary experience" were further defined as having a background of experience that would enable the RRS to perform such tasks as the following:

1.  Contribute expertise needed to coordinate the school's total reading program.

2.  Provide individual diagnostic testing to improve approaches for classroom instruction.

3.  Assist content area teachers in incorporating reading skills as an integral part of all subject areas.

4.  Provide inservice training in reading strategies to school staff members.

5.  Participate in team teaching with classroom teachers.

6.  Interpret the reading program for parents and community.

Barnard & Hetzel (1986) identified ten characteristics of an effective RRS, which are adapted as follows:

### TIPS · CHARACTERISTICS OF AN EFFECTIVE RRS

*   Be a professional—avoid gossip at all costs, do not evaluate teachers, and be fair and businesslike with all.

*   Smile in a friendly, respectful manner when carrying out your duties.

*   Develop listening skills so that other teachers feel comfortable in asking you for assistance. Avoid falling into the "yes, but" routine of being ready with a rebuttal before you have truly listened.

*   Provide options such as demonstrating lessons, trying a new approach together as a team, making classroom visits with feedback, or meeting outside the classroom. By allowing the teacher to choose, you convey respect for individual goals, style, and expertise (Wollman-Bonilla, 1991).

*   Learn to analyze problems systematically without jumping to conclusions before the situation is clearly defined. Offer alternative choices as answers so that teachers can feel they have taken part in the solution.

*   Be visible and available to assist teachers at their request.

- Have a positive attitude and approach, emphasizing what *can* be accomplished rather than what cannot be done.

- Be flexible and adaptable to the differing needs of administrators, teachers, and students.

- Be sensitive to and aware of public opinion in order to project a sincere, competent, and efficient image.

- Be involved with everyone in and around the school.

## The Job Interview

The interview is an opportunity to put your best foot forward. Walk in with the attitude that you are now on the job. When asked questions, do not concentrate on what you have done in the past (unless you are specifically asked about past experience), but incorporate your experiences in answers that focus on what you will do in the future.

Resource teachers must know the latest trends in reading research. When you answer questions, a few well-placed references to current authors or texts can reflect your knowledge base. In addition, as discussed previously, references that reflect your awareness of the importance of interpersonal relationships within the staff will be crucial.

What kinds of questions will be asked? Before the interview, you should try to anticipate the types of questions that will be included. Bean and Wilson (1981) suggest three different question types that will generally be asked:

1. *Surface questions* ask about your teaching experience and qualifications for the current position.

2. *Deep questions* involve probes concerning your philosophical beliefs about the reading process, testing, and so on.

3. *Questions that require a commitment on your part* include your commitment to using cooperative learning techniques, implementing sustained silent reading programs, and the like.

Bean and Wilson suggest that, before the interview, you formulate and answer three or four questions that are important to you. These may relate to the school duties required of you, outside responsibilities, your evaluation, and other similar topics. In this manner, you will be prepared if questions of this nature are asked.

**TIPS · THE JOB INTERVIEW, OR PUTTING YOUR BEST FOOT FORWARD**

- Show that you are knowledgeable about the school and the district. This requires doing your homework. Drive and/or walk around the school before the interview to get a feel for the area and the people.

- When you walk into the interview room, radiate self-confidence through

(*continued*)

## TIPS (continued)

your posture, your smile, and your carriage. Shake hands firmly if and when a handshake is appropriate.

- Remember that nonverbal communication may account for up to 82 percent of your image (Grant & Hennings, 1971). People will largely make up their minds about you before you even open your mouth, so be sure they like what they see (see pages 4–5 for additional ideas).

- During the interview, listen extremely carefully before answering any question, and be sure you know exactly what was asked. Be sincere and honest in your answers. Deceit is almost always detectable. Use eye contact as much as possible, and answer clearly and distinctly—be articulate!

- Listen for hidden questions. For example, a question on how you would deal with a department head who was subverting your efforts might really be a way of ascertaining how you see yourself interacting with the principal and/or assistant principal.

- Always be prepared to answer questions like "What is your greatest strength?" and "Why do you think you're the best person for this job?"

- Remember to be enthusiastic! Even if your answers are excellent, they lose credibility if delivered in a monotone. Change your tone of voice to indicate interest and enthusiasm.

- If a negative question is asked ("What is your biggest weakness?"), minimize your weakness by choosing something of little consequence. An example of a good answer to this question is, "I work too hard."

- If a question is asked for which you have no immediate answer, ask your interviewer(s) to return to the question later in the interview. This technique gives you extra thinking time, and the question may be eliminated if you run out of time at the end of the interview.

- If you don't know the answer to one of the questions, say so. Then describe who you would ask in order to determine the answer.

 - Finally, be prepared to *ask* questions when the time is right.

In Palm Beach County, Florida, questions are used that ask you to describe personal situations depicting your skills in leadership, organization, time management, and interpersonal relations. You can ask for copies of the questions in advance so that you can prepare your answers thoroughly. You might even tape record yourself answering potential questions and then listen to the recording for self-evaluation. These questions require careful study before you enter the interview. Although you don't want to sound rehearsed, you should have at least one answer readily available for each question.

It is not a good idea to take notes during the interview, but you should jot down the questions you remember following the interview. Keep your answers in mind so that you can follow up on programs you suggested or ideas you had during the interview. Also note the names of your interviewers if they are unfamiliar to you. If you are selected for the position, you might eventually want to express appreciation for their confidence in selecting you. If not, your notes will help you prepare for the next interview you tackle.

## Learning about the School Culture

Congratulations! You have been hired as the school's new RRS. You are now ready to proceed toward establishing a strong working relationship with other members of the faculty and administrative staff. One of your first steps to success in your new position is to understand the inner workings, or the *culture,* of the school.

Schools may be viewed as social systems that are bound together by shared "secrets" about the staff, students, and/or students' families (Bean & Wilson, 1981). The seasons of the school year revolve around predictable events such as vacations, sports, or instructional topics covered at different times of year. To deal effectively with the school culture, the RRS must take these "seasons" into account when planning for the year ahead.

What is the school culture and why should you be concerned about it? The importance of understanding the interpersonal relations within the school cannot be overlooked in preparing for your job as RRS. Understanding the school culture involves understanding the nature of the formal and informal cliques that exist, and this knowledge could help to make or break you in your new role.

Try to find out who the "old guard" members of the faculty are and whether or not they are respected by their colleagues. Cultivate the interest of the most respected teachers so that they use their influence in endorsing you when speaking with their peers. Always be aware of the underlying groups within the school. Visiting the area will help you to determine information about the people among whom you will be working. Following are some ideas for becoming familiar with the area:

### TIPS · IDEAS FOR BECOMING FAMILIAR WITH THE SCHOOL CULTURE

- Drive through the streets surrounding the school.

- Visit the feeder school areas.

- Subscribe to the local newspapers or magazines and watch the local television stations for ideas about the community.

- Tour the school to become familiar with the floor plan and to get a feel for the school culture.

- Speak with as many people at the school as possible—this means secretaries, custodians, teachers, administrators, volunteers, students, and parents.

- Learn the names of teachers, administrators, and other resource persons in your area. Identify department heads, class and club sponsors, coaches, and others. Locate an old yearbook and use it to help you attach names to faces.

- Ask people to tell you their names as often as you need to at first. It gets more embarrassing to ask as time goes on.

- Spread out your transparencies as you make them, either in the media center or in the lounge, in order to arouse curiosity and generate interest. You will have to analyze this strategy in your particular school to determine whether the lounge or the media center is an appropriate place to "drum up business." In some schools, the lounge is considered a place where

(*continued*)

**TIPS (continued)**

teachers accomplish very little. In other circumstances, the best teachers may get together in the lounge to discuss lesson plans or grading policies.

 • Throughout the year, attend faculty and Parent—Teachers Association or Parent—Teachers Organization (PTA/PTO) meetings, and school sporting and social events.

## Conclusion

As mentioned earlier, the culture of each school will vary, and you will need to determine the best course of action in each setting. We know of one elementary teacher who ate lunch with a stack of trade books by her side because she was going to read the books to a class after lunch. When the woman sitting next to her asked her about the books, a friendly book talk discussion resulted at the lunch table.

Your competencies and your enthusiasm during the job interview will help you to obtain the job of RRS. Once you have been appointed, however, you should continue to learn about the school, the personnel, the students, and the community in all of your endeavors.

# 2

# Developing the School Program from September to June

| The First Steps | Time Management | Evaluating the Program | Outside Resources |

**A**S YOU START to plan your time for the year, you will probably be swimming in a sea of questions. Will I be able to have an impact on every teacher in the school? How do I decide what to do first? What if there are days with nothing for me to do? What if I commit to doing more than is feasible? How will I keep track of everything? This chapter will keep you treading water as you learn to live with these uncertainties.

## The First Steps

Your first steps as an RRS should be exciting, although you may feel apprehensive about your acceptance by the staff. Resentment can easily occur if teachers see you as having no students scheduled and therefore as having a "plum" job. Many teachers will be busy orienting their students to the course work during the first month of school and may not be ready to invite you into their classes. Public relations (PR) should be a main priority at this point. Diagnosis may be another key area if your job requires work with students or if the school requires pretest student data for any of its reading programs. Whatever your task, you must take great care to plan so that you constantly have high visibility without getting in any teacher's way.

### TIPS · FIRST WEEK OF SCHOOL

- Find out about the school's philosophy and goals. Dig if necessary. See the section on "The School's Philosophy of Literacy Education" in Chapter 5.

- Get a feel for the school's climate. Is morale generally high? See the section on "Learning about the School Culture" In Chapter 1.

- Learn about the lines of authority at the school. Some secondary resource teachers report to the language arts department head. In other schools, the RRS reports directly to an assistant principal so that the RRS is not limited to only one subject area. Find out about the division of labor among all administrators at the school.

*(continued)*

9

### TIPS (continued)

• With the permission of your administrators, contact any supervisor or director responsible for curricular decisions. A request for an interview in a supervisor's office or in the school will show the supervisor how serious you are and can help give you direction about the school history, about your responsibilities, and about personal and material resources to which you can turn.

• Locate existing materials and distribute materials on request. Learn budgetary constraints and ordering procedures for items needed. Materials may be nonexistent or, on the other hand, may be lost in unlikely places. You, of course, can not rummage around teachers' rooms. But it's amazing how much farther existing materials can go when everyone knows they're around. In terms of your own materials, find out if you're responsible for ordering your own paper, transparencies, and the like.

• Help beginning teachers get their feet on the ground. With elementary teachers in particular, it's a good idea to spend several days in a row with each of them to help them fit all the pieces into the puzzle of the school day.

• Distribute a Teacher Request Form listing the types of services you can provide (see Appendix A). If you write a monthly newsletter, be sure to include this form in each edition.

• Use your time to *network, network, network!* Ask permission either to telephone or to visit resource specialists both within and outside the district. Contact those recommended by the district supervisor(s) or by others. These specialists will usually be flattered that you see them as leaders and will give of their time generously. Use these teachers as a resource for *yourself*.

• Take notes and collect as much information as possible. The fact that you are willing to ask questions shows that you are secure, yet not a know-it-all. Remember to remain nonjudgmental while evaluating the information.

• Request that an administrator introduce you at the first faculty meeting to outline what your duties will be. If appropriate, request a ten-minute block of time at each subsequent faculty meeting to present a short overview of a selected reading strategy.

• Attend any committee meetings (grade-level, department head, project meetings) that can help you network. Volunteer to help as much as possible.

• Begin a high-visibility project. If the climate is right for an activity that would entail teacher support, try a project like "Word of the Day." Florida RRS Joanna Cocchiarella (1985) uses the first week of school to prepare words for the Word of the Day for the first month. You gain instant recognition among students and faculty by announcing the Word of the Day, its meaning, and a sentence in which it is used during each day's morning announcements. All teachers are asked to write the word on a board at the front of the room each morning and to reinforce student learning by using the word throughout the day. If there is a moving-letter sign in the school, it too can be used to highlight the word. Following the first month of school, teachers are asked to submit five words that they would like to see used. These words then become the bank from which the RRS can draw for the rest of the school year.

- As time permits, begin on activities listed under "Quiet Days" in this chapter.

The first few weeks will be time for clarifying your role while remaining as helpful and interested as possible. Smile at everyone you meet!

Who will invite you, the new RRS, into a classroom? If you are not invited into any classrooms, how will you get your foot in the door? You will need to develop a tough skin to avoid letting one or two negative teachers get you down. Some suggested activities that every RRS needs to know in order to gain admittance into classrooms are listed in the Tips box that follows. Other activities can be found throughout this text.

## TIPS · SUGGESTED CLASSROOM ACTIVITIES

- *Teacher requests:* Use or modify the Teacher Request Forms in Appendix A as tools to gather teacher requests.

- *Research papers:* Provide students and teachers with information on writing research papers. Include the correct forms for footnotes and the bibliography. Present information on notetaking, paraphrasing, and outlining (see Pauk, 1983).

- *Computer assistance:* Familiarize yourself with the computers and software in the school so that you can offer assistance to other teachers as they introduce their classes to the computer. Through the county office, your colleagues, or printed reviews, research the various computer programs appropriate for your school. See Chapter 8 for help in analyzing software. Work with administrators or the media specialist to order these programs. Try to acquire general-purpose programs such as Print Shop (Broderbund), Crossword Magic (Mindscape), or M_SS_NG L_NKS (Sunburst), and offer to help teachers use these programs to prepare class activities.

- *Vocabulary/comprehension/study skills strategies:* Offer to teach specific lessons in which you focus on helping students to grasp a greater understanding of the text. The possibilities are endless (see Chapter 7).

- *Test-taking strategies:* Provide helpful hints on test taking to students. Be sure to include ideas on taking essay, multiple-choice, matching, and cloze tests. See Chapter 9 and "Test-Taking Tips for Students" in Appendix B.

- *Writing development:* Encourage writing across the curriculum by improving understanding of the writing process (Chapter 6), developing extension activities for content area classes, and helping teachers with ideas for publishing (see "Magazines and Contests that Accept Young Writers' Work" in Appendix B).

- *Listening skills practice:* Develop short activities to promote listening awareness, and ask the principal for permission to read these aloud over

(*continued*)

**TIPS (continued)**

the intercom (see "Listening Habits Inventory" in Appendix B). Remind teachers that you are available for follow-up lessons in their individual classrooms.

- *New materials:* Provide teachers with any promising new materials you may receive from a fellow RRS, publishers, or others. If the materials work well, suggest that they be shared with other members of a grade level or department (see Chapter 8).

- *Reading Committee:* Establish a Reading Committee (see Chapter 5).

- *Individualized instruction or small-group instruction:* Offer to work with individual students or with small groups when an additional person is needed in the classroom. Be careful, however, not to let this become your entire job if it is intended that your role be one of an RRS.

- *Demonstration lessons:* Begin demonstration lessons when the climate is right (see Chapter 11).

- *Inservice session for teachers:* Teach an inservice session for teachers who need reading credit for renewal of their teaching certificate before or after school or during planning periods (see Chapter 11).

## Time Management

You might be surprised at some of the people around you who seem to be so well organized. A simple notepad that you always carry with you can be a lifesaver if you use it to jot down things to do as you think about them at home, in the car, at work. A calendar that you carry with you in order to write down appointments can also help you organize your time and make your job easier. Some people who are not inherently well organized have trained themselves to make such efforts that they have ultimately excelled in this area.

Changing from the norm of having assigned classes to what may seem to be a lack of structure can be frightening. Making sure you stay busy but not becoming overwhelmed can be a real balancing act. Eventually, you will find that you are busier than you have ever been before, but that may not happen right away.

Time management as an RRS is much like time management for anyone else. It's a matter of setting priorities and following a plan to complete each of them in turn.

It's human nature for you to want to feel that you have accomplished a lot each day. Thus, every day you may be tempted to complete several low-priority items that don't take much time in order to "get them out of the way." If you're not careful, though, this strategy may mean that you never get to items that are higher on your priority list and that require more concentration, time, and energy. Following are some suggestions that may help.

 **TIPS · TIME MANAGEMENT**

- Make a "to do" list using the 80–20 rule that Alan Lakein (1973) describes in *How to Get Control of Your Time and Your Life:* 20 percent of the items on the list should yield 80 percent of the value. In a list of ten items, find those two and have a plan for getting them done. Other suggestions for "to do" lists are as follows:

—Keep your lists in *writing,* arranging items in order of priority and crossing them off as they're accomplished.

—Write down things that might not otherwise get accomplished, not routine items.

—Include both long- and short-term projects.

—Avoid making too long a list.

· Even better than a "to do" list is a bulletin board. One of us keeps a small bulletin board with, perhaps, 4 × 4 rows of Post-it notes. Each column represents a different strand of professional responsibilities. These could include professional organizations, inservice sessions, administrator or teacher requests, and long-term projects. As projects are completed, the Post-it notes are removed.

· Be flexible, yet focused. Change your schedule as legitimate needs arise. For example, the district office may ask for a comprehensive report (due yesterday). You may need to restructure the whole day's plans in order to complete the report. But don't allow this type of interruption to upset your schedule regularly. This is easier said than done. However, you do need to stay focused. Learn how to delegate and network. Can someone else do all or part of the project? Find out what help you can get from an aide, a volunteer, a parent, a student, a fellow teacher, or an administrator.

· Start with beginning teachers, a group whose members generally need help and tend to be quite open. Another priority, if handled carefully, can be to include teachers who have received unsatisfactory evaluations; their motivation stems from their need for better evaluations.

· Focus on a grade level with particularly low test scores, or, alternatively, on classes that contain the middle-level students; it is their scores rather than those of either high- or low-achieving students that will raise median scores on standardized achievement tests.

· Focus on a particular grade or, in the secondary school, on a department that needs strengthening or, on the other hand, one that is particularly receptive.

### Keeping a Written Schedule

Why should you keep a written schedule? By preparing a schedule of your daily and/or weekly itinerary, you will organize your time and help to avoid difficulties with administrators and with other teachers.

One RRS we know posts the schedule on the door of her office each day. Other teachers always know where she can be found, and administrators can easily evaluate her performance. Everyone can see at a glance just how busy she is and where she has spent her time each day.

Some of the resource teachers we know place a monthly schedule with open time slots in each teacher's mailbox and ask teachers to fill in the dates and times during which they would like the RRS to visit. This system could cause conflicts in a large school but might work nicely for an RRS who works with teachers at only one grade level or in one department.

Other teachers keep logs of their activities to help them remember which strategies they used with any given teacher(s) and what the results appear to have been. A sample Strategy Log can be found in Appendix C.

Tables 2.1 and 2.2 show two sample weekly schedules. Appendix C contains Sample Year-Long Schedules (constantly evolving) of programs developed by teach-

**TABLE 2.1 · Sample Elementary Schedule**

This schedule was written by Carol Francia while she was a primary resource specialist at Rainbow Park Elementary, a lower socioeconomic school in the Dade County Public Schools (Miami, Florida). Carol's schedule was structured in that she was to assign herself to different teachers during each time block.

| Time | Monday | Tuesday | Wednesday | Thursday | Friday |
|---|---|---|---|---|---|
| 8:30–9:00 | Morning exercises and preparation for day's acitivities | | | | |
| 9:00–9:30 | | | | | |
| 9:30–10:00 | | | | | |
| 10:00–10:30 | | | | | |
| 10:30–11:00 | | | | | |
| 11:00–11:40 | Lunch | | | | |
| 11:40–12:15 | | | | | |
| 12:15–12:30 | Supervise Reading Reentry[a] aides | | | | |
| 12:30–1:00 | | | | | |
| 1:00–2:00 | Supervise Reading Reentry aides | | | | |
| 2:00–2:30 | Planning | | | | |

[a] Reading Reentry is a one-to-one tutorial program for at-risk first-graders, modeled on Reading Recovery (Pinnell, DeFord, & Lyons, 1988).

**TABLE 2.2 · Sample Secondary Schedule**

This schedule was written by Lois Meyer while she was a resource specialist at Edison Senior High, a lower socioeconomic school in Dade County Public Schools (Miami, Florida). Note that Wednesday periods are shortened to allow time for Sustained Silent Reading.

| Period | Monday | Tuesday | Wednesday | Thursday | Friday |
|---|---|---|---|---|---|
| 1 | | | | | |
| 2 | | | | | |
| 3 | ESOL (English for Speakers of Other Languages) reading class, grade 9 | | | | |
| 4 | | | | | |
| 5 | ESOL reading class, grade 10 | | | | |
| | Lunch | | | | |
| 6 | ESOL reading class, grade 10 | | | | |
| 7 | | | | | |

ers at different levels. Most of these teachers were not tied to as much structure as we showed in Carol Francia's Sample Elementary Schedule in Table 2.1. But each sample year-long schedule could be adapted for both full-time and part-time situations, regardless of the level of structure expected.

## Quiet Days

There will always be days when teachers do not want to see you—for example, the first and last days of school or the days just before winter recess. Save as much paperwork as can wait for these days so that you can be readily available to teachers the rest of the time. Test yourself on the following checklist to get a picture of how diligent, dedicated, and dynamic you are.

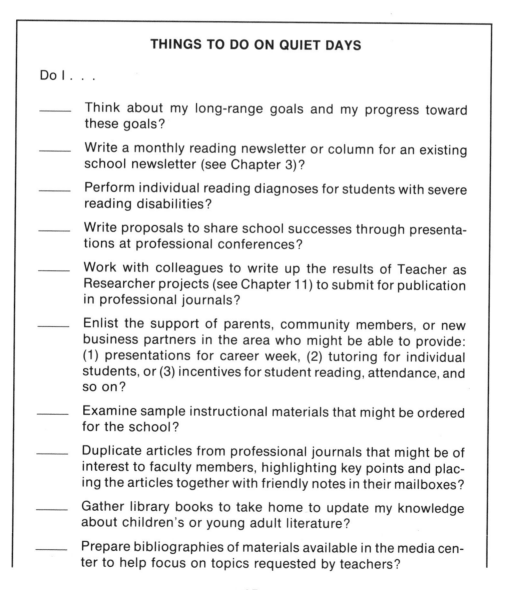

**THINGS TO DO ON QUIET DAYS**

Do I . . .

_____ Think about my long-range goals and my progress toward these goals?

_____ Write a monthly reading newsletter or column for an existing school newsletter (see Chapter 3)?

_____ Perform individual reading diagnoses for students with severe reading disabilities?

_____ Write proposals to share school successes through presentations at professional conferences?

_____ Work with colleagues to write up the results of Teacher as Researcher projects (see Chapter 11) to submit for publication in professional journals?

_____ Enlist the support of parents, community members, or new business partners in the area who might be able to provide: (1) presentations for career week, (2) tutoring for individual students, or (3) incentives for student reading, attendance, and so on?

_____ Examine sample instructional materials that might be ordered for the school?

_____ Duplicate articles from professional journals that might be of interest to faculty members, highlighting key points and placing the articles together with friendly notes in their mailboxes?

_____ Gather library books to take home to update my knowledge about children's or young adult literature?

_____ Prepare bibliographies of materials available in the media center to help focus on topics requested by teachers?

_____ Send my district supervisor samples of what I have done during the year?

_____ Develop plans for and/or monitor reading activities such as Sustained Silent Reading or Visiting Reader Day?

_____ Offer to tape portions of text for teachers working with low-achieving students?

_____ Prepare units on study skills strategies on topics such as goal setting, getting organized, time management, listening skills, following directions, textbook overviews, prereading, test-taking tips, and notetaking (see Chapter 7)?

_____ Update test preparation materials banks?

_____ Update and purge my files?

_____ Prepare an annotated summer reading list for schoolwide distribution (after checking first with school and local libraries to be sure the books are available)?

## Evaluating the Program

 Ongoing program evaluation gives you feedback on current efforts and helps you plan for the future. Good evaluations also serve as a public relations tool to ensure continuation of a resource teacher position. Note that, as you might expect, you will see some overlap between the following Tips box and Chapter 9 on "Assessing Student Performance."

## TIPS · EVALUATION OF PROGRAM

- Plan your evaluation when you plan the school's reading program. Start with required testing and record keeping, and then consider going beyond these. This might be the perfect time to ask your administrator if you can invite your reading supervisor/director to help you define goals and the means of evaluating them. An invitation at such a nonthreatening time can lay the groundwork for future helpful visits.

- Consider your audience: Is it district and school-level administrators, teachers, parents, community, students? Selection of the type of evaluation will depend partly on the audience.

- Use varied forms of evaluation and groups of evaluators. The more variety, the more valid the picture that emerges. There is sometimes a tendency to examine only standardized test scores, even though this measure may be the least likely to show a difference. Examples of forms of evaluation are:

—Solicited and unsolicited verbal and nonverbal feedback as the year progresses (from administrators, supervisors, peers, parents, students)
—Any classroom-based research to document the effectiveness of a given strategy (see the "Teacher as Researcher" section in Chapter 11)
—Norm- and criterion-referenced test scores
—Frequency counts (e.g., number of books checked out of the library, number of students participating in a motivational reading program)
—Portfolios with writing samples, completed projects across the curriculum, lists of books read, "I can do" lists, and the like
—Student attendance and grades
—Self-evaluation
—Observations
—Questionnaires
—Interviews

 • Be critical of your program—but not too critical.

You also need to pat yourself on the back (especially if no one else does). See Appendix D for a number of assessment options that you may wish to use or adapt as you conclude the year:

• *Letter to highlight accomplishments and Checklist of accomplishments:* Share both within and outside the school.

• *Content and process self-evaluation checklists:* Have some colleagues (not just your friends) fill them out also and see how your perceptions compare.

• *Program review form:* Adapt or use this form for self-evaluation or outside evaluation of the school program.

## Outside Resources

You are not alone. There is a network of professional resources beyond your school that can empower you, invigorate you, and provide a forum for you to share your successes and problem-solve your challenges.

### District Office

What your district can provide you will vary, of course, from district to district. Often, however, schools do not know of or think to use the resources that do exist. The district director/supervisor can help you in ways like these:

• Give you names of other RRSs who have projects similar to yours or who simply have some good ideas. We have seen joint grant proposals, joint presentations, cloning of one school's ideas throughout a district, and other exciting results from such networking.

• Send literature on a needed topic. As this is being written, just this week, one RRS said that a book on study skills that one of us had loaned her had really "saved her life" this year.

- Suggest libraries of films, professional resources, computer software, and other instructional materials for preview or loan.

- Provide information on everything from names of schools that have tried innovative programs to locations and dates of professional conferences.

- Answer questions ranging from state or district requirements to names of businesses that might support your program. Some RRSs keep this line open on a regular basis.

- Help solve problems. One RRS we know was concerned about the copyright laws. Although she had read through the information in her files, she was still confused about certain points. She contacted the district supervisor, who set up a meeting with the school board attorney and the RRS.

- Plan inservice sessions to suit your needs. If there is a topic you'd like covered, don't keep it a secret.

- Suggest curriculum support staff who can visit teachers, do grade-level or school presentations, and the like.

- Visit your school. Maybe you want your director/supervisor to attend a reading celebration, or to be an advocate with the principal for your program, or to give advice about the reading program at your school, or simply to stop by to keep in touch. Regardless of the reason, if you'd like a visit, ask for it!

Remember—the more information you have at your fingertips about district resources, the better your program will be.


## Community

More and more community agencies and businesses are becoming educationally conscious. Consequently, providing grants for innovative projects and sponsoring recreational reading activities have become fashionable. Pick up on this trend! If you need funding for a special program or activity, ask. The answer may be "no." It may even be "no" over and over again. But there is a "yes" out there. It just takes persistence.

When you approach community agencies and businesses, be specific about what you want to do and how much it will cost. Let your potential sponsor know what he or she can gain from the collaboration. Maybe you can provide a public "thank you" in a school newsletter. Maybe you can display student work in the corporate office. Maybe the project can get some publicity in the local paper.

Reach out to the public libraries in your vicinity. It may be that you can create joint projects such as book lists, reading incentive programs, visits from noted authors, library tours, and library card registration campaigns.

Your local newspaper may be involved in Newspaper in Education activities or may have special thematic supplements available to schools. Be certain you are on the mailing list and be sure to have a contact person at the newspapers. Also, be aware of the procedure for getting publicity and recognition for your special programs in the newspaper. Of course, you will have a better shot with a neighborhood paper or supplement than you will with the big dailies. Newspapers are interested in off-the-wall projects. For example, we know of one elementary school that had an all-day pajama party. Students and staff went to school with pajamas, a favorite bedtime storybook, and a stuffed animal.

Also, reach out to the community to enlist volunteers (see "Interactions with Volunteers" in Chapter 3). Some volunteers may serve on an ongoing basis to help with particular teachers or children. Others may get involved for one-shot deals—to lend an extra hand during special reading programs and the like. Local celebrities can also be enlisted for one-shot read-aloud sessions. Think big! Once again, many "no"'s can lead to a "yes"!

## Professional Organizations

Other than a personal regimen of wide reading in professional literature, the best way to keep up to date on issues and trends in education is through involvement in professional organizations. Interactions with other professionals at the local, state, regional, national, and international level broaden your horizons, heighten your awareness of what's new, and provide a forum for you to share your good work.

Many organizations strive for a balance between university-based and school-based leadership. Thus, the opportunities for involvement are open at all levels. These involvement opportunities include the following:

- Assuming leadership roles as officers and committee members

- Attending/presenting at conferences

- Making arrangements for conferences

- Sharing your successes through professional journals and newsletters

One valuable benefit of membership in professional organizations is access to publications. The output of high-quality books, monographs, journals, newsletters, videotapes, audiotapes, and brochures among professional organizations seems to mushroom each year.

• *International Reading Association:* The International Reading Association (IRA) is an organization devoted to literacy improvement. IRA has several periodical publications: *The Reading Teacher* (elementary), *Journal of Reading* (secondary, postsecondary, and adult), *Reading Research Quarterly* (a prominent research journal), *Lectura y Vida* (a Spanish-language journal focusing on literacy issues), and *Reading Today* (a bimonthly newsletter). In addition, the IRA publishes numerous books. The IRA sponsors local reading councils throughout the world, which support grass-roots educational and service efforts. In addition, the IRA sponsors annual regional conferences and a World Reading Congress. The primary meeting, however, is the IRA conference in May.

International Reading Association
800 Barksdale Road
P.O. Box 8139
Newark, DE 19714

• *National Council of Teachers of English:* The National Council of Teachers of English (NCTE) focuses on improving the teaching of reading and the language arts. Its publications include *Language Arts* (elementary) and *English Journal* (secondary), as well as many books. The NCTE offers many opportunities for professional growth through membership in local affiliate groups, regional conferences, and summer institutes. NCTE's major annual conference is scheduled in November.

National Council of Teachers of English
1111 Kenyon Road
Urbana, IL 61801

• *National Reading Conference:* Membership in the National Reading Conference (NRC) is a must for anyone interested in keeping up with literacy research. NRC has two major publications, *Journal of Reading Behavior* and the *NRC Yearbook.* The NRC annual conference is held in December.

National Reading Conference
11 East Hubbard Street
Chicago, IL 60611

• *Association for Supervision and Curriculum Development:* Membership in the Association for Supervision and Curriculum Development (ASCD) enables busy professionals to keep up to date on trends, issues, and research in general education. The ASCD journal, *Educational Leadership,* summarizes key findings from a variety of disciplines in a user-friendly, classroom-oriented manner. The ASCD annual conference is held in March.

Association for Supervision and Curriculum Development
1250 N. Pitt Street
Alexandria, VA 22312-1403

• *Whole Language Umbrella:* Whole Language Umbrella (WLU) is a confederation of whole language teacher support groups. Its purpose is to provide a forum for networking among teachers interested in the whole language movement. WLU has a newsletter that is published three times a year.

Whole Language Umbrella
Debbie Manning
4848 N. Fruit
Fresno, CA 93705

• *American Library Association:* As an RRS, you are not likely to be a member of the American Library Association (ALA), but elementary RRSs should be aware of *Book Links: Connecting Books, Libraries, and Classrooms,* a popular ALA thematic publication issued six times a year.

*Book Links* Subscriptions
P.O. Box 1347
Elmhurst, IL 60126-1420

## Conclusion

Have we kept you treading water in this chapter as we promised? It can be daunting to swim through the icy waters of a year-long program, often without any lifeguard or posted rules to help you manage your time and resources, but it can also be exhilarating. We hope this chapter gives you the gumption to plunge in again and again and again.

# 3
# Developing Communication Techniques

| Enthusiasm and Positiveness | Assessing Your Image |
| Communication Skills | Marketing Your Program | Reading Newsletter |

**D**EVELOPING COMMUNICATION TECHNIQUES should be one of your main priorities. Administrators, teachers, students, and parents will be more receptive and responsive to you if you are enthusiastic, positive, and articulate. You should also realize the importance of nonverbal communication. In addition, you will need some clever ideas for marketing your program, including the development of a reading newsletter. Read on for some suggestions on developing these important skills.

## Enthusiasm and Positiveness

The traits of positiveness and enthusiasm often accompany each other. People with these strong characteristics are stimulating to be around. If you are not usually enthusiastic or positive, try to develop these traits within yourself. See the following "Do's & Don't's" list for additional suggestions:

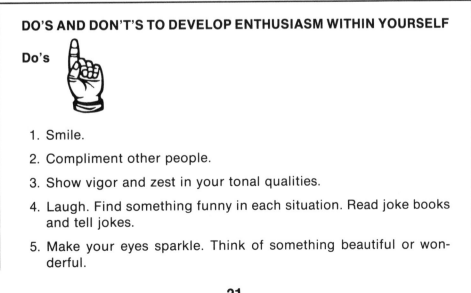

**DO'S AND DON'T'S TO DEVELOP ENTHUSIASM WITHIN YOURSELF**

Do's

1. Smile.

2. Compliment other people.

3. Show vigor and zest in your tonal qualities.

4. Laugh. Find something funny in each situation. Read joke books and tell jokes.

5. Make your eyes sparkle. Think of something beautiful or wonderful.

6. Walk with enthusiasm.

7. Associate with lively, interesting people.

8. Read, read, read—books of all kinds, inspiring, humorous, biographical.

9. Volunteer to work with people who get things done—"movers and shakers."

10. Make your successes visible. Keep a chart or talk this over with a friend.

11. Reward yourself. Do things that are fun.

12. Exercise to get out of the doldrums and relieve stress.

13. Eat healthful foods—not too much fat or sugar.

14. Look at your students and think of their potential and your part in releasing it.

15. Look at each day as being new and challenging—even in mundane things.

16. Remind yourself that you are the important one, and actively seek ways to do things because of this realization.

17. Get enough rest.

18. Identify with characters in books you are reading and let yourself be carried away to another world.

19. Express enthusiasm in body language through facial expressions, heightened voice tone, leaning forward, direct eye contact, and hand movements.

20. Become a role model, and speak encouraging words to those around you.

21. Use a favorite soap, cologne, or perfume.

22. Wear a favorite piece of clothing or jewelry.

23. Have a little chit-chat with a friendly colleague.

24. Dance—ballroom, rock 'n' roll, square dancing, jazzercise, whatever.

25. Watch a favorite movie.

26. Listen to music you especially enjoy.

27. Learn something new or try something new. Begin a new project such as gardening, cooking, decorating, or planning a trip.

28. Go to a lecture and stimulate your mind.

29. Take time to be quiet so you can think things through and know your goals in life.

30. Meet and talk to friends who have a positive attitude about things they are doing.

31. Sing a favorite song.

32. Anticipate doing something you enjoy, and begin planning for it.

33. Think of someone who loves you.

34. Do something to help someone.

35. Listen carefully!

**Don't's**

1. Frown.

2. Be negative.

3. Speak in a monotone.

4. Associate with the school complainers.

5. Hide away and become inaccessible.

6. Overextend yourself and get so tired that you get little satisfaction out of anything.

7. Gossip about anyone or anything to anybody.

8. Disappear and fade into the woodwork so that no one knows what you are doing.

9. Be too aggressive or pushy.

10. Become frustrated or disappointed with teachers who don't invite you into their classrooms. Focus instead on those who do want you in their classrooms.

11. Wear clothes that are too formal—they may categorize you as part of the administration.

12. Wear clothes that are too casual.

13. Be unavailable.

14. Wear inappropriate or uncomfortable shoes that look messy or dirty.

15. Carry a bag of materials that is overstuffed with junk.

16. Wear anything spotted, snagged, or frayed.

17. Be provocative—wear anything too tight or too short.

18. Look sloppy. Avoid tennis wear, sweatsuits, and shorts for normal school days.

19. Avoid eye contact.

20. Act unfriendly.

Source: Adapted from J. Stanchfield, *Ways to Develop Enthusiasm within Yourself* (Gold Coast, Australia: International Reading Association World Congress, 1988).

## Assessing Your Image

An important aspect of your overall image is how you are perceived by your colleagues and the students in their classes. First and foremost, your colleagues should perceive you as a professional. Many of the most successful people in business and industry are those with the strongest organizational skills. If you tend to be disorganized, start a personal campaign to improve! (see "Time Management" in Chapter 2 for suggestions).

In order to present this image, you must take pride in both your appearance and your manner of speaking. It has been said that teaching is 95 percent presentation and 5 percent content. Teachers and students will react more to the way in which they see something presented than to the actual words you use. For instance, try this demonstration activity with a group of teachers to emphasize the importance of visual presentation:

> Ask all teachers to place their thumb and forefinger in a circle, as in the "O.K." sign. Now direct all participants to place their fingers, in the same position, on their chins. As you say this, have them watch you as you place your fingers on your cheek. Most of the audience will do what they see rather than what you say.

If school employees, staff, and students are to think highly of you, what is the image you wish to present? If those outside the school are to think highly of you, specifically what do you want them to think?

If you could choose, what words or phrases would people use to describe you and your teaching style?

_____    _____

_____    _____

_____    _____

What overall image would they have of your presentations?

_____

Do you have a goal that can be put into slogan form? (See below for examples.)

_____

_____

_____

| *Goal* | *Slogan* |
| --- | --- |
| 1. Promote improvement in test scores. | 1. Meet the challenge . . . make the grade. |
| 2. Tell the community you are concerned about pupils. | 2. Caring to learn . . . learning to care. |
| 3. Communicate high expectations. | 3. Reach for excellence. |

The students and teachers you work with are your salespersons, your image, and your best or worst advertisement. Marketing yourself will help to present your most positive image. By deciding on a goal and developing your own unique slogan, you will effectively promote your program. Easily remembered and meaningful slogans can enhance your overall image and promote awareness of your program.

## Physical Appearance and Body Language

Physical appearance can play a large part in the acceptance you receive as an RRS. Because everyone will be watching what you do, you must be particularly careful to project a neat, clean, and appealing image. Pay attention to specific colors or styles which are attractive on you. Your chances for success can increase if you are neat and attractive in your appearance. You will be visiting a great many classes, and it seems likely that some students (and perhaps other teachers as well) may try to emulate you as a role model.

We all know that the way we put words together, or our diction and grammar, influence our credibility. Research indicates that our body language also strongly affects the way others respond to what we are saying (Kindsvatter, Wilen, & Ishler, 1988). There is little doubt that actions speak louder than words. Yet most people are unaware of the pervasive effect of nonverbal communication on their everyday lives (Goleman, 1986).

It is vitally important that you become aware of your own nonverbal messages and their impact on others. Your facial expressions, gestures, posture, tone of voice, and position in the classroom all may connote more than your words alone. Your nonverbal communication often expresses information you would never state aloud.

Moving your hands in certain ways can indicate nervousness, self-assurance, impatience, or boredom. Nervous teachers often play with the change in their pockets, pick at their hair or clothing, or fiddle with jewelry. These are signs that students notice immediately!

Body language also involves awareness of personal space. Distance and closeness have special meanings. Some students, especially those who have experienced any kind of physical abuse, may experience discomfort if you stand too close to them, invading their personal space. On the other hand, elementary students brought up in cultures where personal space is small have been found to perform better on exams when a teacher sits close to them (Power, 1988).

In any form of nonverbal communications, make sure that your words and your actions are congruent. For example, if you are supposed to be listening to a teacher or student, but you are reading at the same time, you will give the impression that you are uninterested or even bored. Noncongruent classroom messages result in "signal jamming" or "mixed messages" (Ginott, 1969). Using noncongruent messages may cause others to view you as insincere and untrustworthy. Here are some hints for using body movements effectively:

## TIPS · USING BODY MOVEMENTS EFFECTIVELY

- Pointing your finger at a student may make him or her feel uncomfortable. Instead of pointing, turn your palm upward and use your entire hand to gesture toward the student. The open hand presents a picture of openness and seems warmer and more accepting than the pointed finger.

(*continued*)

### TIPS (continued)

•   Standing with folded arms may make you look as though you are barricading yourself away from others. This posture may be perceived by others as one of dominance, impatience, and/or superiority.

•   Using your hands when interacting with students may help to increase your effectiveness (Power, 1988). When directing students' attention to key points, emphasizing important information, or presenting new concepts, remember that using hand motions has been found to improve students' attitudes and their test scores as well (Power, 1988).

•   Leaning away from your listeners may cause you to look as if you are uninterested in what is being said. Leaning toward them can make them feel that you are interested in what they have to say.

### Eye Contact

A common quote is that "the eyes are the windows of the soul." Use of effective eye contact is one way of enhancing your communication with others. By looking into another person's eyes, you convey interest in what he or she has to say. When another person is speaking and you are looking directly into his or her eyes, you convey a message of agreement, even if you don't fully agree (Kindsvatter et al., 1988).

Research (Knapp, 1974) indicates that we tend to use eye contact to a greater degree when speaking with people who support and care about us. Therefore, using eye contact with parents, faculty, and students can generate feelings of warmth, interest, and support. We hope that those with whom we engage in more eye contact will develop positive feelings about us.

Eye contact helps us to interact with others. In a restaurant, when you catch the waitress's eye, you usually get an immediate response. Similarly, when you catch the student's eye, you signal that you are expecting the student to be attentive and responsive (Knapp, 1974).

When communicating messages with your eyes, you must be particularly careful to avoid any negative messages you might convey. If you look away when someone is speaking to you, you may communicate a message that says you are not interested in the speaker or in what he or she has to say. If you fail to meet another person's eyes, you may cause the person to experience a feeling of exclusion (Fast, 1979).

Trial attorneys say that members of a jury, after completing their deliberations, often avoid looking at the defendant if they have arrived at a guilty verdict. In this way they express their negative feelings and place distance between the defendant and themselves. In this same manner, by avoiding a teacher's or student's eyes, you close the channels of communication and place distance between the two of you.

The duration of your eye contact with another person should not exceed ten seconds or you will be likely to cause the other person some discomfort. In some instances, however, prolonged eye contact may serve as a deterrent to misbehavior. The more aggressive the student, however, the less success you will have using eye contact alone to stop the misbehavior (Knapp, 1974).

Some cultural differences exist with regard to eye contact (Evertson & Emmer, 1982). In some cultures, it is preferable to avoid eye contact. If you are speaking to a student from such a culture, you might cause problems by using or expecting direct eye contact.

The eyes can be used to share a private thought, as when winking at another person; they can be used to reprimand, as in a stern, angry expression; or they can be used to designate feelings, as in a roll of the eyes at something we feel is foolish. We might narrow our eyes in suspicion or look away in disbelief (Evertson & Emmer, 1982). A warm glance or a cold stare may convey all the meaning necessary without the use of a single word.

## Communication Skills

Your speaking style is an integral part of your success as an RRS. What happens if you use a style that is too aggresive? Walking up to people and speaking into their faces may be perceived as too pushy and can cause others to feel uncomfortable. What happens if you use a mumbling, head-down style? Depending on cultural background, this may make you appear weak and discredit you as having nothing important to say.

Be well organized in your speaking. Before you say anything, organize your thoughts and try to express yourself logically and concisely. Teachers will run from you if they think you will monopolize their time. Remember also that your tone of voice is important in the total package. Your tone can project emotions ranging from enthusiasm to boredom and is an essential element in the total image you wish to project.

In this same manner, it is imperative that you realize the extent to which grammar, diction, and vocabulary usage influence your credibility. Careful enunciation and articulation can instill feelings of trust in those around you.

Written communication is another area in which you most obviously project your image. Be totally aware of your writing style, and write carefully and clearly at all times. Your grammar and punctuation must be impeccable, whether in formal memoranda or in informal notes. Specific ideas for writing notes, newsletters, and the like are provided throughout this chapter.

Are you friendly, persuasive, helpful, attentive, knowledgeable, positive, and sincere? If you can answer affirmatively to most of these questions, you are on your way to becoming a successful RRS. Check yourself out with each of these traits:

- *Friendliness* will entice other teachers to use your services. A smiling, cheerful face can be your greatest asset.

- *Persuasiveness* will help you to convince your colleagues of the importance of allowing you to demonstrate the inclusion of reading strategies in their classrooms.

- *Helpfulness* can provide you with an entrance into a teacher's classroom. You may be able to assist with a difficult lesson or with a group of students having trouble comprehending a particular concept. Once your helpfulness (not intrusiveness!) has been established, your reputation will quickly spread.

- *Attentiveness* is an essential characteristic for an RRS. By listening carefully to a teacher's needs and by responding appropriately, you will develop a following among your colleagues. One RRS always repeats the teacher's requests in order to display understanding of the situation. Another listens first, places the requests in writing, and then follows up by reviewing the requests with the teacher.

- *Awareness of personality differences* among the members of your faculty is essential. Remember to give specific compliments whenever possible, emphasize points of agreement while minimizing points of disagreement, and avoid embarrassing teachers at all costs. If you are dealing with a teacher with a superiority complex, indicate respect for his or her position and ask for his or her view. Begin with those who will work with you and not against you, rather than starting with those who are indifferent or apathetic. Some of the most effective staff development programs in the country (e.g., Ohio State's Reading Recovery and the University of Miami/Dade County Public Schools Writing Institute) have begun with those who would be most likely to implement the change. Others will soon follow suit.

- *Positiveness* is sometimes a difficult attitude to maintain. You may find that teachers are reluctant to invite you into their classrooms because you may be viewed as an "administrator in disguise." Teachers may also feel that they have to give up classroom time when you enter their classes. Sometimes a lesson may not work as successfully as expected. These pitfalls and many others may cause you to feel inadequate or unappreciated. Remember to smile bravely through any difficulties—all of these are learning experiences, and tomorrow will be a better day!

- *Sincerity* can provide the thread that winds through all of your interpersonal skills. If your colleagues feel that you are genuinely interested in helping them, your role as an RRS will be secure.

- *Collegiality* can help you get your foot in the door. If the RRS has a "Here I am, you lucky people—I'm the one with all the answers" attitude, he or she is doomed to failure. We can and should be willing to empower each other.

- *Thoughtfulness* should always be a part of the RRS's day. In order to thank the teachers with whom she works, one RRS we know gives out lollipops. Another RRS uses special notepaper to write thank-you notes to teachers and to classes in which he has made presentations.

As you continue your work as as RRS, you will find that many other interpersonal skills are necessary. Those delineated here are the most crucial when first entering the field. In addition to these skills, you may want to consider the skills that are important and specific to your daily interactions with administrators, other resource personnel, teachers, volunteers, students, parents, and the community.

## Interactions with Administrators

In any communication with administrators, try to convey as much positive information about your program as you possibly can. After all, you are your own best advertisement—let the administrative staff know about your successes.

Always remember to maintain your professional image. Because you will be on the move a great deal, shifting gears from class to class, you will sometimes feel overwhelmed. Try to remain calm and cool as you encounter members of the administrative staff throughout your daily travels.

## TIPS · COMMUNICATION WITH ADMINISTRATORS

- Make your message clear and concise. Administrators are busy and may not appreciate having their time monopolized.

- Use newsletters, memos, bulletin boards, needs assessment results, and/ or an annual report to share what you have accomplished with the administration (see Appendix D).

- Be sure that any written communication is carefully written, neatly typed (when appropriate), and professional looking.

- Make appointments to speak with administrators when you feel it is necessary. Be brief and concise during your meetings.

- Seek approval for new projects. Make sure your administrators know the big picture and approve of your ideas.

- Solicit ideas from administrators and give them credit if you use their ideas.

- Seek out administrators for their assistance in planning and carrying out programs, but try not to burden them with too many additional responsibilities.

- Report your successes as they develop!

## Interactions with Other Resource Personnel

In order to establish a good working relationship with other resource personnel, such as counselors and media specialists, initially, you may want to set up individual appointments to get to know these valuable colleagues. Be sure to specify the length of the meeting, and try not to exceed your meeting time limit. Introduce yourself and your program. An outline of your goals for the year might also be included in this meeting.

Throughout the year, you may need to check with counselors concerning a student's standardized test scores, or you may want to consult the media specialist about ordering resource materials for the media center. Professionalism is essential in all of your daily encounters.

## Interactions with Teachers

All the points mentioned previously are relevant when working with teachers. In addition, you will want to publicize the services you can provide through a regular newsletter or letter. You should also plan to consult with the teachers regularly concerning their needs and the information or materials you are providing.

Teachers may feel threatened by your presence at first. To overcome this feeling, you will need to be extremely convincing and helpful. Enter the classes of the friendliest teachers first. Don't confront those who do not want you in their classrooms. As your successes occur and your reputation spreads, invitations will follow. Other tips for interacting with teachers will occur throughout this book.

### Interactions with Teachers in Pull-Out Programs

Most schools have pull-out programs to meet the needs of diverse student populations. Resource rooms to serve students who qualify for English as a Second Language (ESL), gifted, special education, and compensatory education are present in both elementary and secondary settings. Even if the RRS is not primarily responsible for these programs, he or she can play a role in involving students in schoolwide reading programs and in assisting general education teachers in planning and making adaptations for special-needs students.

Because the special education, ESL, remedial reading, and gifted education teachers are the professionals responsible for monitoring students who have been identified for special programs, it is vital that the RRS work collaboratively with them. To initiate a program without collaborating with the teachers of pull-out programs only serves to alienate fellow professionals and fragment the school's literacy program. Communicate to the special services teachers that you are eager to help them supplement an already good program.

Following are ways that you can collaborate with the teachers of pull-out programs. See also the tips for working with learning-disabled students in Chapter 7.

## TIPS · WORKING WITH TEACHERS OF PULL-OUT PROGRAMS

- Invite the teacher(s) to be members of the Reading Committee (see Chapter 5). It's a good way to communicate and coordinate.

- Start an information exchange. Chances are these specialists receive publications from professional organizations other than your own. Make a habit of swapping articles with each other.

- Keep the teacher(s) informed of all schoolwide reading programs. Often the resource classes are inadvertently left out. Talk with the teacher or teachers in advance to make certain that their scheduling makes participation feasible.

- Work cooperatively with the teacher(s) to plan a series of inservice workshops to provide teachers with specific suggestions for making such adaptations for diverse student needs in the classroom. Classroom teachers report that their knowledge, skills, and confidence in planning and making adaptations for special needs students in their general education classes is quite low (Schumm & Vaughn, 1992).

- Coordinate the curriculum with the teacher(s). These teachers may or may not be familiar with the literacy instructional strategies employed in the general education classes at your school. You can help provide this valuable information.

### Interactions with Volunteers

Volunteer efforts are on the rise in the United States. Many high schools and universities now include a community service component as a graduation requirement. Religious and service organizations and organizations of retired professionals have become actively engaged in volunteer efforts. Yet, despite this upsurge of volunteerism, many schools are not prepared to accommodate volunteers who may show up at the doorstep. Frequently volunteers are delegated tasks such as running off copies or grading papers. These tasks are necessary, but some volunteers wish to make a contribution in other ways than by doing clerical tasks.

Volunteers may be those who serve on an ongoing basis to assist with particular teachers or children. Volunteers may also get involved in one-shot efforts, lending an extra hand during special reading programs and the like. Local celebrities can also be enlisted for one-shot read-aloud sessions. Think big! Once again, many no's can lead to a yes! There is much more than meets the eye to having a successful volunteer program. The following section addresses this issue.

If you are serious about enlisting volunteers, then your efforts must be intentional and well structured. An effective volunteer program needs to incorporate plans for enlistment, training, placement, monitoring, evaluating, and recognizing.

• *Enlistment:* Initially, a multifaceted recruitment campaign is the best way to assure results. As prospective volunteers contact you for details, ask how they heard about your program and keep a tally of their responses. This will help you track the best method for recruiting volunteers in subsequent campaigns. Some suggestions for volunteer recruitment include:
　　—Letter to parents
　　—Ad in the newspaper
　　—Radio or television news spots
　　—School district volunteer office
　　—Sign-up table at major school event (carnival, PTA meeting, etc.)

• *Training:* For a volunteer program to function smoothly some training is essential. Volunteers need to be made aware of their roles and responsibilities. Training should focus on an overview of the school environment and routines. Procedures for signing in and out of the school should be detailed. Expectations should be clarified. Procedures for maintaining student confidentiality and trouble shooting should also be clearly delineated. Depending on your plan to involve volunteers, your training can range from an informal chat to a series of training workshops. Here is an example of a workshop series for a volunteer read-aloud program:

*Session 1:* Orientation (overview of the program, roles and responsibilities, introduction to the school environment)

*Session 2:* How to read aloud to children

*Session 3:* How to encourage students to respond to reading through writing, art, and discussion

*Session 4:* How to select appropriate books

*Session 5:* How to motivate the reluctant reader and writer

• *Placement:* With large volunteer programs, placement can be particularly challenging. A strategy for placement of volunteers can be outlined and procedures verified with administrators and teachers. Animosity can arise if all teachers who *want* volunteers cannot *get* volunteers. Conversely, volunteers should not be assigned to teachers who prefer to work alone.

• *Monitoring:* Often, once a volunteer has been assigned to a teacher or a child, that's the end. After that, volunteers are left to their own devices. A system for periodic monitoring of the volunteers is necessary to make certain that they feel comfortable in their role and have the support they need.

• *Evaluating:* Volunteers do not need to be graded, but they do need the opportunity to evaluate the program. End-of-year or exit interviews are one way to glean information about program pros and cons. This monitoring can be done by you, an administrator, another teacher, or an experienced volunteer whose responsibility is to serve as a liaison between the volunteers and you.

• *Recognizing:* Volunteers give of their time and talent for altruistic reasons, and most would say that thanks are not necessary. But they are. Unless volunteers receive recognition on an ongoing basis, they may begin to feel that their services are not valued. Thank-you notes from children, teachers, and the RRS are always appreciated. Certificates, buttons, and recognition in the school newspaper are other ways to show that volunteer services are valued. Formal recognition of volunteers at a function at least once a year is also a must.

## Interactions with Students

In structuring reading programs and classroom practices, we often ask administrators, teachers, and parents about what they think is best or about what might work. Although we have not been in the habit of asking students what they think, research has indicated that students have definite opinions about instructional adaptations teachers make (Vaughn, Schumm, Niarhos, & Gordon, in press), teaching strategies teachers use (Schumm, Vaughn, & Saumell, in press), and the nature of their own reading problems (Miller & Yochum, 1991). Not only do students have definite opinions, but their opinions are often sensitive and insightful, and can contribute to instructional practice.

It is important to hear what students have to say, and the RRS can take a lead in the school in hearing the students' voices. When students' opinions are sought, it is important that evaluation of strategies and practices be divorced from individual personalities as much as possible. The purpose of the inquiry is to find out what helped students to learn best. The purpose is not to evaluate individual teachers.

When you are working with other teachers' classes, students should be aware of your role as RRS. At first, you may need to precede the lesson with a brief description of your role. This will become unnecessary as the year progresses and students become more familiar with you.

Students should look forward to seeing you in their classes. To develop this anticipation on the part of the students, additional ideas will be provided in the rest of this chapter as well as in the section on classroom demonstrations (see Chapter 11).

## Interactions with Parents and Community

As in your communications with administrators, you will want to convey as many positive thoughts about your program as possible. You may want to drum up financial support for your program through the business contacts you either already have or those you develop within the community.

One RRS involved both parents and community members in her RRS program by beginning a Guest Reader Day. She invited radio and television announcers, school board members, school administrators, lawyers, doctors, presidents of local companies and universities, and well-known political leaders to read their favorite books to students. One reader was assigned to each classroom for half an hour. Over 80 participants helped motivate students to read in the course of this interesting and innovative program. The sections on "Outside Resources" in Chapter 2 and on "Parent Involvement" in Chapter 5 will give you other ideas to add to your "bag of tricks."

## Marketing Your Program

As in a successful business advertising campaign, you will want to make students, teachers, administrators, and the community aware of your program. Ideas for marketing and enhancing motivational reading programs can be found in Chapter 10 ("What's on the Market?"). Ideas for marketing and enhancing your program overall include the following tips:

### TIPS · IDEAS FOR MARKETING YOUR PROGRAM

- Make up bumper stickers or buttons.

- Prepare and make visible a calendar of your schedule for each month, one-quarter of the school year, or an entire semester (see "Sample Year-Long Schedules" in Appendix C).

- Develop a newsletter with current reading research, classroom action research, information on practical reading strategies, and the like (see the section entitled "Reading Newsletter," which follows).

- Design paper with your name and a logo that you will use on all communications with students and teachers. This does not have to be expensive. One way to accomplish this easily and quickly is to use clip art books that may be duplicated. These are available from a variety of publishers—ask your media specialist for suggestions or check your local craft or book store. One RRS developed a logo using the outline of a book within which she typed her name. She copied the logo onto a ream of paper and used these sheets for all her communications. Another RRS found a book containing reproducible borders and claimed one as her own. Other options include asking for help from a friend who does calligraphy, using computer graphic capabilities, or calling on the expertise of the art teacher.

- Choose notepaper of a particular color that teachers instantly recognize as yours. Use this paper consistently for communications with other faculty members. Whenever a goldenrod sheet (for example) appears in their mailboxes, teachers will immediately know that you have sent them a note.

(continued)

## TIPS (continued)

- Ask the media specialist to provide one bulletin board on which all the reading news can be publicized. Or ask to use the electronic memo board in the cafeteria if one is available.

## Reading Newsletter

A reading newsletter can help you spread the word about your program quickly and efficiently. Through your newsletter, you can make teachers aware of new or unique teaching techniques and increase teacher interest in requesting your services (Beers, 1986b).

Before you begin, however, be organized and have a plan. Determine the size, shape, length, and number of issues at the start. If you plan to publish a monthly newsletter, be sure you have the time to gather materials and prepare them in a timely fashion. If time is at a premium, you may decide instead on a quarterly newsletter. Once you decide on the plan, try to stick to it.

A critical facet of your newsletter is its name! Try to select a name that is tasteful, lively, and appropriate. A sample newsletter (see Appendix A), entitled "Reading Between the Lines," includes one line above and one line below the title for its visual representation.

The next most important part of your newsletter is the front page. Because this is the first thing readers see, it needs to grab their attention. The reader's first impression must be a positive one. If a newsletter looks boring, no one will bother to read it. In determining the layout, pay particular attention to the design of the first page.

You may wish to keep a file folder with clippings, cartoons, and interesting articles that you can use in future newsletters. One RRS we know keeps articles in folders according to the topic and publishes newsletters on a theme. For example, one month's issue may contain only information on graphic organizers; the following month may be limited to the explanation and use of the "One-Sentence Summary." Another approach is to include a variety of information about interesting happenings within your district and/or your school.

A note of caution involves the use of materials with a copyright (refer to "Copyright or Copy Wrong" in Appendix C). A particularly resourceful RRS we know called the local newspaper for the address and then wrote to Hank Ketchum, author of the "Dennis the Menace" cartoons. She requested permission to reprint one of his cartoons and received a letter entitling her to do so. If you have the time and the inclination, you may be surprised at some of the requests that will be granted.

Many excellent software packages may be purchased to format your newsletter. Some of these software packages include the following:

For elementary and secondary newsletters:
—The Children's Writing & Publishing Center, The Learning Company
—Newsmaster II, Unison World
—The Newsroom, Spinnaker

For middle and senior high school newsletters:
—Aldus PageMaker, Aldus
—Express Publisher, Power Op!
—MacWrite II (for Macintosh only), Claris Corporation
—-Word Perfect, Word Perfect Corporation

## How-to's, or Putting Together the Parts

*Typing:* You will need to make initial decisions about margins, spacing, type-writer versus word processor (the latter is preferable), and the type and size of paper and typeface to be used. Obviously, these decisions will be based on what is available to you. Whatever you decide, however, always maintain a high-quality image for the finished product. Your newsletter should be neat, should be in a typeface that is easy to read, and should be printed on good paper. If you don't think it's worth doing well, why would anyone else want to read it?

*Headlines:* If you use a word processor, you may be able to include larger, bolder type for headings. If your computer or typewriter does not have this capability, you can type out headings on a separate sheet of paper and enlarge them on a photocopier. You can attach them by using a waxer (see the section on "Paste-up" later on) or glue. Try not to use too many different kinds of type; more than two or three different type styles can be distracting. Be consistent in your use of headlines. If one headline is bold and centered, all should be bold and centered. Make sure they are large enough and dark enough to be noticed, and try to make them clever enough to capture your readers' attention.

*Mastheads:* Include the school address, your name as editor, and the room number or extension at which you can be reached.

*Photographs/visuals:* Add interest and break the monotony of straight type by including light and/or whimsical clip art, photographs, captions, boxed enlarged quotes, cartoons, and/or illustrations. Remember to leave a lot of space around the visuals.

*Logo:* If you design a logo, make it simple, easily recognizable, and eye catching. If you need help, ask the art teacher in your school or ask the students for ideas. One RRS we know uses a specific border around each page of her newsletter as well as on every page she produces. As a result, her material is instantly recognizable.

*Color:* The color of the paper you use may affect readability. Best choices include pale pink, beige, light green, and light blue. You may be torn between a desire to be ecologically sensitive (by using white paper) and a desire to have your newsletter (and perhaps all your communications) stand out and be instantly recognizable. One RRS we know settled for white paper with students coloring in the border. If your photocopier offers a choice of ink colors, be sure that there is enough contrast between the paper and the ink color you choose. For example, blue ink on blue paper may be difficult to read.

*Layout:* Your layout choice should invite reader interest. A single column is most often used in business but causes difficulty when you try to include photos or illustrations. A two-column format is clean and easy to read. A three-column format provides flexibility for including artwork, but calls for much more care in designing the page.

*Design:* Don't overcrowd the pages. Leaving lots of space around text increases readability. Try to keep your pages simple and balanced. Put larger or longer passages near the middle of the page and smaller, shorter passages near the edge. Because our eyes move naturally from upper left to lower right, put the most important items in the top left-hand corner of the page. Use a box around passages you want to emphasize. Keep article length to no more than one page. Most people will not continue reading an article that continues onto a second page.

*Proofreading:* If you use a word processor, be sure to use the spell check feature! Otherwise, ask at least one other person (and preferably more than one) to read the material carefully while looking for typos, spelling, usage, style, and so on. Remember to proofread and edit in order to discard nonessentials. Be sure to keep sentences and paragraphs short and to the point. Make it interesting!

*Paste-up:* For best results, create a camera-ready dummy copy of your newsletter. We have used an electric waxer, available from art supply stores, for pasting up the finished copy. Using the waxer, as opposed to glue, enables you to place items on the page and then lift them up and continue to move them around until you are pleased with the design.

*Tools and supplies:* Clean, uncluttered surface; Exacto knife; editor's blue (non-reproducible) pencil; sharp scissors; white correction fluid; ruler and/or triangle; templates for drawing lines, arrows, and circles; supply of borders, border tape, letters, and other transfer materials; paste-up board or graph paper; waxer; photocopy of text; artwork; headlines; and anything else you may find helpful.

## Content: Contributions from Teachers and Students, Reports on School Projects, and New Ideas

The best way to guarantee contributions from the faculty and the student body is to develop a form on which articles and/or ideas can be written. You might include the form in your newsletter as a tear-off sheet, or it might be distributed to teachers in their mailboxes or at faculty meetings.

You may wish to ask teachers to include the newsletter form as a class assignment, and then you can select from among the submissions. Teachers might ask students to write annotated bibliographies of favorite books they have read and include these as a regular feature of your newsletter.

Students who so desire may want to be included in your newsletter by reporting on interesting school projects. Again, you will most likely need to solicit this information through the classroom teachers. If you are in a middle or senior high school, you may want to work in conjunction with the journalism teacher to encourage students to submit articles for your newsletter.

New ideas can be found everywhere around you. Items of interest appear in the daily paper, on television and radio, and in your school itself. One RRS we know was watching the Academy Awards show on television when Steven Spielberg commented, "Only a generation of readers will spawn a generation of writers." She quickly grabbed a pen and wrote down the quote, which she made the focal point of her next newsletter! Be sure to network with other RRSs to share newsletter ideas. Exchanging newsletters with other RRSs in your district, your region, or your state can give you numerous ideas for the future.

Your newsletter can become a marketing tool that promotes your program as an important resource in the school. By producing a high-quality product with pertinent information, you will alert others about the importance of the RRS position.

## Conclusion

The communication techniques we have explored in this chapter will help you carry out and market your program. In time, you will see these skills develop not only for you but for your faculty as well.

# 4
# Becoming a Change Agent

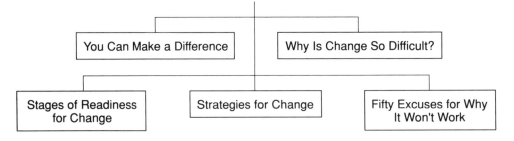

As a CHANGE AGENT you will be a combination of politician, energizer, manager, detective, salesperson, and hero (Carnine, 1988). Much of what appears elsewhere in this book regarding the general role of the RRS and your role in staff development applies also to your role as a change agent.

Sometimes we are indifferent or resistant to change, but we may not recognize this in ourselves. It has been said, in fact, that the only people who like change are wet babies. It's not that we need change for change's sake, but, like plants, either we are growing or we are dying. We cannot stand still. Inasmuch as teaching is an art, we never fully achieve mastery. It is not so much the product but the process of change that is important. You should thrive on change that results in growth.

## You Can Make a Difference!

Trust that, working with your faculty, you can be a powerful instrument of change. John Manning (Samuels & Pearson, 1988, p. v) tells us that the realities of social, cultural, and educational improvements are more closely related to individual accomplishments than to national movements. He reminds us that it was the accomplishments of Martin Luther King, Jr., that defined the noble goals of passive resistance to racial segregation, and that it was the stubborn will of Eleanor Roosevelt that kept alive the liberal conscience of the American people before, during, and after World War II. You should be among those who ask not "Why?" but rather "Why not?"

Littky and Fried (1988) say that to be lured out of their inertia people need change agents, people with great gobs of energy and enthusiasm, people with a passionate vision who have fires of school reform burning in their bellies. They warn that as enthusiastic amateurs you can get your heads handed to you. Even more likely, you may be patronized—thanked for your earnest efforts and sent back to where you belong. On the other hand, you *will* win some battles.

## Why Is Change So Difficult?

Despite the truism that "you don't have to be sick to get better," there is often much resistance to the idea of change. Here are some of the reasons why change is difficult:

- In teaching, we have no absolute answers as to what will work. Research findings may seem to say one thing one year and another thing the next. Moreover, research findings are sometimes translated into checklists of desirable behaviors, which teachers may have to follow regardless of their appropriateness to the teaching situation (Anders & Levine, 1990). Often, being forced to follow prescribed behaviors results in cynicism and resistance to change (Fraatz, 1987).

- The act of teaching is continually oversimplified (Anders & Levine, 1990). Some skills require as many as twenty-five practice episodes to master (Good, 1981; Showers, Joyce, & Bennett, 1987). Furthermore, change will often involve more than Piaget's assimilation; it may well involve replacing one paradigm with another. This process requires time.

- Change results in stress, something we have enough of already. Because of the stress inherent in change, change efforts often are restricted to safe areas, such as the purchase of a new set of materials (Pincus, 1974).

- Change involves risk taking. Not everyone is a risk taker.

- Schools, as opposed to private industry, may lack competition for clients. In most public schools there is no struggle for survival. Like the domesticated cat, a school is fed and cared for. Its existence is guaranteed (Carlson, 1964).

- Change may result in attacks to the implicit curriculum. For example, O'Brien and Stewart (1990) describe how teachers often see the structure of the secondary school as immutable. Secondary teachers who are stereotypically more discipline-centered than they are child-centered may fight changes such as content area reading or interdisciplinary instruction because they support an implicitly unchangeable curriculum.

- Teachers may be unsure about administrator commitment (Anders & Levine, 1990). Administrators may (1) not give a clear expectation for change, (2) not have a reputation for following through, (3) view change as only something being implemented in response to "central office pressure," and/or (4) give mixed signals regarding what is important.

One way of looking at blockages to change is Carnine's (1988, pp. 62–66) description of discrediting, delaying, distorting, and, ultimately, discontinuing tactics.

- *Discrediting:* Innovations are usually discredited through activities such as:
  —Attributing their success to unique factors not found in other settings ("Sure, let's just see that work with *my* kids!")
  —Objecting to the values represented by the innovation

—Questioning, criticizing, and ignoring any evaluation that judges the innovation to be effective ("Just goes to show, you can prove *anything* with research.")

—Claiming that the innovative practice has already been incorporated into current practices

—Simply ignoring the innovation's success.

- *Delaying:* The widespread adoption of an educational innovation can take at least ten times as long as the adoption of a new drug (Carlson, 1964).

- *Distorting:* Although a process of adaptation seems reasonable for an untried innovation, adaptation may become a euphemism for distortion. A district may adapt only part of an innovation and then attribute the subsequent failure to the entire innovation. Or a practice may be implemented in name only.

- *Discontinuing:* Rowan (1977) found that innovations that had nothing to do with instruction had the greatest likelihood of survival. Those that dealt with instruction were terminated most quickly. Sometimes termination of a program is a reflection of political rather than pedagogical realities.

Meyer, Scott, and Deal (1979, p. 3) explain that schools are not organized around a knowledge base for delivering quality instruction:

> It is most crucial for a school, in order to survive, to conform to institutional rules—including community understandings—defining teacher categories and credentials, pupil selection and definition, proper topics of instruction, and appropriate facilities. It is less essential that a school make sure that teaching and learning activities are efficiently coordinated.

Fraatz (1987), a sociologist who did extensive observations in schools and gave us an enlightened outsider's perspective, discusses why it is so difficult for reading specialists, for district-level personnel, for principals, and for parents to effect change. What follows is a gross oversimplification of her thesis, but a key problem for resource specialists and principals is that you can be effective only if you have cooperation. To achieve that cooperation, you need to compromise, often to a fault. Because principals and resource teachers rely so much on teachers' good will, Fraatz finds teachers to be the real power base in the school. Onore and Lester (1985) also argue that "if change is ever to occur, it is the teachers themselves who must carry it out" (p. 11). Teachers have the power to ignore you. You cannot be effective without them, but they can often be effective without you.

## Stages of Readiness for Change

Do you remember the first time you heard of some new term, like *whole language, metacognition,* or *cooperative learning?* Were you instantly ready to implement the new notion in a variety of settings? Of course not. We all go through stages of readiness for change. The challenge is to realize that others will be at different stages of readiness at different times.

If you didn't know better, you might suppose that change is easy once people have "seen the light." This, of course, is not the case. Gilbert (1978) illustrates this point by telling the story of a training course for Korean War soldiers on how to avoid trenchfoot and frostbite, greater sources of casualties than gunshot wounds. The point of the lecture was "Keep Your Socks Dry!" Even after watching movies of toes falling off, soldiers simply would not go to the trouble to keep their socks dry. (If you think you're immune, think about the food you eat or the tobacco you smoke even though you know better!).

## TIPS · DETERMINING THE NEED FOR CHANGE

When evaluating the need for change, consider the following:

- State the change you want to introduce.

- Identify the state of affairs that helped you to conclude that a change is desirable.

- Decide what others in the school have to gain or lose if the change effort is successful. If, for example, the desired change is for teachers to spend more time with a low group than with a high group, then if you know that it is more satisfying for many teachers to work with the high group, you will be prepared for possible resistance.

- Determine what effect would be felt by the whole organization if the change were successful. Consider the price tag in terms of dollars, time, and faculty morale as well as student achievement.

## Strategies for Change

You know that your students must be strategic learners, that they need to learn when, where, why, and how to apply each strategy that they learn. The same applies to change agents. You cannot expect that simply because you are competent, you will automatically be able to effect change. You should use strategic wisdom in planning: Know what to do and what not to do, know why you are doing something, and know when, where, and how to do it.

## TIPS · STRATEGIES FOR CHANGE

- Try to work with an interested group rather than an individual. Because change is stressful and stress actually results in the brain's inhibiting teacher creativity and openness to change, you will have a better chance of success when there is group support (Caine & Caine, 1991, pp. 64–67, 175).

- Set a collaborative tone. The idea is to learn from one another.

- Remember that a group should have (1) ownership and (2) knowledge regarding the change effort. Without these, teachers may try your idea

*(continued)*

### TIPS (continued)

without understanding why they are doing so. If an idea is not immediately successful, it may well be promptly dropped. To win a group over to change, you may spend more time on rapport building than you spend in actual assistance.

*   Realize that ownership is greatest when teachers have control of when and how change is implemented in their classrooms (see Wollman-Bonilla, 1991).

*   Use people's personal agendas. Some respond to praise, others to the opportunity to lead. Remember that we all march to different drummers!

### Force Field Analysis

Use Force Field Analysis (Kast & Rosenzweig, 1974) to help you identify the forces for and against change in your building. You will always have both. The key is to maximize the former and minimize the latter.

---

**FORCE FIELD ANALYSIS**

Follow these pointers:

*   Define the change goal precisely enough that action can be planned.
*   List forces *for* and *against* change. Examples of the former include clearly set goals; time, effort, and product worth the amount of change accomplished; and change seen as betterment of self, students, professionals, and program. Forces against change can include cynicism, lack of trust, and lack of motivation.
*   Decide which forces are most important, hardest to deal with, and most amenable to change with your influence.
*   Choose a strategy: Decide on action that is required to (1) weaken or eliminate hindering forces, (2) strengthen helping forces, or (3) add new helping forces.

---

Following is an example of Force Field Analysis:

*Goal:* The principal is enlisting your support in implementing a whole language curriculum in the computer lab.

| *Forces for the change* | *Forces against the change* |
| --- | --- |
| You agree with the principal about this change. | Faculty is unsure about the program's potential for effecting positive change. |
| Faculty will be informed about the change and given a chance to vote on it. | The computer lab aide may be reluctant to maintain the added communication with the teachers that would be needed for an effective program. |

There is sufficient hardware and software.

There is little knowledge at the school about how to make this work.

School-based management has had the effect of increasing openness to change.

There is little time for training on this program.

There are contingency funds that can be used.

The assistant principal is seriously ill and will not be able to help.

You have good rapport with all concerned parties.

The PTA doesn't want any such newfangled program to interfere with the current computer lab operation.

There is no rush to start the program.

*Strategy:* After weighing the items in both of these lists, you consider whether to use persuasion or coercion, knowing full well that sometimes what is needed is a combination of both. Coercion can be a powerful tool—think of school attendance as a driver's license requirement, for example. But you opt to emphasize persuasion. You smile as you think of people you know who got much more accomplished with a carrot than with a stick—for example, the supervisor who left a rose on her superintendent's desk every week and who received unbelievable support for her resource teachers.

1. You recognize that the faculty can probably be convinced once they know more about the program. You know that once the faculty is sold on the program, it won't be as hard to turn the PTA around.

2. You can take advantage of the forces working for you by trying to get a promise for contingency funds for substitute teachers so that staff development will be possible during the school day, when teachers are more receptive. Knowing of this fund availability will influence some teachers' votes. Moreover, teachers can be reassured that the program would not begin until they have received the proper inservice training.

3. You know that it is a good strategy to enlist the help of reluctant staff members. For example, you take advantage of your good rapport with the computer aide and your understanding of her hidden agenda (reluctance to spend additional time communicating with teachers). You work out a form for written communication, emphasizing that the use of written communication will cut back on the time needed for oral communication. You also offer to help as a communications link, realizing that this will give you an "in" with some of the teachers you haven't yet reached. You may not completely change the aide, but at least you have neutralized the situation.

4. You have a meeting with key PTA players and key faculty members soon after the teachers agree to give the program a shot. You invite the PTA members to visit the lab once it has been in operation for one month. You promise to meet with the PTA members after their visit to the lab if they so request.

5. Recognizing that it is always comfortable to go back to old ways, you systematically monitor and support this change throughout the school year.

### Rosabeth Moss Kanter Model

Rosabeth Moss Kanter (1989), a professor at Harvard, author of *The Change Masters,* and consultant for Fortune 500 corporations, uses *Alice in Wonderland* as a metaphor for the change process. Like Alice in the croquet match, she says, we may feel as if we're sometimes trying to drive evasive hedgehogs through constantly moving wickets while the Queen of Hearts bellows new and contradictory orders at whim. How do you convince colleagues to design a more appropriate curriculum when the state or the district keeps changing mandates or curricular guidelines?

Kanter cites some "F's" for change, among them that change should be *focused, flexible,* and *friendly:*

*Focused:* Kanter cites the example of Brigham Young, who didn't say, "I'll go West for awhile, and if that doesn't work I'll try another direction." Nor did Martin Luther King, Jr., say, "I have a few ideas; let's start a few committees." Rather, such leaders had focused visions and tenaciously pursued their dreams.

*Flexible:* As teachers, we are masters of flexibility. Kanter gives a business example of flexibility: a CEO who had his board of directors arrested by security guards and taken out of the board meeting before he helicoptered them to a new location. His point? They were not to start being bogged down by old ideas. The new location symbolized a fresh start. Kanter speaks also of kaleidoscope thinking—rearranging resources to form a myriad of possibilities. We should not, however, be so flexible that we lose focus.

*Friendly:* Contrary to popular belief, this is not an "each man or woman for him- or herself" world. We need each other to effect change.

Kanter then adds two more "F's" for good measure: *family* and *fun.* We should remember to keep room in our plans for our families and for fun. Kanter cites the Massachusetts Institute of Technology (MIT) as an example of a place where fun—via a playful, irreverent attitude—fosters a great deal of creativity.

### TIPS · ADAPTATION OF ROSABETH MOSS KANTER MODEL

- *Be focused.*
  —Post your school's philosophy (or goals) on the wall if that's what it will take to stay focused.
  —A slogan can help achieve focus. "We Make a Difference" campaigns in Florida ("Teachers make a difference" "Students make a difference," etc.) have been effective. Or think of "Just Say No to Drugs."
  —An Action Plan will help you keep on target (see Appendix C).

- *Be flexible.* Our resources may not vary, but we can vary the way we arrange them. We remember one office clerk who was a reading zealot. When she was on lunchroom duty, she read to the previously rowdy students and told them knock-knock jokes. You could have heard a pin drop in the cafeteria.

- *Be friendly.* It's hard for people to fight a friendly face. Your friendliness will go a long way toward effecting change.

## Sales Agent Model

Your role as a change agent is partly one of sales promotion. You send information into the free marketplace of ideas in the hope that it will be purchased. You act like a traveling salesperson who tries to drum up business through personal techniques as well as through the quality of the product. You offer advice in response to a client-initiated need, and ultimately a product or service is negotiated (Gallagher, Goudvis, & Pearson, 1988).

# TIPS · SALES AGENT MODEL

Use techniques of the business world when dealing with teachers' "sales resistance" (Burgett, 1976). This includes speaking the customer's language:

- Use the terminology of shop, home economics, or special education classes, for example.

- Change the labels associated with the product in order to sell it. "Reading" strategies can be translated into "learning" or "thinking" strategies.

Sometimes your sales efforts will have greater effect for ambitious, demanding programs than for a routine project. Teachers are willing to take on extra work if they believe their efforts will make them better teachers and will help their students (Samuels & Edwall, 1976).

---

### FIFTY EXCUSES FOR WHY IT WON'T WORK

We can always find excuses as to why something won't work.
Use the following list (from the Connecticut newsletter of the Association of Children and Adults with Learning Disabilities) as comic relief if you want to avoid hearing excuses:

1. We tried that before.
2. Our system is different.
3. It costs too much.
4. That's beyond our responsibility.
5. That's not my job.
6. We're all too busy to do that.
7. It's too radical a change.
8. There's not enough help.
9. We've never done it before.
10. We don't have the authority.
11. There's not enough time.
12. Let's get back to reality.
13. That's not our problem.
14. Why change it? It's still working O.K.

15. I don't like that idea.
16. You're right, but . . .
17. You're two years ahead of your time.
18. It isn't in the budget.
19. We're not ready for that.
20. Sounds O.K. but impractical.
21. Let's give it more thought.
22. That's my bowling day.
23. That doesn't affect me or my child.
24. Nobody cares about that.
25. We've always done it this way.
26. It might not work.
27. Not that again!
28. Where'd you dig that one up?
29. We did all right without it.
30. It's never been tried before.
31. Let's shelve it for the time being.
32. I don't see the connection.
33. What you are really saying is . . .
34. Let's not be the first.
35. Maybe that would work in your class but not in mine.
36. The administration will never go for it.
37. It can't be done.
38. It's too much trouble.
39. It's impossible.
40. You're not here to think.
41. Can't teach an old dog new tricks.
42. Let me think about that and I'll get back to you.
43. Let's wait until the next administration.
44. State says (I can't remember who) we can't do that.
45. We can't fight City Hall.
46. That's old/new business and can't be discussed now.
47. That's too serious a subject.
48. No one is interested.
49. It's too early to think about it.
50. It's too late to start.

Yet, excuses notwithstanding, change can be rewarding. Wollman-Bonilla (1991) quotes one experienced teacher: "For the first time in my life I feel like shouting from the tops of buildings about something that's happening in my classroom!" (p. 120), and asserts that, with effective staff development, many more teachers can be moved to feel this exuberance.

## Conclusion

To the original roles of change agent as politician, energizer, manager, detective, salesperson, and hero, we must add the role of juggler. As you juggle all these roles, keep a close eye on the task at hand. Return to this section for a periodic refresher course as your faculty progresses through stages of the change process.

# PART TWO

# The Resource Role: The Content

The second half of the handbook focuses on the content that the RRS needs to know. The graphic organizer below gives you a picture of these key areas.

**THE RESOURCE ROLE: THE CONTENT**

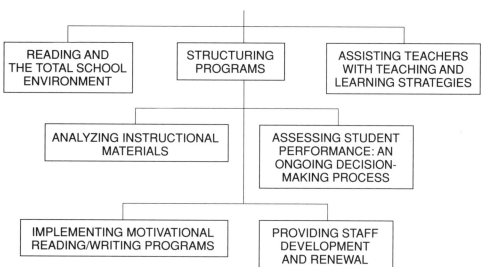

# Reading and the Total School Environment

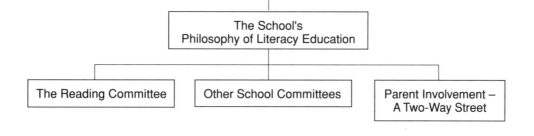

**A**S AN RRS YOU ARE of course involved with the total school environment. If the school's philosophy of literacy education is a jigsaw puzzle frame, then you are one of many essential jigsaw puzzle pieces. Make yourself invaluable to as many committees as you can possibly manage. Be a team player.

## The School's Philosophy of Literacy Education

You might question the value of philosophy, because philosophies are sometimes written and then forgotten. But we have seen great success when businesses or school staffs pull together and then march in the same direction. One high school we know won the meritorious high school award for the county three years in a row. Although they did not specifically start with a philosophy, they did spend an entire planning day each year coming up with a schoolwide project. The resulting sense of ownership was quite powerful. In the case of an elementary school, schoolwide decisions concerning the need for a basal reading series or concerning which series to use can be quite traumatic when everyone is going his or her own way. Having a literacy philosophy drafted by a reading committee (to be discussed below) and then modified by the staff can pave the way for less traumatic decisions.

Your work as an RRS should be based on the overall school philosophy and program. One of your responsibilities may be helping to ensure that classroom organization matches the school philosophy. If, for instance, a school is moving into a whole language orientation in which reading is integrated with other subject areas, this philosophy will dictate changes in student scheduling from what might have existed previously. Following are three scenarios:

- If elementary students were cross-grouped for reading within a grade in order to reduce the range of levels in each reading class, they might now be cross-grouped for a longer reading/language arts period rather than for reading alone. This might require that you help teachers reexamine their use of language arts and reading textbooks.

- If a middle school adopts a Nancie Atwell (1987) philosophy of using coordinated reading and writing workshops, the same teacher might be assigned to both reading and language arts periods, with these periods scheduled back to back. This would then require that you train teachers whose expertise might be in only reading or writing, but not in both (more about this under "Secondary School Models" in Chapter 6).

• If you are a secondary RRS and your school works from a departmental perspective, then you might be called upon to assist counselors in placing students into tracked classrooms (see the "Secondary School Models" section in Chapter 6).

## The Reading Committee

You may well find more support for a project requested by a reading committee (Anders, 1985) than for one of your own design. A wise RRS will try to work through a reading committee made up of influential people in the school. The committee might include an administrator, parents, students, grade chairs or department heads, a union representative, an exceptional education teacher, and well-respected teachers overall. Be sure to invite any other reading teachers in the school, and structure meetings to allow for an open-door policy. Be prepared with ideas about the outcomes you would like to see emerge from the committee so that you can help lead the committee in these directions. Use an Action Plan like the one in Appendix C to guide your efforts.

## Other School Committees

As an RRS, you should be highly visible on school committees. One RRS who began with a reluctant principal now has the principal solidly on her side. She owes this to the fact that she is a team player. She is willing to work behind the scenes whenever she is needed. Committee work also gives an RRS more opportunities to slip in his or her message. For example, if a middle school RRS serves as a permanent member of one interdisciplinary team or as a resource to several teams, this work can provide opportunities to bring up pertinent reading strategies or journal articles, and simply to increase rapport with the faculty.

## Parent Involvement—A Two-Way Street

We give parents mixed messages. We want their help with our reading programs, as we do with all our efforts, but we don't always make them feel welcome. This can be particularly problematic for parents who experienced difficulty in school themselves and who therefore may avoid the school as adults. Use the following tips as you work with your administrators and teachers to encourage parent support and involvement.

### TIPS · THE RRS AND PARENTS

• Have inservice sessions for teachers on how to get parents to attend PTA/PTO meetings. Here are a few ideas:
  —Have students perform.

—Make arrangements for the children (such as a storytelling session in another room).

—Remember the refreshments!

—Address topics that will be of interest to parents. Aside from the usual topics such as understanding test scores, look for timely topics such as finding time to read to your child when you are a single parent. A special meeting for fathers may help bring in those who normally let their wives attend. In some areas you might need a session on gangs, AIDS, or crack cocaine. Do whatever it takes. Once the parents are there, you can supplement the program with reading-related issues.

- Have inservice sessions for teachers on how to communicate with parents.

—Call parents early in the year before there is any reason for a complaint. This establishes a positive rapport and may help avoid the assumption that any call from the teacher must be bad news.

—*Listen* to parents! They have agendas just as teachers do. Find ways in which teachers can help parents with *their* agendas.

—Meet parents side by side. Sitting authoritatively behind the desk is as bad as sitting authoritatively behind educational jargon!

—Brainstorm with teachers on how to make parents feel a part of the school community so that they will be involved on an ongoing basis.

—Find ways in which working parents can help out. Maybe they can help with some paperwork at home. Maybe they can encourage neighbors to send their truant children to school. Maybe they can take off a day or give up a lunch break to come and speak on Career Day or to serve as a field trip chaperone.

- If possible, principals may require that parents pick up report cards. This could be used as a drastic measure for getting parents of secondary students into the school and making sure they see these report cards.

- Educate parents and keep them informed with regular newsletters, flyers, or radio/television announcements for those who can't read. In multicultural communities, use the media from each cultural group. We know of one secondary school which provided parents with a flipchart of information on study skills, interpretation of test scores, and the like.

- The principal can involve parents in decision-making, advisory, or service committees. Make clear the parameters of these committees' roles to avoid any misunderstandings.

- The principal can have community school activities after school. Parents who get used to coming to the school for flower arranging or aerobics may be more willing to come on other occasions. One inner-city Philadelphia principal went so far as to install washing machines for community use!

- Plan activities that specifically relate to reading.

—Parents can have a "lunch bunch" reading club (an award-winning PTA project) with small groups of students who read and discuss the same books.

—Parents can receive literacy training while students participate in a homework club.

(*continued*)

**TIPS (continued)**

—Parents can help with incentive reading programs, mounting displays, gathering rewards from the community, and the like.

—Parents can sign contracts specifying that they will read aloud to their children on a daily basis. Volunteers can help fill out certificates or help plan a spaghetti dinner for children and parents who complete their contracts.

• Consult the section on "Outside Resources" in Chapter 2 or references such as Edwards' (1990) Parents as Partners in Reading program for further ideas.

## Conclusion

As you have seen from this chapter, you can be a key to setting the tone for the total school environment. Collaborating with everyone within and outside the school can help to build stronger commitment. Be visible and enthusiastic, and watch the improvements occur!

# Structuring Programs

| Physical Design and Appearance of Classrooms | Curriculum | Student Placement and Grouping |

**U**NTIL CLASSROOMS ARE STRUCTURED, little else can be accomplished. And what goes on in the classroom is often intimately linked with the classroom's structure. Changes in classroom structures can be traumatic because they affect discipline and classroom control. Your role in this area can be a critical one.

## Physical Design and Appearance of Classrooms

One of your first steps as an RRS with some teachers may well be to help with the physical design and appearance of a classroom. Classroom arrangement can have a lot to do with student engagement. Anyone walking into the room makes an initial judgment of the teacher on the basis of what is seen. But you should move with care. Changes in classroom structure can be traumatic because they affect discipline and classroom control. Remember that it is the teacher who will live in the room, so the teacher will have to buy into any new arrangement.

Your help to teachers may take several forms:

- Discussing alternative arrangements and possibly showing teachers classrooms arranged differently

- Brainstorming ways to involve students in planning their environment

- Helping teachers gather needed materials (e.g., free carpet squares at carpet outlets, needed furniture that you have seen sitting unused elsewhere in the school)

- Physically helping with any rearranging

Questions to ask include the following:

- Are materials laid out for easy access?

- Can all students see the board?

- If students sit in rows rather than at tables or clusters of desks, is there any other provision for cooperative learning—maybe carpeting so that students can sprawl on the floor?

- If there is a thin divider with another classroom, is furniture arranged

53

so that each teacher's voice will tend to carry into his or her own room rather than into the adjacent room?

- Are accommodations made for students with physical handicaps?

Once you have attended to the basic physical design, look at the overall appearance.

- Is your first impression one of a classroom "marinated" in literacy, or is it one of piles of dittos?

- Are the bulletin boards student-made rather than store-bought? How about student-made borders for bulletin boards?

You can encourage school administrators to rotate faculty or committee meetings in attractively decorated rooms. This strategy can work wonders in motivating teachers to keep rooms bathed in literacy.

Beyond questions of physical design and appearance of classrooms are those which relate to the school as a whole. A dull library and dreary hallways do nothing to enhance enthusiasm. An RRS can enlist the aid of students, a rotating committee of teachers, or an art teacher to liven things up. Visitors can readily evaluate school priorities if they see:

- Teacher writing as well as student writing on display

- Permanent murals painted by students

- An attractive library shelf of books authored by students

- A rack with books and other material for students and parents to read when in the office—with one of your cards and a "Read while you wait" sign!

## Elementary Schools

Calkins and Harwayne (1991, pp. 11–12) admonish us to not "rush about filling the room with a variety of paper, bulletin boards, conference areas, editing checklists, and an author's chair—these will all come in time—but, instead, to fill the classroom with children's lives." They suggest that, "instead of stapling scalloped edges and cardboard horns of plenty onto our bulletin boards, we might let youngsters use bulletin boards as a place for announcements, jokes, news about ticket sales, [and] displays of artwork, writing, quotes and posters, maps and photographs."

Authentic print-rich environments should be taken one step at a time. Gradually, you may be able to help teachers come to see the need for elements such as the following. The list will, of course, vary by grade level:

- Do classroom arrangements provide for a variety of groupings?

- Does classroom management use print? Is/are there . . .
  —a mailbox(es)?                  —a message board?
  —labels and printed signs?       —daily routines posted?
  —helper charts?                  —attendance charts?
  —center assignments?             —a calendar?

- Are there displays of words that might be helpful in writing?

- Is recent work from every student readily visible? If writing is displayed, is it individual writing or are all the papers "carbon copies"?

- Has an effort been made to hang student writing at student eye level?

- If display space is limited, are creative solutions found (e.g., clotheslines with writing clipped to them, walls outside the rooms used as bulletin boards)?

- Do classrooms have learning centers: a listening center, a reading corner, a writing center? Are centers logically placed? For example, a quiet reading corner would not work well next to a noisier kitchen center. Are the centers well designed? If not, children will not use them.

- Does the reading corner stand out when someone first enters the room?
  —Does it display the covers of some books?
  —Does it have a comfortable feel to it (e.g., bean bag chairs, area rugs, an old sofa, a bathtub, a rocker)?
  —Is it well stocked with a variety of age-appropriate and ability-appropriate material?
    - at least five to eight books per child?
    - multiple copies of favorite books?
    - appropriate reference materials (illustrated dictionaries, encyclopedias, maps, directories, etc.)?
    - a variety of magazines (e.g., *Sports Illustrated for Kids, Highlights for Children,* a nature magazine)?

- Is the writing center well planned? Are there
  —index cards for students' own words?
  —materials for making books?
  —postcards, stationery, envelopes, and stamps?
  —various colors and sizes of papers?
  —various kinds of markers and pencils?
  —spelling aids for high-frequency words?
  —story stimulators and motivators?
  —a typewriter?
  —scissors, glue, tape, old magazines?
  —alphabet chart, tactile letters?
  —writing folders?

- How about a day-to-day print center with newspapers, restaurant menus, coupons, and the like? Or a unit center focusing on a current theme? Or ad hoc centers that change throughout the year?

Try having contests for the best library corners or the best bulletin boards; be sure to use judges from outside the school. And remember to take photographs or arrange walk-throughs of winning rooms for all to enjoy.

## Secondary Schools

Design and appearance of secondary classrooms gives clues to whether cooperative learning is encouraged, whether celebrating student writing is important, and whether reading of trade books, magazines, and newspapers is a major part of the instruction. Secondary teachers must often share classrooms. When there is no ownership in the classroom, its appearance may be no one's concern. Even when the room belongs to one teacher, the appearance can sometimes be improved. The RRS can make tactful suggestions or can help with room appearance—for example, by hanging up student work. The RRS can suggest that teachers who share a room rotate responsibility for its decoration. Of course, student help can be enlisted as well.

You can also attend to the appearance of the school as a whole. We know of one senior high school in which one sports trophy case was used to display prizes for a reading lottery (Lubell, 1991). At this same school, bookworm displays with additions for each book read were unabashedly hung all over the outside walls.

## Arrangement of Students in the Classroom

As an RRS, you should note where different students are placed within classrooms.

- Where are the lower and higher achievers sitting? You probably know that students seated in the front and center of the classroom are more likely to be noticed and asked to respond than are those on the room's periphery (Miller, 1988). Low-performing students might be enticed to participate if they are seated close to the teacher in the front of the classroom.

- Are students' seats grouped by reading level? This may be necessary if teachers are using ability groups and are in small rooms in which there is no space for students to gather around a table or on the carpet. But grouping by reading level further aggravates the problems inherent with ability grouping (see the section on "Student Placement and Grouping" later in this chapter).

- Are students grouped in cooperative heterogeneous groups—for example, two pairs of desks facing each other? This arrangement allows stronger students to help weaker peers and promotes cooperation among all students.

- Are mainstreamed exceptional education students or disruptive students isolated? This can be helpful for brief time-out periods, but it is damaging to the student's self-esteem when done for long periods of time.

In your role as an RRS in another teacher's classroom, you probably will not want to reassign students' seats. However, you might want to request using a semicircle or some other different seating pattern on the days you visit the class. Just by changing the seating pattern slightly, you may find that some of the less capable students respond more positively toward you. If you do move chairs, be sure to move them back at the end of the lesson. Changing the normal classroom configuration of space involves risk taking on your part, but it could provide more teacher–student interaction during the class. In addition, you would be modeling a technique that the classroom teacher might want to replicate to stimulate classroom discussion and students' motivation to learn.

## Curriculum

To some extent, your curriculum is probably set by state and district rules and by past practice. It is beyond the scope of this book to cover curriculum in depth, but a few issues do need to be mentioned in the context of structuring programs.

### Literacy Instruction

Philosophy for literacy instruction will be a key factor in determining your school's curriculum. At the elementary level, there may be a tug-of-war between traditional basal reading and more integrated holistic approaches. On the other hand, teachers may have found a comfort zone in using holistic approaches with whatever material they are provided—holistic basals, trade books, a combination, or whatever. Parallel situations could be envisioned at the secondary level.

We find ourselves avoiding the term *whole language* because it means so many different things to different people. Whole language myths abound (Newman & Church, 1991). The classic one is the notion that no phonics is taught with whole language. Bergeron (1990) surveyed 64 articles in an attempt to define whole language and found different definitions in each. Help your teachers sort through these issues by keeping abreast of current literature. Some of the sources you can turn to for updated coverage of curriculum issues are Heinemann, Scholastic, and Owen publishers, the National Council of Teachers of English, and the International Reading Association (see "Suggested Readings" in Appendix C).

If, as is true in most of the United States and other English-speaking countries, your school is moving toward a more integrated approach, there are several terms with which you will want to be very familiar. The following Whole Language Glossary may help:

---

**WHOLE LANGUAGE GLOSSARY**

*Whole language (our definition):* A philosophy of education at all grade levels in which listening, speaking, reading, and writing across the curriculum are integrated and are taught with a whole-to-part rather than a part-to-whole skills-based perspective; a political movement of empowering teachers and students to make decisions based on ongoing observation; a child-centered perspective that bases learning on authentic reading and writing experiences.

*Writing process:* Although there is really no universal process of writing, the field refers to the writing process as a recursive, not linear, process in which writers go through the following stages, with teacher and peer conferencing anywhere along the way:

- *Prewriting:* Thinking about what to write, perhaps based on material found in experiences or in books, perhaps with help from activities such as free writing and clustering.

- *Drafting:* Getting something down on paper.

- *Revising:* Improving the content (not yet the mechanics!) of the

---

draft—perhaps a better beginning sentence, an improved sequence, or an increased use of truly descriptive language.

- *Editing:* Correcting spelling and mechanics.

- *Publishing:* Sharing one's writing through reading it aloud, mailing it to someone, posting it on a bulletin board, and the like. See "Magazines and Contests that Accept Young Writers' Work" in Appendix B.

*Invented spelling:* We find that the term *temporary spelling* goes over better with parents. It fosters the understanding that children go through a set of predictable levels in learning to spell just as they do in learning to walk or to talk. Indeed, a book written by a teacher (Barron, 1990) that makes that point to parents in a very user-friendly manner is: "I IAEN TO RAed AND WRT Th WA I LAEN TO Tak."

*Literature-based (as contrasted to skill-based):* A curriculum that starts with the literature and pulls skills from the literature, at its best without overdoing the skill work and without neglecting expository reading.

### Literacy across the Curriculum

Reading and writing should occur across the curriculum. To facilitate this, teachers may have to resequence their textbooks. For example, an elementary teacher doing a basal unit on animals at the beginning of the year might move up an end-of-the-year science chapter on animals to correlate this instruction. We know of one middle school in which sixth-grade science and social studies departments decided with the reading teacher which of their objectives could be covered in reading class. The content teachers gave the reading teachers some materials to help with this instruction. We know of one senior high school that reorganized its sequence of novels to match the social studies curriculum. Your job responsibilities will probably include helping your school find their own way of integrating literacy across the curriculum.

## Student Placement and Grouping

As an RRS you may be asked to provide suggestions for student placement and grouping. A number of parameters should be considered in making these decisions. A key issue is, of course, your school philosophy. Following are discussions of some other important issues.

### Heterogeneous versus Homogeneous Grouping

One issue on which you are likely to find strong opinions is that of heterogeneous versus homogeneous grouping. When we group students homogeneously, it has been with the intention of better meeting their needs through different materials, pacing, and techniques. However, ability grouping and tracking work better for the high achievers than for their peers (Slavin, 1987a). Yet, there is some evidence that high achievers often do as well in heterogeneous groups as they do in homogeneous groups (Oakes, 1986). For social and academic reasons, high achievers should probably spend some time in both settings.

Strict homogeneous grouping is unquestionably damaging to low achievers (Keating & Oakes, 1988; Oakes, 1986; Slavin, 1987a; Wilkinson & Calculator, 1982). It is discriminating (albeit unconsciously) in the following ways:

- Lower self-esteem and expectations from the student, the teacher, and the parent

- Greater emphasis on isolated skills

- Less homework assigned

- Less actual instructional time

- Fewer high-level questions and shorter wait time for questions (which, in turn, leads students to realize that, if they wait long enough, the teacher will call on someone else and they'll be off the hook)

- More discipline problems

- Less likelihood of having requests responded to appropriately by other students

- Greater likelihood of receiving information on procedures and materials rather than on content

- Often, a lower degree of teacher enthusiasm

- Often, assignment to less qualified teachers

- A feeling of learned helplessness on the part of the students

All this results in a widening achievement gap, which is harder and harder to remedy as students move from grade to grade. E. D. Hirsch uses a snowball metaphor for this phenomenon: A big snowball will gather much more snow (information) than will a little one. It behooves us to make those snowballs big from the very start.

You may face quite a challenge in fostering an understanding of these problems. One effective weapon in your arsenal can be audiotapes for use by teachers who wish to monitor their treatment of different groups. Teachers who listen to their lessons on tape can compare their questioning techniques, level of enthusiasm, and instructional time with lower and higher achieving students.

Schools considering the elimination of special classes for high achievers need to realize that this is an unpopular move with most communities. Thus, they should consider the research cited here as well as local politics before undertaking a plan that could result in vocal community dissatisfaction.

Following are sections on (1) cooperative learning, a strategy that can be most helpful especially in working with heterogeneous groups of students, and (2) some specific elementary and secondary models that go beyond the issue of heterogeneous versus homogeneous grouping to look at grouping from a number of additional angles.

## Cooperative Learning

Cooperative learning is a method by which small heterogeneous groups of students work together to achieve a common goal. As you will see in reading this section, cooperative learning is not the same as the valuable technique of peer teaching, in which one student is the teacher and one is the learner. Nor is it the old-fashioned group project in which one student does all the work and the others act as "hitchhikers." As an instructional leader, you should be sure to read at least one of the many books that have been written on cooperative learning (e.g., Johnson, Johnson, & Holubec, 1990). In a multipurpose book like this one we can't give you all the information you'll need to help teachers do it well. Following are a few basic pointers (Johnson & Johnson, 1989):

1. *Positive interdependence:* This is the "sink or swim together" idea. Students must believe that they are responsible for both their own learning and the learning of the other members of their group. Thus, for example, each student can get a bonus on a spelling grade if each student in the group meets a preset goal.

2. *Face-to-face interaction:* Students have the opportunity to explain what they are learning to each other and to help each other understand and complete assignments.

3. *Individual accountability:* Each student must demonstrate mastery of the assigned work. Thus, at least some of the grades should be individual grades.

4. *Social skills:* Each student must communicate effectively, provide leadership for the group's work, build and maintain trust among group members, and resolve conflicts within the group constructively. Social goals are set ahead of time just as academic goals are. Some modeling and role playing of cooperative and noncooperative activities will be helpful. Groups may then be rewarded for specified verbal or nonverbal behavior (see also the section on "Content versus Process" in Chapter 11).

5. *Group processing:* Groups must stop periodically and assess how well they are working and how their effectiveness may be improved.

Cooperative learning is one of the few issues in education in which the research does not say, "It depends." A massive base of research on cooperative learning says that, when it is carried out well, for a part of student instruction, it can be very effective in terms of both social and academic goals for students of all ages and all socioeconomic groups (Johnson, Johnson, & Holubec, 1990). One caution: Lower achievers wear their disabilities on their sleeves during cooperative activities. Because they cannot fade into the woodwork as they can during whole class activities, they may not enjoy the group work. As the RRS, you can help teachers find ways of working around this problem—for example, by finding roles that each group member can carry out successfully.

Following are some suggestions for easing the way into cooperative learning:

• Brainstorm solutions to potential problems. Possible solutions to a noise level problem, for example, include the following:
—Install carpeting to muffle classroom noise.
—Teach students to use a twelve-inch voice when speaking in a group

(Johnson & Johnson, 1989); that is, their voices should not carry beyond twelve inches.

—If appropriate to the activity, have pairs of students sit in chairs that are side by side, facing in opposite directions, so that they can hear each other when speaking in a very low volume.

—Teach students to respond to signals. "Quiet" might be signaled to elementary students with lights out, or to students of any age with, "If you can hear me clap once, if you can hear me clap twice, . . ." Rarely will you need to go beyond "clap three times" before you have the group back with you.

—Reward groups that display the appropriate behavior.

—Remember that noise can be a sign of a productive classroom environment.

• Become a group member to role-play appropriate and inappropriate group behaviors.

• Make sure that the teacher's roles are those of careful planner, monitor, and cheerleader. Encourage students to solve problems within their groups. Johnson and Johnson (1989) tell the story of a student who came to the teacher complaining that a fellow student wouldn't get out from under the table. The teacher sent the student back to solve the problem with his peers. Next time the teacher looked over that way, the whole group was busily working under the table! If necessary, you might give a group a choice of ways to solve a problem. But let *them* make the decision!

• Explain to parents the reasons for cooperative learning. Parents of brighter students sometimes object to its use. They should understand the role of metacognition—that is, the importance to their children of being able to understand and explain their own thought processes. These parents also can be told of a Harvard study (Coons, 1989) in which college graduates reported that the most serious omission in their education was a failure to learn to work cooperatively in groups. The more competitive our society, the greater the need for cooperation. However, cooperative learning and peer tutoring should not be abused. Teachers should make sure high achievers are not overused as tutors and that their grades and learning do not suffer.

• Arrange grading carefully, including individual and group grades, to make it possible for all groups to experience success. Using extra points rather than grades for group work helps students develop a positive attitude toward the group work; students will then be less likely to feel penalized because of the work of their fellow group members. Be careful about using extrinsic rewards, however. Kohn (1991) makes a strong case that extrinsic rewards take away intrinsic student motivation.

• Start with simple and/or quick activities involving pairs (particularly for teachers afraid of losing class control).

—Students take turns reading to each other.

—Students take turns (1) giving an answer to a computer screen and (2) approving the answer and punching the appropriate key (this helps eliminate guessing).

—Students help each other with varying stages of the writing process.

—Use a Think-Pair-Share, a Listen-Think-Pair-Share, or a Think-Pair-Share-Write variation (McTighe & Lyman, 1988). This strategy (see Chapter 11) produces much more student involvement than when only one student answers the question. As Kohn (1987) has pointed out, "It's hard to get left out of a pair."

• Expand to groups of three of four. Form groups that are heterogeneous by gender, ethnicity, and ability. Authorities differ about the best size for such groups. It depends in part on the nature of the task. Groups of more than four, however, may not provide enough opportunities for all students to interact.

• Form groups that can be expected to work well as a team. Then keep the groups at least until they do function well together. Initial problems of "I don't want to work with him or her" can be handled by reminding students that the groups will rotate. The arrival of a new student in the room can be used as the pretext for disbanding a group that is not working well. Often, despite any initial problems, the children in a group become so friendly that they help each other on homework as well as classwork.

• Use isolation as a strategy for a student who will not work with a group. Losing the privilege of working with the group can sometimes help students see the light.

## Elementary School Models

*Traditional Grouping:* Elementary students generally have been either grouped heterogeneously into three groups for reading instruction, or cross-grouped. Both these models evolved from a desire to meet individual needs, but both involve homogeneous grouping, the problems with which have been discussed. Additional pitfalls particular to low reading groups are:

- More interruptions of oral reading rather than letting the student read on and go back to self-correct

- More interruptions with "Sound it out" than with "Does that make sense?"

- Slower pacing

- Fewer words in each selection

- Fewer opportunities for silent reading

- More use of "round robin" reading, with a resulting decrease of time on task

As Allington (1977, p. 57) aptly points out, "If they don't read much, how they ever gonna get good?"

With cross-grouping, students who are grouped heterogeneously in their regular classes are regrouped into different teachers' classes to narrow the range of reading levels during the reading block. Thus, teachers A, B, and C would redistribute their students according to reading level for this period of time. The disadvantage of cross-grouping is that it breaks the continuity of instruction on the part of a teacher who might otherwise integrate material across subject areas throughout the day. To minimize this problem, it is crucial that teachers who cross-group meet and plan together on a regular basis. You can periodically assist with this planning.

*Joplin plan and success for all:* A seldom-used but effective (Slavin, 1987b) variation of cross-grouping is the Joplin Plan, in which intermediate students are regrouped for reading instruction across grade levels (Floyd, 1954). Grouping across grade levels has been successfully extended into the primary grades in the Success for All program (Slavin, 1990).

*Flexible grouping:* Elementary teachers implementing a holistic philosophy may teach an entire class of heterogeneous students from the same trade books or may use a "core selection on grade level" approach from a basal series. Because little has been written about flexible grouping, and because it is a model being adopted by so many school districts, we will discuss it here in depth.

As noted previously, there is much research that questions ability grouping (e.g., Barr, 1989; Hiebert, 1983). And there is initial research regarding the effectiveness of plans such as the "core selection on grade level" approach (Cunningham, 1991b; Cunningham & Hall, 1991; Martin, 1991; Paratore, 1991; Radencich et al., 1992). Teaching all students with the same material can give the teacher more time to integrate subject areas than would be possible using ability groups. Teachers across the country report that low achievers try harder when they have the opportunity to work with their peers. Using this model can help teachers avoid the pitfalls of homogeneous grouping mentioned earlier.

For this model to be successful with both high and low achievers, however, *it cannot be simply one big reading group. Low achievers must be exposed on a daily basis to reading material with which they are comfortable. It is also crucial that flexible grouping be part of the plan.* Thus, a given classroom might, during the course of a week, have a variety of different types of groups.

Even in schools where the bulk of the instruction is delivered through in-class or between-class ability grouping, there should be some flexibility. You can help teachers structure their classes using various types of groups. If teachers are using only one type of group, you can start by helping them incorporate one additional type into their overall class structure.

Note the overlap among the group types that follow:

1. *Cooperative groups:* Cooperative groups are small, mixed-ability groups in which every member plays a specific role in completing a task. (See the section on "Cooperative Learning" earlier in this chapter).

2. *Interest groups:* Interest groups are a form of cooperative groups that are ideal for completion of theme projects. Students self-select their groups. You and the library/media specialist can help gather theme-related material.

3. *Partner groups:* Pairs are the easiest form of cooperative grouping for teachers to manage. Following are some ideas for paired activities:
   - *Buddy reading:* Students take turns reading to each other. Repeated readings are especially important for lower achievers. Each buddy can choose to read either a paragraph or a page.
   - *Peer editing:* Students read their writing to one another and help each other in various stages of the writing process.
   - *Completion of tasks:* Pairs of students can help each other with worksheets, computer software, spelling lists, and the like.
   - *Think-Pair-Share:* See the section on "Content versus Process" in Chapter 11 for details.

4. *Skill/strategy groups:* Teachers may pull groups of students who need work on a particular skill or strategy. These groups could include both high- and low-achieving youngsters who happen to need the same skill. You may need to model for teachers so they can see how, after pulling skills out of context, they can put them back in context before a lesson is over.

5. *Ability groups:* Ability groups are another type of flexible group that teachers will want to use periodically. Possible uses of ability groups are as follows:

   • Preteach students needing extra help. This can take place one or two days before the introduction of a unit to give the students a head start with background knowledge, vocabulary, and/or a read-aloud. We call this strategy "early bird." It is particularly effective in that it gives students who normally don't shine a chance to show off when the selection is introduced to the whole class, because there may be something that *they* now know that others do not. The early bird strategy can be used by the teacher, a volunteer, an aide, a pull-out teacher, or an RRS. Users tell us that "It works!"

   • For lower achieving students, supplement the core selection with a predictable language book or other simple text that is a logical extension of the selection (e.g., same author, same topic, same genre). You can be instrumental in locating this type of material. It might mean borrowing from a teacher of younger students, making books, or borrowing from a colleague at a neighboring school.

   To accommodate students who are particularly weak readers, you can reduce the amount of material that they practice. They can do repeated readings (Samuels, 1979) on the first and last pages, on the first page, on the first paragraph, or if necessary on a summary of the selection. This gives them the opportunity to hear themselves fluently read through a part of each selection.

   • Rotate a couple of high-achieving visitors to a low group.

   • Ask high achievers to extend class reading—for example, to read an entire book when the basal reader includes only a chapter or to read related books when the class is already reading an entire trade book. Teachers can pull these students together for instruction relating to such assignments.

Following is one specific flexible group model:

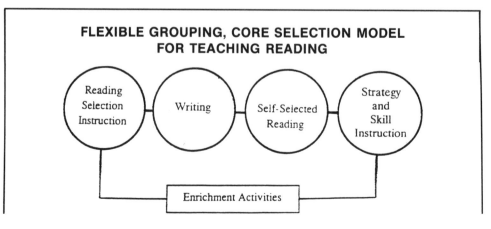

**FLEXIBLE GROUPING, CORE SELECTION MODEL
FOR TEACHING READING**

Reading Selection Instruction — Writing — Self-Selected Reading — Strategy and Skill Instruction

Enrichment Activities

The instructional framework used in Pinellas County, Clearwater, Florida, to teach reading with flexible grouping is symbolized by a "four circles" model. The essential elements of the model—reading selection instruction, writing, self-selected reading, and skill and strategy instruction—are linked by enrichment activities. The parallel placement of the circles signifies the equal importance of the four elements. They may be taught in any order. Interrelated and interdependent, the elements frequently overlap, and teachers often integrate them.

It is the intent that each of the four instructional elements be taught daily. Together, the four circle activities may fill the time a teacher would have devoted to the teaching of reading using ability groups, or they may fill the district's entire two-and-a-half-hour reading and language arts time block. The materials teachers use for reading include (1) a core selection, which is a grade-level text or paperback that all students use, and (2) a wide range of supplementary paperbacks and other reading materials. Following is a description of the model in detail.

*Reading Selection Instruction*
During the reading selection instructional time period, which occupies about one-fourth of daily reading time, the teacher instructs all students from a single on-grade-level text. The selection chosen may be from the basal text or a trade book. In most cases, the teacher delivers instruction initially to the whole class. This instruction is frequently followed by heterogeneously paired reading, cooperative group work, and/or small-group teaching. Instruction moves alternately between whole-group instruction and flexible grouping. The activities typically used in reading selection instruction can be grouped under four headings: (1) Preparing to Read, (2) Reading and Rereading, (3) Discussion, and (4) Skill Instruction and Practice. It usually takes two to three days to complete all four of these kinds of activities for one story.

*Preparing to read (primarily whole class).* Preparing to read is usually a whole-class activity. The teacher begins by building background and eliciting predictions in the traditional manner, and then often reads all or part of the text aloud to the students. New vocabulary is introduced through activities such as semantic mapping, and the teacher encourages students to ask questions about the selection. This activity takes about 15 to 20 minutes.

*Reading and rereading (primarily small flexible groups).* Students break into a wide variety of grouping patterns for reading and rereading. For example, some students might read the selection independently and write in response to what they have read, some students who need extra help might meet with the teacher for a guided reading lesson, and some students might listen to the selection on audio tape and write or draw in response to the selection. Next, all students who wrote or drew in response to the selection might meet with the teacher while the other students meet in pairs to review vocabulary words.

The entire class might then participate in partner oral reading of the grade-level text and rereading of familiar stories. Frequently teachers start reading and rereading activities on one day and complete them the next day. These activities will typically consume a total of about 45 minutes.

The number and kinds of groups a teacher employs are limited only by a teacher's ingenuity. Flexibility is the key. A teacher might meet with a group working on a theme-related project while the rest of the class participates in oral reading with partners. At another time the teacher might divide the class into three groups, one reading independently, one working with partners writing in response to reading, and one working at centers. The teacher circulates and intervenes as necessary.

Although students are generally grouped heterogeneously in a flexible grouping model, there are times when grouping by ability is appropriate. For example, less skilled readers might need to meet with the teacher to participate in teacher-guided oral reading activities such as assisted reading and repeated reading. At this time, students might use easy-to-read material or selections previously read from the basal. They are not taken out of the grade-level text, however. Some highly skilled readers might be working on a cooperative writing project that requires teacher direction. Whatever the activity, it is essential that groups do not become static. There should be no "Eagles," "Bluebirds," or "Buzzards."

*Discussion (primarily whole class).* Discussion is primarily a whole class activity that follows reading and rereading. During this time, students may confirm predictions, retell the story, summarize, and/or compare the selection to selections previously read. This activity is similar to the kind of discussions teachers formerly conducted with ability groups, but it has the advantage of allowing interaction among students at all levels. Discussion generally takes about 15 to 20 minutes.

*Skill instruction and practice as needed (whole class and/or small flexible groups).* The flexible grouping, core selection model has not eliminated the need for skill instruction. Now, this instruction most often follows rather than precedes the introduction and reading of a story, and it is taught in context rather than in isolation. The teacher may introduce a skill to the whole class, but because not all students need practice in all skills, follow-up instruction and/or practice is usually accomplished in small groups. These groups may be cooperative groups, heterogeneous pairs, or teacher-directed extra-help groups. Frequently students work together on workbook pages or other written work. The time devoted to skill instruction is held to a minimum.

*Meeting the needs of above-level and below-level students using a grade-level text.* The question is often asked, "How can a teacher using a grade-level text meet the needs of above-level students and below-level students?" Pinellas County teachers have found that it can be done through differentiating instruction. Rather than place students in static ability groups, teachers find ways to help less skilled readers use grade-level materials, and they provide extension activities for more skilled readers. Below-level students are helped to succeed in a grade-level text through hearing stories read aloud, rereading in a variety of settings, participating in discussions with groups of students of varying abilities, having numerous opportunities to practice in connected text, and receiving extra help from the teacher and other students. Students eligible for Chapter 1 and state compensatory education receive preteaching instruction. Moreover, because reading is not necessarily learned sequentially, below-level students can participate successfully in many of the same classroom reading activities as above-level students. For above-level students, the discussion, extended writing, and cooperative group activities related to the grade-level text provide an opportunity to expand their learning. Use of a grade-level text imposes no ceiling on critical discussion and writing.

*Writing*

Writing is an integral part of the teaching of reading. Every student at every grade level writes every day. Writing occupies at least one-fourth of daily reading instruction. Pinellas County uses a process writing approach, in which students work individually, in cooperative groups, and in small teacher-directed response groups. Students keep their drafts and revisions in writing folders and publish in a variety of formats, from student-bound books to audio tapes.

*Writing in response to reading.* Writing in response to reading is a critical component of the flexible grouping model. It is as important to the teaching of reading comprehension and critical thinking as it is to the teaching of writing. In addition to the usual writing on teacher-suggested topics, students at all levels frequently write personal responses inspired by the reading or rereading of all or part of a selection.

Students often write two or three responses to a single selection or part of a selection. The initial response is the first reaction a student has upon hearing or reading a story. The teacher frequently asks, "What does this passage make you think about?" or "How does this story make you feel?" Teachers treat this first response as journal writing and often engage in a written dialogue with the student. The student's second response is a focused response to one element (e.g., character, setting, word choice, use of detail) of the passage. A teacher might reread a portion of a selection that describes a character and ask, "What does this rereading make you think about?" Discussion specific to the character might follow the second writing.

The third response is a new student-generated topic, associated directly or indirectly with previous readings, in which students relate literature to their lives.

*Other writing.* Aside from response to reading, other regularly used types of writing include journal writing, narrative writing (including both personal and fictional narrative), and project and report writing. Students have pen pals as far away as China and as close as the class down the hall. From kindergarten through grade 5, the emphasis is on purposeful, authentic writing.

*Sharing.* Students share unfinished pieces of writing as well as finished work, and they share frequently. They share in small groups and with the whole class, and each time, the student follows his or her reading with two questions: ''What do you like about my story?'' and ''Do you have any questions?'' The answers to these questions give the writer positive reinforcement and provide direction for revising. Sometimes the teacher helps students see the similarities and differences between their own work and work of other authors.

*Self-Selected Reading*

During self-selected reading, which occupies about one-quarter of daily reading instruction time, students read silently in materials that are on their independent or instructional levels. Students are encouraged to choose selections that are of interest to them. The sports section of the local newspaper is just as acceptable as *Little House on the Prairie.* When students have difficulty finding materials of interest at their reading levels, teachers guide them.

It is impossible to overemphasize the importance of daily self-selected reading for students at *all* levels. It gives below-level readers critically needed practice in reading connected text that they can read with success independently. It gives above-level students the opportunity to read in materials that are on a much higher level than either the grade-level text or the above-level basal texts they were given when they were ability grouped.

*What does the teacher do during self-selected reading?* In the past, teachers frequently read along with their students during sustained silent reading time. Although such modeling is still considered important, teachers will just as often interact with students during self-selected reading time. Some teachers conduct individual or group book chats. Others circulate and conference with students. Some call up individual students to read orally. Some meet with a small group for activities such as assisted reading, echo reading, and/or rereading familiar selections. Some may meet with a small heterogeneous group to discuss the elements of plot, character, or setting in the students' various selections.

*Sharing.* Students talk to each other daily about what they are reading. They do not wait until they finish a selection to share. Sharing causes students to summarize what they have read, continually exposes other students to good literature, and promotes oral language development and critical thinking skills.

Teachers frequently group students in small cooperative groups or pairs for sharing. The sharing activity takes only about five to ten minutes. Sometimes students turn their chairs around and briefly tell what they have read that day. One teacher calls this time ''popcorn sharing'' to encourage students to be brief and allow each person a turn. Some teachers use timers.

*Skill and Strategy Instruction*

While skill and strategy instruction is frequently given to individual students and small groups, there are some skills and strategies that teachers find are important to work on with the total class. Some teachers, for example, may conduct a whole-class manipulative phonics activity such as *Making Words* (Cunningham, 1991) or a whole-class sight word activity such as *Word Wall* (Cunningham, 1991). Other teachers may teach the whole class the strategy of summarizing. Following whole group instruction, teachers sometimes divide the class into small groups for cooperative or teacher-directed practice. As often as possible, skill and strategy instruction is given within the context of what the students are reading and writing.

Teachers have found that they must be careful not to sacrifice self-selected reading time and writing time for skill instruction. Skill and strategy instruction, both small group and whole class, makes up no more than one-quarter of the time devoted to the teaching of reading. The typical basal reader contains more skills lessons than can be taught in the course of one school year without infringing on the time that is needed for more critical reading activities. Teachers must be selective.

Source: Adapted with permission from Lyn McKay, Pat Nelms, and Pam Moore, Pinellas County Schools, Pinellas County, Florida (Radencich et al., 1992).

This entire section may raise the question of the optimal balance of whole-group, flexible small-group, and individual activities. The answer is in the question: The issue is *balance*. Grouping choices will vary as a function of the task and of student need. In helping teachers balance whole-group, small-group, and individual activities, remember that teacher attention is critical for learning (Medley, 1977; Rosenshine, 1979; Stallings, 1975).

You can help teachers who provide support (Chapter 1, lab, etc.) fit into flexible structures. If you are responsible for student instruction, you too can find ways of fitting in. Think broadly. For example, teachers responsible for remedial students may work with classroom teachers in a variety of types of groups rather than working only with the low achievers. In this way they provide a better overall environment and, in the process, better service to the remedial students.

## Secondary School Models

In the shadow of public concern about illiteracy, dropout rates, declining SAT scores, and growing numbers of college students in reading courses, secondary schools struggle with how best to provide literacy instruction. Will groups be homogeneous or heterogeneous? Will groups sizes vary? Will there be a "school within a school"? Such decisions are, of course, made within the boundaries of each school's philosophy and goals.

Comprehensive programs involve the orchestration of "interrelated components consisting of human, material, and procedural factors which influence the extent to which institutional objectives are realized" (Samuels, 1981, p. 256). The wide range of reading ability among secondary students (Conley, 1989), the well-documented resistance to content area reading among subject area teachers (O'Brien, 1988; Smith & Feathers, 1983), and difficulties in communication in departmentalized settings (Bean, 1989) are only a few of the challenges facing the implementation of effective reading programs.

Following is a decision-making framework that can be used or adapted in structuring secondary reading programs (Schumm & Radencich, 1991). Also provided are vignettes describing reading programs that have successfully met the challenge.

1. *Decision-making framework:* When designing a secondary school reading program, a number of decisions need to be made. These include scope, instructional approach, personnel, time and place of instruction, methods and materials, and program monitoring and evaluation.

• *Scope:* The first decision is to define the scope of the reading program in terms of curriculum and the target student audience. How to plan for a reading program at a new school, how to change or revitalize an existing program, what materials to order, what courses to offer, and how to place students in these courses are all decisions related to program scope. Roe, Stoodt, and Burns (1978) propose that program "phases" are useful in defining the program scope—*basic or developmental, corrective or remedial, content area,* and *recreational.* To these we have added a fifth, an *enrichment phase* of instruction that advances literacy competencies beyond a minimal level—for example, with a middle school Junior Great Books program or a high school reading course for the college-bound.

In addition to these five sometimes overlapping phases, the school's perception of literacy instruction defines program scope. Many literacy programs do not limit their curricular range to reading. Rather, reading, writing, listening, and speaking are merged in programs of a more holistic nature (Roehler, Foley, Lud, & Power, 1990). Other programs add areas such as computer literacy and study skills to the overall plan.

• *Approach:* The approach refers to the program's philosophy. A remedial lab might not match a school where the philosophy is one of stretching all students to work in heterogeneous groups as they explore literature and content area material. Moore and Readence (1983) reported four basic approaches to content area reading instruction:

1. *Presenting isolated skills:* Students are taught basic reading skills with an underlying assumption that learning to read is a linear rather than a recursive process. Materials generally focus on the skill itself and not on the *why, when,* or *how* of its application to content area reading.

2. *Aiming at content:* "Aiming" directs students to salient information in textbooks. Teachers tell students what to look for when reading or probe to see if the students located the information. No specific instruction is provided about *how* to locate the information.

3. *Guiding toward content:* Students are provided with a study guide to instruct them in what to look for when reading and how to find it. "Aiming" differs from "guiding" in that students may be provided with

models of how to gather the appropriate information. Skills instruction is incidental.

4. *Presenting skills and content concurrently:* Reading strategies are taught with subject content. Teachers are concerned with developing mature reading patterns (process) as well the designated curriculum (product).

In our experience, most reading programs adhere to one or more of these four approaches. The balanced fourth approach, presenting skills and content concurrently, is probably the one supported most consistently in the literature (e.g., Katz, 1982; Peters, 1990). It promotes transfer of skills to genuine textbook material. Decisions regarding approach, however, should take into consideration local priorities and accountability factors as well as your school's philosophy.

• *Instructional personnel:* The question is not only "Who will teach?" but also "How will multiple instructors interact with each other?" Roe, Stoodt, and Burns (1978) suggest that four types of individuals should be involved with literacy instruction—administrators, the reading consultant, the reading teacher, and content area teachers. The reading consultant or RRS may teach students with special needs or serve in a resource role to consult with regular classroom teachers (Bean & Wilson, 1981). Reading and language arts teachers may teach whole classes. Peer tutoring (Ehly & Larsen, 1984) and cross-age tutoring ( Juel, 1991) are models that promote student involvement with instruction. Finally, volunteers including parents provide instructional assistance either during or outside of school hours.

When more than one instructor is involved in teaching reading, role confusion can result (Bean & Wilson, 1981; Vacca, 1989). Faculty members should be clear about specific responsibilities, accountability, and curriculum coverage. Systematic, ongoing communication is imperative and should be built into the program design, for example through a Reading Committee (see "The Reading Committee" in Chapter 5).

• *Time and place of instruction:* Timing can refer to the length of a reading course. When given the option, middle schools should weigh the advantages and disadvantages of offering courses on a rotating quarterly exploratory "wheel," for a semester, or for an entire year. A "summer special" in Dade County (Miami, Florida) Public Schools has allowed at-risk middle school students to explore reading and writing experiences in a summer camp atmosphere.

Place of instruction is often determined by the designated personnel. A reading specialist who teaches reading will probably do so in a reading classroom or a resource room. One variation is for an entire content class (including the teacher) to go into a reading lab for instruction that is to be followed up in the content class. Another model is for an RRS to teach *in* the content area classroom with the teacher present, or even to team-teach. In this way the RRS can focus on material from *real* textbooks, something that does not always occur in a reading class (Peters, 1990). Also both the students and the content teacher may be more likely to see the relationship between the reading strategies and their subject area if they are taught in their content classroom rather than in a special reading room. This model can even be carried out with team teaching over an entire semester.

Peer tutoring or after-school reading programs may take place at the school (e.g., in classrooms or the library), or at locales that are not as likely to be associated with failure in school, such as churches and YMCAs. A final option is closed circuit television, particularly in areas, such as some remote rural areas, where a regular instructor is not available.

• *Methods and materials:* Secondary teachers today have available an unparalleled array of methods and materials for literacy instruction (Irwin & Baker, 1990; Tierney, Readence, & Dishner, 1990). The initial decision, however, is not specifically what methods and materials to use but, rather, who will make the selection and how that decision will be made (Schumm & Doucette, 1991). Will the decision be made by individual instructors or by district and school-based administrators? Will there be any coordination between middle schools and the senior high schools? Such articulation can ensure that the same levels of the same materials are not used in both the middle and the high school. If teachers are involved in the decision making, will individual teachers select methods and materials on their own, or will a cooperative effort be made to coordinate instruction on a departmental or schoolwide basis? When methods and materials are specified, students can also help evaluate and perhaps field-test them. Whoever makes the decision, it is important that it be made with care (see Chapter 8).

One key consideration is determining grouping structures. Research is by no means unanimous in recommending one best grouping pattern (see Barr, 1989, for a review). Secondary students are generally placed homogeneously in all content areas according to teacher recommendations and scores on traditional norm-referenced group achievement tests such as the Stanford Achievement Test (1989) or the Degrees of Reading Power test (1984). But these popular tracking plans have been heavily criticized in recent years. Fortunately, recommendations for grouping patterns that can enhance student achievement and self esteem are now being promoted (Au, 1991) and should be considered. As a first step, schools that place students primarily on the basis of performance on a norm-referenced test might at least group the lowest achievers with some average students. This can result in a decrease in the number of levels of a course—perhaps from four or five down to two or three—and thus in an amelioration of some of the problems mentioned earlier; for example, it can increase the expectations for the class and decrease discipline problems.

• *Program monitoring and evaluation:* Monitoring and evaluation are essential for program success. Considerations of *when*, *how*, and *who* need to be addressed. This role may be assumed formally or informally by district and school-level administrators or by individual reading and content area teachers (see the "Program Review Form" in Appendix D). Peer observation and counseling and student surveys and interviews may also be used for ongoing program evaluation (see Chapter 9, "Assessing Student Performance," and "Evaluating the Program" in Chapter 2).

2. *Vignettes:* Following are vignettes of secondary organizational models in action. For each, we'll provide a profile based on the decision-making framework. Other program profiles can be found in Condon and Hoffman (1990) and Valencia, McGinley, and Pearson (1990).

• Middle school interdisciplinary teams

| | |
|---|---|
| *Scope:* | Developmental, corrective, and content area |
| *Approach:* | Teaching skills and content concurrently |
| *Personnel:* | Middle school faculty, students |

| | |
|---|---|
| *Time and place:* | Content area classrooms |
| *Methods and materials:* | Team decisions; heterogeneous grouping, cooperative learning, content area materials |
| *Monitoring and evaluation:* | Completion of team projects; individual achievement on tests |

A middle school interdisciplinary team typically includes teachers of required subjects who can meet regularly *Before* and *After* instruction to plan for the group of students whom they all share (Arhar, Johnston, & Markle, 1988). A second type of team can be a similar group of teachers of elective courses. This type can be problematic because students have different patterns of interests.

Assignment of students to classes and teams should be done with care. Two reasons for not grouping students by reading ability are the problems inherent in tracking (discussed earlier) and the fact that levels of reading might well not coincide with levels of performance in other subjects. Students are not grouped randomly, either, because many teachers and parents are uncomfortable with grouping that is completely heterogeneous. Rather, the grouping is done with knowledge of the students involved and regard for overall manageability.

Some of the lessons are tied to thematic team projects; others are individual teacher assignments. You can rotate among teams to help them decide on strategies and themes on which to focus, and to help the teams develop lessons. If team projects are new to your school, start with just one the first year. The school can gradually expand in subsequent years.

• Atwell's *In the Middle* (1987)

| | |
|---|---|
| *Scope:* | Developmental, corrective, recreational/integrated language arts |
| *Approach:* | Teaching skills and content concurrently |
| *Personnel:* | Language arts/reading teacher, students |
| *Time and place:* | Reading/language arts classrooms |
| *Methods and materials:* | Teacher/class decisions; homogeneous or heterogeneous grouping, cooperative learning |
| *Monitoring and evaluation:* | Portfolios; informal assessments |

Nancie Atwell's (1987) success as an eighth-grade teacher has led middle school teachers and others throughout the country to emulate her reading and writing workshops. In Atwell's model, reading and writing periods are scheduled back to back. Both reading and writing activities are plentiful throughout the combined period. Skills are introduced as they fit into the reading and writing tasks. Assessment is primarily handled through portfolios, although other types of assessment can be used as needed. Teachers who are adept at reading or writing instruction but not at both may well need your help to make this model a success.

• LEAP for Success

| | |
|---|---|
| *Scope:* | Developmental, corrective, content area |
| *Approach:* | Teaching skills and content concurrently |

| | |
|---|---|
| *Personnel:* | Content area teachers; parents |
| *Time and place:* | Content area classrooms; homes |
| *Methods and materials:* | Teacher decisions; whole-class instruction |
| *Monitoring and evaluation:* | Peer review |

The Learning Environment and Attitude Program (LEAP) at Louisiana State Laboratory School is designed to enhance personal and academic success for middle school students through involvement of students, faculty, and the home (Cowart & Fabre, 1986). Some classroom instruction time in each academic discipline is used to teach basic reading/study strategies in which all faculty members are trained. The strategies are used consistently in all academic classrooms throughout the school year. Thus, students grow to "own" the strategies and learn to use them automatically as appropriate. For example, all faculty require that Cornell Notetaking (Pauk, 1983) be used in taking notes during their lectures. Regular workshops, along with a parent handbook, are used to orient parents to the basic strategies used in each class and to train parents to help their children at home. The program's effectiveness depends on close cooperation of all faculty. This cooperation is enhanced by peer observation of strategy presentations.

For another secondary program that organizes strategies by grade level, see Simmons-Wolpow, Farrell, and Tonjes (1991).

- Teaching for Transfer

| | |
|---|---|
| *Scope:* | Content area; enrichment |
| *Approach:* | Teaching skills and content concurrently; isolated skills |
| *Personnel:* | Content area teacher; reading specialist |
| *Time and place:* | Content area classrooms; reading lab |
| *Methods and materials:* | Teacher decisions (weekly meetings) |
| *Monitoring and evaluation:* | Peer evaluation; student evaluations |

This high school reading/study skills program evolved because of an American history teacher's concern. She lamented that although her students were not performing as well as she would like, she simply did not have the time to teach reading and study skills.

Because all high school juniors were required to take a one-semester course on "Reading for the College-Bound Student," the reading specialist and the American history teacher decided to join forces. The content of the reading course did not change with respect to ACT (American College Testing) familiarization objectives (isolated skills), but the reading/study skills focus changed to Teaching for Transfer. When the reading specialist taught reading and study strategies, practice exercises were completed using the American history textbook as reading material.

The approach of Teaching for Transfer was a combination of isolated skills and teaching skills concurrently. The reading specialist and the history teacher worked cooperatively to implement this program in both the reading laboratory and the content area classroom. Methods and materials were determined during weekly meetings between the two. Monitoring and evaluation were conducted through teacher and student evaluation.

In the days when materials-driven models were the norm in secondary school programs, little school-based decision making was necessary. Basals or reading kits dictated the program. With the focus on the role of teachers as decision makers (Stern & Shavelson, 1983) and on that of students as active participants in the learning process (Ericson & Ellett, 1990), it is imperative that we explore frameworks for making such decisions.

## Reading Labs

The role of the reading teacher has often been that of a lab teacher. Students are pulled out of regular classes and attend a lab for remediation. As has just been described in the secondary models section, there are effective ways of using labs. However, Allington (1985) and others have argued convincingly about the typical problems with labs:

1.  *The classroom teacher may feel less responsibility for the student's instruction, resulting in lessened efforts when the student is in the regular classroom.*

2.  *There is often little coordination between the classroom teacher and the reading teacher. Thus, the students who can least afford it wind up with a program that is quite fragmented.*

3.  *Lab students are penalized when they are grouped together by being subjected to the problems with ability grouping discussed earlier.*

4.  *Students may believe that what they learn in the lab is to be applied there only. They may have difficulty understanding that they are to transfer this learning to their regular classes.*

5.  *A reading teacher who is in a lab the entire day can serve only a limited number of students. Typically, middle and high achievers will be excluded. In explaining this problem to principals, we often resort to bringing up test scores. The only way that median percentile scores for a school can be raised is if the students in the middle improve.*

To repeat, however, our section on "Secondary School Models" earlier in this chapter indicates that labs do not have to look like this. The point is well taken for elementary schools as well. One alternative model we have seen is that of regularly rotating all seventh-grade English classes through a lab throughout the year, with English teachers accompanying their classes. The reading teacher teaches a strategy first in "reading" materials of limited length and later through content area texts. Teachers and students are expected to apply the strategies when regular classes resume. Psychologically, however, there is probably not as much transfer from what is learned in a room other than the regular classroom. Thus, we prefer the model where an RRS models lessons in students' classrooms rather than in labs. One selling point for our position that we have found to be effective with principals is that this model involves freeing up a classroom, which could then be used for other purposes.

A variation on this approach is a computer lab through which students rotate. It might be taught by a computer teacher with periodic assistance from the RRS. This is another model that shows some promise.

## Conclusion

So, was there more to structuring programs than you thought? Every step—from the physical layout of the classroom to the choice of curriculum to the use of grouping patterns—is as essential to a well-oiled classroom as the physical layout of your kitchen, your choice of ingredients, and the way you combine ingredients is to the success of your cooking. As you do with cooking, experiment a little, expect a bit of a mess, but look forward to some new treats as well!

# 7

# Assisting Teachers with Teaching and Learning Strategies

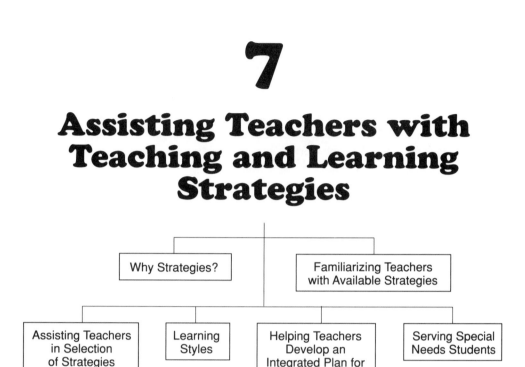

- Why Strategies?
- Familiarizing Teachers with Available Strategies
  - Assisting Teachers in Selection of Strategies
  - Learning Styles
  - Helping Teachers Develop an Integrated Plan for Strategy Instruction
  - Serving Special Needs Students

**A** MATURE, INDEPENDENT LEARNER is a learner with a plan. The learner knows what to do, how to do it, and when to do it. Even when the original plan falls through, the mature learner has a set of alternative plans or a system for problem solving that enables him or her to keep going. As educators, we all hope that our students become mature, independent learners. For this to happen, we need to structure opportunities for students to become learners with a plan—strategic learners. This chapter provides a rationale for strategic literacy learning and explains how the RRS can help classroom teachers to empower their students (particularly those with special needs) to become strategic learners.

## Why Strategies?

The notion that textbooks are often difficult (Johnson & Vardain, 1975) and uninteresting to students (Baldwin, 1985; Baldwin & Leavell, 1991) is not new. As early as 1932 Bartlett observed that the type of writing contained in textbooks not only made it difficult for readers to derive information from the text, but also impeded their ability to organize that information.

What is new is the growing heterogeneity in classrooms throughout the United States. The advent of school desegregation, the influx of various cultural groups into U.S. society, and the onset of mainstreaming of special education students have all broadened the range of cultural, linguistic, and academic diversity in the classroom. As a consequence, textbooks that didn't quite fit before are even more frustrating now. Students have a difficult time extracting the most important information from textbooks and learning that information for tests.

In response to the belief that textbooks are not user-friendly and are written beyond the reading level of many students, teachers have been encouraged to make adaptations that allow them to integrate the teaching of specific strategies to enhance textbook comprehension (Herber, 1978; Schumm & Strickler, 1991). Paris, Wasik, and Turner (1991, p. 610), while recognizing that there is some ambiguity in the definition of reading strategies, nevertheless offered the following working definition, which we will use here: Strategies are a "wide range of tactics that readers use to engage and comprehend text" (p. 610). You will see in our Strategy Matrix later in this chapter that we distinguish between teaching strategies (teacher-initiated) and learning strategies (student-directed) (Alvermann & Moore, 1991).

A textbook strategy is really an action plan for trying to (1) decode an author's message, (2) comprehend an author's message, (3) remember an author's message, or (4) relate and apply an author's message to personal experience. Some strategies are multifaceted and are designed to do all four. Most strategies can be easily adapted to any reading level—even for emergent readers—in that "reading" strategies can become "listening" strategies.

Research demonstrates the effectiveness of strategies to enhance students' learning from textbooks (see Alvermann & Moore, 1991; Alvermann & Swafford, 1989; Swafford, 1990; Swafford & Alvermann, 1989, for reviews). Despite this evidence, teacher resistance to strategy instruction is well documented (Hinchman, 1987; Ratekin, Simpson, Alvermann, & Dishner, 1985; Smith & Feathers, 1983). This is particularly true at the secondary level. Even when teachers have completed university course work in content area reading, their use of strategies is often limited. This resistance is more than a simple aversion to William S. Gray's adage that "Every teacher is a teacher of reading." Because teachers are accountable for course content, they tend to focus on product rather than process (Schumm, Vaughn, & Saumell, 1992). Indeed, teachers find many content area reading strategies to be highly desirable, but their implementation is not feasible given the realities of today's classrooms. This is particularly true in the case of instructional practices that require a great deal of preparation time for individual students. (Schumm & Vaughn, 1991).

Wood and Muth (1991) discussed the discrepancy between "what is" and "what should be" regarding instructional practice in the middle grades. This disparity between best instructional practice and what actually occurs in the classroom is a concern for both teachers (Schumm, Vaughn, & Saumell, 1992) and students (Schumm, Vaughn, & Saumell, in press). The voice of students is particularly compelling. In a survey of approximately two thousand urban middle and high school students, students reported that they were not getting the instructional support they felt they needed to read and comprehend textbooks. This was true for both lower and higher achieving students (Schumm, Vaughn, & Saumell, in press).

The task of the RRS is a challenging one. Students want and need assistance in learning from difficult textbooks. Some classroom teachers, particularly at secondary levels, are preoccupied with content coverage and plagued with class sizes that inhibit their ability to deal with individual student needs. The RRS should work collaboratively with classroom teachers to empower them to explore different ways to promote student learning. As the RRS you can (1) familiarize teachers with available strategies, (2) help teachers select strategies, and (3) help teachers develop an integrated plan for incorporating strategies in their regular instructional routine.

## Familiarizing Teachers with Available Strategies

There are two basic ways to familiarize teachers with strategies: mentioning and modeling. You can mention strategies through inservice training sessions, provide teachers with strategy summaries, and share highlighted reprints of journal articles. Mentioning is an important aspect of your job because classroom teachers often do not have the time to pore over a variety of professional journals and texts in search of resources. Once you know your teachers' concerns, you can keep an eye out for strategies that would be helpful.

Mentioning is vital, but modeling is much more powerful. If you model a strategy during an inservice workshop or (better yet) during an actual elementary or secondary class session, teachers can see the strategy in action. Suggestions for implementing strategies in the classroom are provided in Chapter 11 on "Providing Staff Development."

The number of reading/study strategies seems to grow with each issue of each professional journal. Our "Strategy Primer," to be discussed in this chapter, only scratches the surface. Fortunately, strategy anthologies for use in elementary and secondary classrooms are readily available. Complete references are available in the "Core Professional Library" list in Appendix C. If you supplement these strategy "cookbooks" with regular reading of professional journals, you'll have quite a repertoire of suggestions for teachers. Our favorite strategy collections are the following:

Bragstadt, B. J., & Stumpf, S. M. (1982). *A guidebook for teaching study skills and motivation.* Boston: Allyn and Bacon.

Cunningham, P. M. (1991). *Phonics they use: Words for reading and writing.* New York: HarperCollins.

Irwin, J. W., & Baker, I. (1990). *Promoting active reading comprehension strategies.* Englewood Cliffs, NJ: Prentice-Hall.

Monahan, J. N., & Hinson, B. (1988). *New directions in reading instruction.* Newark, DE: International Reading Association.

Schumm, J. S., & Radencich, M. C. (1992). *School power—Strategies for succeeding in school.* Minneapolis: Free Spirit.

Tierney, R. J., Readence, J. E., & Dishner, E. K. (1990). *Reading strategies and practices: A compendium,* 3rd ed. Boston: Allyn and Bacon.

Vacca, R., & Vacca, J. (1989). *Content area reading,* 3rd ed. Boston: Little, Brown.

Wilson, R. M., & Gambrell, L. B. (1988). *Reading comprehension in the elementary school: A teacher's practical guide.* Boston: Allyn and Bacon.

For strategies for working with special education students, we recommend:

Bos, C. S., & Vaughn, S. (1991). *Strategies for teaching students with learning and behavior problems.* Boston: Allyn and Bacon.

For strategies for working with ESL students, we recommend:

Gunderson, L. (1991). *ESL literacy instruction: A guidebook to theory and practice.* Englewood Cliffs, NJ: Prentice-Hall.

## A Strategy Primer: A Bibliography of Reading/Study Strategies

*Anticipation/reaction guides:* A pre- and postreading strategy used to highlight major concepts in a chapter and stimulate critical thinking about these concepts. These guides consist of chapter-based statements designed to generate student opinions about the topic. Before reading the chapter, students decide if they agree or disagree with each statement (anticipation). After reading the chapter, students revisit the statements and once again decide if they agree or disagree (reaction).

Readence, J. E., Bean, T. W., & Baldwin, R. S. (1992). *Content area reading: An integrated approach,* 4th ed. Dubuque, IA: Kendall/Hunt.

*Concept mapping:* A graphic learning tool that enables students to see relationships among key concepts in text.

Heimlich, J. E., & Pittelman, S. D. (1986). *Semantic mapping: Classroom applications.* Newark, DE: International Reading Association.

*Cornell notetaking system:* A strategy for helping students take two-column notes from lectures and summarize the notes for study purposes. Originally developed for college students, it has also been used successfully with upper elementary and secondary students.

Pauk, W. (1983). *How to study in college.* Boston: Houghton Mifflin.

*DR/TA (Directed Reading/Thinking Activity):* A comprehensive guided reading strategy to help students preview assigned readings, make predictions based on the preview, and confirm predictions through reading and discussion. Can also be used as a listening strategy (DL/TA; Directed Listening/Thinking Activity).

Stauffer, R. G. (1969). *Directing reading maturity as a cognitive process.* New York: Harper & Row.

*Frayer model:* A model for helping students learn critical features of key concepts. Elements include essential and nonessential characteristics, examples and nonexamples.

Frayer, D., Frederic, W. G., & Klausmeier, H. J. (1969). *A scheme for testing the level of concept mastery.* Working Paper No. 16. Madison: Wisconsin R&D Center for Cognitive Learning.

Also in:

Tierney, R. J., Readence, J. E., & Dishner, E. K. (1990). *Reading strategies and practices: A compendium*, 3rd ed. (pp. 215–219). Boston: Allyn and Bacon.

*GIST:* A reading/writing tool for helping students activate their prior knowledge about a topic, synthesize that information with cues from the text, and write a summary statement about the passage. The acronym GIST stands for Generating Interactions between Schemata and Text.

Cunningham, J. W. (1982). Generating interactions between schemata and text. In J. A. Niles & L. A. Harris (Eds.), *New inquiries in reading research and instruction,* Thirty-first Yearbook of the National Reading Conference. Washington, DC: National Reading Conference.

*K-W-L:* A reading/thinking strategy that focuses on what a student Knows about a topic, what a student Wants to learn, and what the student Learned from reading.

Ogle, D. (1986). K-W-L: A teaching model that develops active reading of expository text. *The Reading Teacher, 39,* 564–570.

*List-group-label:* Word relationship activity that helps students categorize key terms. Can be used as a before- or after-reading activity.

Taba, H. (1967). *Teacher's handbook for elementary social studies.* Reading, MA: Addison-Wesley.

Also in:

Tierney, R. J., Readence, J. E., & Dishner, E. K. (1990). *Reading strategies and practices: A compendium,* 3rd ed. (pp. 200–204). Boston: Allyn and Bacon.

*Mnemonics:* A set of memory-training techniques used to improve retention of text material. Mnemonics include associational learning strategies such as acronyms, acrostics, and pegwords.

Mastropieri, M. A., & Scruggs, T. E. (1989). Constructing more meaningful relationships: Mnemonic instruction for special populations. *Educational Psychology Review, 1,* 83–111.

Roe, B. D., Stoodt, B. D., & Burns, P. C. (1987). *Secondary school reading instruction: The content areas,* 3rd ed. Boston: Houghton Mifflin.

*PORPE (Predict, Organize, Rehearse, Practice, Evaluate):* A five-step strategy for preparing for essay tests. Initially developed for college students, it is appropriate for middle school and high school students as well.

Simpson, M. L. (1986). PORPE: A writing strategy for studying and learning in the content areas. *Journal of Reading, 29,* 407–414.

*Pyramiding:* A graphic learning tool that helps students to arrange main ideas and details in logical categories.

Maring, G. H., & Furman, G. (1985). Seven "whole class" strategies to help mainstreamed young people read and listen better in content area classes. *Journal of Reading, 28,* 694–700.

*QAR (Question Answer Relationships):* A strategy for teaching students how to answer reading comprehension questions by demonstrating the question answer relationships ("right there," "think and search," "author and me," "on my own").

Raphael, T. E. (1984). Teaching learners about sources of information for answering comprehension questions. *Journal of Reading, 27,* 303–311.

*RAFT:* A writing strategy that can add sparkle to composition assignments. Before beginning to write, the student determines the following: Role, the writer's role (e.g., a toaster, a computer, Thomas Edison, a police officer); Audience, to whom the writing is being addressed (e.g., a slice of bread, a parent, a Supreme Court Justice); Format, the form the piece will use (e.g., letter, FAX memo, diary), and Topic plus a strong verb.

Holston, V., & Santa, C. (1985). RAFT: A method of writing across the curriculum that works. *Journal of Reading, 28,* 456–457.

*Reciprocal teaching:* An interactive teaching strategy that serves as a dialogue between the teacher and students. The strategy has four components: summarizing, question generating, clarifying, and predicting.

Palincsar, A. S., & Brown, A. L. (1986). Interactive teaching to promote independent learning from text. *The Reading Teacher, 39,* 771–777.

*ReQuest:* An interactive reading strategy that enables teachers to demonstrate effective self-questioning. The teacher asks students questions, but students ask the teacher questions as well.

Manzo, T. V. (1969). The ReQuest procedure. *Journal of Reading, 11,* 123–126.

*Semantic feature analysis:* A chart or grid that can be used to demonstrate similarities and differences among key concepts.

Johnson, D. D., & Pearson, P. D. (1984). *Teaching reading vocabulary.* New York: Holt, Rinehart and Winston.

*SQ3R:* A classic study strategy designed to enable students to become actively engaged with text. The basic framework of SQ3R (Survey, Question, Read, Recite, Review) has served as the seed for a variety of strategies.

Robinson, F. P. (1961). *Effective study,* rev. ed. New York: Harper & Row.

*Story mapping:* A diagram that can be used as a plan for writing a story or as a tool to identify the major components of a story students have read or heard. A story map consists of a set of questions that pertain to the basic elements of a story (setting, characters, plot, etc.).

Beck, J., & McKeown, M. G. (1981). Developing questions that promote comprehension: The story map. *Language Arts, 58,* 913–918.

*Think-alouds:* A modeling strategy that enables teachers to demonstrate how good readers monitor their reading and use fix-up strategies when comprehension breaks down. Elements can include oral hypothesizing, rereading, expressing confusion, relating to prior knowledge, and other metacognitive processes.

Davey, B. (1983). Think aloud: Modeling the cognitive processes of reading comprehension. *Journal of Reading, 27,* 44–47.

Table 7.1 on page 84 is a strategy matrix listing the various types of strategies and their possible uses.

## Assisting Teachers in Selection of Strategies

Literally hundreds of strategies are available for content area teachers. Which one should be used? How does the teacher decide? The RRS can assist classroom teachers in strategy selection. We know of one RRS who decided to introduce a new strategy every week. We can only imagine the confusion created by this strategy deluge!

With strategies, less is better. We offer the following tips for helping teachers to choose from the strategy menu:

## TIPS · SELECTING STRATEGIES

- The strategy should be consistent with the content being taught. For example, not every textbook chapter lends itself to a List-Group-Label activity.

- The strategy should be adapted to more than one content presentation so that you can use the strategy more than once.

- The strategy should allow for more than one level of involvement. High- and low-achieving special needs students should all have the opportunity to be included.

- If the strategy involves much preparation time, the time spent should be worth the potential learning that may take place.

- The strategy should not require prerequisite skills that students do not yet have, or the prerequisite skills should be taught before introducing the strategy.

- If the strategy involves student grouping, a plan for that grouping should be considered.

- The strategy should allow the desired amount of depth and breadth in content coverage.

- The procedures for implementing the strategy should be clear.

- The strategy should promote student independence.

- The strategy should be easy to describe and model.

*(continued)*

### TIPS (continued)

- Teachers should have enough time to provide guided and independent practice of the strategy, if necessary.

- Teachers should provide specific instruction on how to transfer the strategy to new situations, if appropriate.

### TABLE 7.1 Strategy Matrix

| Strategy | Strategy Type | | Possible Uses | | | | |
| --- | --- | --- | --- | --- | --- | --- | --- |
| | Teaching | Learning | Vocabulary | Reading Comprehension | Listening Comprehension | Study | Write |
| Anticipation/ reaction guides | X | | X | X | X | | |
| Concept mapping | X | X | X | X | X | X | X |
| Cornell Notetaking | | X | | | X | X | |
| DR/TA & DL/TA | X | | | X | X | | |
| Frayer model | X | | X | | | | |
| GIST | | X | | X | | | X |
| K-W-L | X | | | X | X | | |
| List-group-label | X | | X | X | X | | |
| Mnemonics | | X | X | | | X | |
| PORPE | | X | | X | | X | X |
| Pyramiding | | X | | X | X | X | X |
| QAR | | X | | X | X | | |
| RAFT | X | | | | | | X |
| Reciprocal teaching | X | | | X | X | | |
| Request | X | | | X | X | | |
| Semantic feature analysis | X | | X | X | | | |
| SQ3R | | X | | X | X | | |
| Story mapping | X | X | | X | X | | X |
| Think-alouds | X | | | X | X | | |

## Learning Styles

The value of using learning styles in the classroom is much debated (Brandt, 1990), but this is all the more reason for you to be familiar with the topic. Classroom teachers eager to choose the right strategies to meet individual needs are likely to ask you questions about learning styles. The most popular learning styles models (Carbo, 1983; Dunn, Dunn, & Price, 1985) focus on the idea that we all learn differently. It is easy to caricature learning style theory by depicting a teacher letting one student read along in the morning, with rock music, in a beanbag chair, with bright light, with a cool temperature, eating carrot sticks, while every other student has a different individualized set of arrangements. But we can't get away that easily.

It would certainly be helpful for all teachers at least to be aware that lecturing, a style often used in teaching, may not be the style from which their students will learn best. Teachers who use a variety of teaching styles are most likely to reach all their students with one or another of these approaches.

There is probably value in letting students in the middle grades, or perhaps even earlier, try to become aware of what works for them. One middle school runs a Reading Habitat, a room staffed by a reading specialist and a middle school specialist. All students in the school rotate through the Reading Habitat for two-week periods as they find their comfort zones. Students are surveyed about the circumstances in which they read best and are given opportunities to explore in the Reading Habitat. They keep logs about the kind of furniture they find most comfortable when reading each of several types of reading material. They write in their logs when studying at home as well. At the end of their time in the Reading Habitat, they are interviewed about their comfort zones, and these results are recorded.

You may want to begin a file of information on learning styles so that you can help your staff decide on the implementation of specific programs.

## Helping Teachers Develop an Integrated Plan for Strategy Instruction

Imagine what would happen if in one elementary school the fourth-grade teacher taught SQ3R and two teachers of other grades taught SQ3R variations (e.g., PQ4R and PQRST). The strategies are similar, but there are slight differences. Imagine what would happen in one middle school if the eighth-grade science teacher required students to use the Cornell Notetaking System, the eighth-grade social studies teacher required mapping for notetaking, and the English teacher required that notes be taken in outline form. Again, there are some similarities. But the students who need these strategies the most—those with learning problems—will probably suffer from strategy confusion.

At the school level, it is helpful if a core of strategies can be agreed on and followed through the grades. Such strategies can be summarized in a booklet for parents so that a few strategies can be used consistently at school (between and among grades) and at home. Moreover, students in pull-out classes can rely on a bank of strategies that are consistent between their general and special education classes. Often mainstreamed students learn one set of strategies in their resource rooms and another set of strategies in the general classrooms (see the section "Secondary School Models" in Chapter 6).

## Serving Special Needs Students

### Students for Whom the Textbook Is Too Difficult

In addition to specific strategies, teachers also often request suggestions for adapting the textbook—what to do when the textbook is too difficult. The section on flexible grouping in Chapter 6 provides some pointers. Following are two frameworks that also address this question.

When the textbook is too difficult, mediated instruction is necessary. Neal and Langer (1992) have developed a Mediated Instruction of Text (MIT) diagram that can serve as a framework. In this structure, the teacher follows different strategies before, during, and after reading. These strategies include the following:

*For activating prior knowledge:*

- Questioning
- Brainstorming
- Posing a problem
- Role playing

*For predicting content:*

- Surveying ideas
- Conducting demonstrations/experiments
- Semantic organizers
- Building word meaning
- Posing purpose questions
- Structured overviews

*For constructing meaning:*

- Responding to purpose questions
- Verifying predications
- Responding to study guide

*For monitoring understanding:*

- Questioning/talking about ideas
- Notetaking
- Student-generated quizzes

*For processing ideas:*

- Summarizing
- Response writing

- Constructing graphic organizers

- Teaching others

- Learning games

- Discussion

*For applying knowledge:*

- Participating in projects, experiments, creative work

Following is a set of suggestions that provides a second framework for responding to the question, "What do I do when the textbook is too hard for my students?"

## TIPS · WHAT TO DO WHEN THE TEXTBOOK IS TOO HARD

*Supplement the Textbook*

- Audio-tape textbook content.

- Read the textbook aloud to students.

- Pair students to master textbook content.

- Use direct experiences/films/videotapes/recordings and computer programs.

- Work with students individually or in small groups.

*Simplify the Textbook*

- Construct abridged versions of textbook content or use publishers' abridged versions.

- Provide students with chapter outlines or summaries.

- Use a multilevel, multimaterial approach.

*Highlight Key Concepts*

- Preview reading assignments.

- Provide students with purposes for reading.

- Provide an overview of an assignment before reading.

- Structure opportunities for students to activate prior knowledge before reading.

- Introduce key vocabulary before reading.

- Develop a study guide to direct textbook learning.

- Summarize or reduce textbook information to guide classroom discussions.

*(continued)*

**TIPS (continued)**

- Reduce length of assignments.

- Provide assistance for answering questions.

- Demonstrate or model effective reading strategies.

- Place students in cooperative learning groups.

- Teach comprehension monitoring techniques.

- Teach students to use graphic aids.

*Help Students Retain Key Ideas*

- Structure postreading activities to increase retention.

- Teach students to record key concepts and terms.

- Teach memory strategies to improve retention of text material.

Adapted from J. S. Schumm & K. Strickler, ''Guidelines for Adapting Content Area Textbooks: Keeping Teachers and Students Content,'' *Intervention, 27* (1991), pp. 79–84.

### Limited English Proficient Students

Limited English proficient (LEP), otherwise known as ESL (English as a Second Language), students are a rapidly growing segment of our population. LEP students present special challenges. This is especially true for the increasing influx of older students who have had little schooling. Following are some helpful hints. For additional ideas see Gunderson (1991) or Nurss and Hough (1992).

### TIPS · LIMITED ENGLISH PROFICIENT STUDENTS

- Suggest that, to provide plentiful access to language, teachers use cooperative learning and buddy systems. The classroom should be active.

- Facilitate extensive use of media: Language Masters, films, tape recorders, filmstrips, computers with clear voice capabilities, and the like.

- Suggest that teachers encourage students to use English outside of school (but they should *not* presume to tell the parent what language to speak in the home). Students can belong to English-speaking organizations such as scout troops. They can watch television programs that are in English. One third-grade teacher we know divided students into groups of three who lived close to each other. The students were to learn a television commercial and act it out in class. It worked wonderfully!

- Encourage teachers to use the language experience approach with comprehensible input (Moustafa & Penrose, 1985). Comprehensible input is language with an understandable message that is interesting and relevant to the LEP learner, offered in sufficient quantity to allow access to the language, and sequenced for meaning rather than by grammatical forms. Language experience with comprehensible input goes beyond regular language experience primarily in that prewriting is more extensive. During prewriting, teachers develop new referents in addition to those that were previously developed. Furthermore, teachers ensure that oral language is developed before they write it down.

• Suggest that, to help students feel free to take risks with language, teachers use masks or puppets. (It's O.K. if the *puppet's* English isn't quite right!) Both elementary and secondary students can identify with masks of faculty members or media stars. You can be helpful in finding or constructing masks or puppets or in locating an art teacher, a student, or someone else who can do so.

• Help teachers plan lessons that cover both receptive and expressive language skills, and that focus on language that will be useful to the student.

• Encourage teachers to highlight the languages and cultures represented in the classroom, using native foods, music, and so forth. Teachers can read from culturally relevant material whenever possible. You can help expand such efforts to make them schoolwide. For example, each room could represent a visit to a different country. Passports could be stamped as students and other guests travel from country to country. These efforts should not be done only during a particular week during the year, but should be interjected on a regular basis. A warm environment can go a long way!

• Help teachers include LEP students in class or group lessons even if the students don't understand a lot; they will learn the language more quickly that way than by sitting alone with an assignment on paper.

• Suggest games with off-the-wall directions, even for secondary students. "Simon Says" can yield all kinds of possibilities (Simon Says, "Yell"), or teachers can try a whisper game in which a child acts out an action whispered by another child. Others try to guess what action is being shown. Teachers should expect answers in complete sentences (Minkoff, 1984).

• Suggest classic games like hangman for spelling, or word lotto or word bingo for vocabulary.

• Encourage teachers to use visual aids as much as possible. For example, older as well as younger students can compose stories for wordless picture books.

• Suggest that teachers teach idioms. Acting out or drawing the literal meaning of idioms (e.g., raining cats and dogs) is always fun. Several trade books play with idioms. Among these are Gwynne's books such as *The King Who Rained* (1970b) and *Chocolate Moose for Dinner* (1970a), and Parish's *Amelia Bedelia* (1986) and its sequels.

• Help teachers of elementary students to find and use predictable language books such as Bill Martin's (1967) *Brown Bear, Brown Bear*. Students experience a quick feeling of success with this type of material. They get needed repetition not through drill but through rhyme and rhythm and fun. Students can then replicate the book's patterns ("Maria, Maria, who

(*continued*)

### TIPS (continued)

do you see, I see José looking at me''). See Appendix B for a sample list of predictable language books.

- Encourage teachers to read aloud frequently to small groups and to tape record themselves reading favorite stories so that students can return to them. Here are some ways you can help:
  — Help teachers find books with good text-to-picture match with pictures that are large enough for the children to see.
  — Model for teachers how to use cueing strategies when reading and how to enunciate clearly.
  — Stop frequently to allow students to talk about the books.

- Model for teachers the use of the repetition in raps and songs as the basis for instruction. *Jazz Chants* (Graham, 1978) and *Sound Expressions* (Darquea, 1988) are two sources of this type of material. Choral reading of this and other material can be most effective (McCauley & McCauley, 1992).

- Help teachers find someone who can translate both oral and written information as needed when communicating with LEP parents.

- Suggest that teachers encourage parents to read to their children, even in the home language. There is much transfer—of story structure, conceptual knowledge, and love of reading.

- Remember that children learn by doing. Help teachers find ways of ensuring that language learning is a joyful experience.

### Students with Learning Disabilities

The Education for All Handicapped Children Act of 1975 (Public Law 94-142) mandates that all mentally, physically, and emotionally handicapped children in the United States are entitled to a free education in the "least restricted environment" possible. In other words, to the degree it is possible, special education students must be placed in the general education classroom, if at all appropriate, for all or part of the day. Most mainstreamed students are students with learning disabilities (LD). The special education teacher will in all likelihood assume the responsibility of monitoring students who are mainstreamed into general education classes. Because you will interact with these students from time to time, the following tips are provided:

 **TIPS · WORKING WITH STUDENTS WITH LEARNING DISABILITIES**

- Remind general classroom teachers with mainstreamed special education students to read each student's IEP (Individual Educational Plan). Research indicates that general education teachers (particularly at secondary levels) rarely read IEPs and are thus unaware of the special needs of these students (Schumm & Vaughn, 1992).

- Help provide these students with a reason for coming to school. When computers were installed in one elementary school, it was the LD class that learned how to use them first. These children then became tutors for the others. Other ideas include giving a student with learning disabilities the responsibility of helping a younger child (or even an adopted grandparent at a neighboring nursing home!), or of listening to a child read.

- If the student is mainstreamed during reading/language arts periods, help the classroom teacher develop activities that are appropriate for the student, are consistent with instruction in the LD resource room, and will promote inclusion in the regular classroom routine.

- In intermediate or secondary settings, organize a corps of student volunteers to tape record textbook chapters. These can be listened to in special education or general education settings, or perhaps in the school media center.

- In secondary settings, organize a corps of "study buddies" who will help tutor during lunch or after school.

- Be prepared to provide classroom teachers who have mainstreamed students in their classroom with strategies to promote social and academic integration of these students. Bos and Vaughn (1991) have compiled a book of strategies that can be quite useful to general education teachers.

- Brainstorm with the teacher(s) about ways to make accommodations in unobtrusive ways. Include these in your newsletter to general classroom teachers. Some recent research (Vaughn, Schumm, Niarhos, & Gordon, in press) has suggested that low-achieving students and students with learning disabilities are reluctant to have adaptations made for them when they are mainstreamed in the general education class because such adaptations may draw attention to their handicaps.

### Low-Achieving Students Who Do Not Receive Special Services

Many low-achieving students do not qualify for special education or compensatory education services. These students pose a special challenge for general education teachers who often recognize the learning difficulties of this group of students but do not have the resources to develop individual instructional programs to meet their needs.

## TIPS · LOW-ACHIEVING STUDENTS

- Encourage teachers to employ flexible grouping practices for literacy instruction that discourage student labeling.

- Work with teachers to identify high-interest, low-vocabulary, age-appropriate trade books that will be appealing to low-achieving students.

- Be prepared to provide teachers with supplementary strategies and materials to help meet the needs of low-achieving students who do not receive special services.

(continued)

**TIPS (continued)**

- Develop a network of volunteers who can help students during and after school.

- Offer to consult with teachers to pinpoint student strengths and weaknesses in literacy learning and to develop an action plan.

- Model reading and writing strategies in class that demonstrate how to engage diverse student learners.

- Help teachers develop a list of practical suggestions for parents to support literacy learning in the home.

- Provide workshops for parents who would like to learn more about how to help their children with reading and writing competencies.

- Provide in-class or after-school mini-lessons in reading, writing, and study skills.

- Work with grade-level or subject area teams to develop strategies, study guides, and audiotapes for content area textbooks.

## Unmotivated Students

Except for those students whose behavior is belligerent and incorrigible, the most frustrating students for teachers are generally those who are unmotivated. When teachers give their best efforts and student engagement is still lacking, it can be extremely frustrating. One way to attack an individual student's lethargy is with cooperative problem solving. Rather than isolated teachers trying to put a spark under a student, the RRS (perhaps in conjunction with the school counselor) can arrange a faculty conference of all teachers who interact with the target student.

The conference can include the development of an action plan. This action plan can be structured using the PARS plan suggested by Forgan and Mangrum (1989):

- *Purpose:* What can each teacher do to promote a sense of purpose for learning? Often, unmotivated students simply do not see the relevance of their course work to their lives. Teachers can make purpose-setting links more easily if they know the students and are aware of students' interests and goals. Thus, interest and attitude inventories (Chapter 9) are critical pieces of information. Adult mentors can serve as role models for unmotivated students and can help students to see the importance of schooling.

- *Attitudes:* What can each teacher do to promote a sense of caring about this student as an individual? What can each teacher do to see that the student has a place to "belong" in the school?

- *Results:* What can each teacher do to provide students with immediate feedback about completed work? What can the teacher do to encourage the student to monitor his or her own work (Brozo, 1990)?

- *Success:* What can each teacher do to design opportunities for student social or academic success? One way to help teachers to work collaboratively with students to set realistic goals is the contract approach (Taylor, Harris, & Pearson, 1988). Contracting is based on the notion that students are more likely to complete tasks if they have the opportunity to participate in selecting and structuring the tasks. Contracts can be made for reading, writing, listening, and speaking goals. Sample Reading and Writing Contracts can be found in Appendix B.

This action plan is simple, but it is not simplistic. Students who understand the purpose for learning, have a positive attitude, see results, and have a feeling of success are less likely to become disengaged.

## Above-Average Readers

As we all know, reading is vital to students' academic success. Because of the heavy emphasis on standardized test scores at both the elementary and the secondary level, even above-average readers can benefit from direct reading and test-taking instruction (Beers, 1986a).

Above-average readers in elementary school must be challenged in reading. In the past, such students were placed in above-level basals. This strategy is falling into disfavor because even above-level basals are limiting in that selections are often only portions of books and are limited in scope. Thus, teachers are often beginning with grade-level selections with the whole class but then going beyond these, particularly with above-level readers, with other chapters from the same book, other works by the same author, or additional works on the same subject (Radencich & McKay, in press). Teachers also assign extra projects and expect more and better writing from students who are more capable.

### Peer Tutors
Above-average readers can serve as peer tutors. Peer tutoring can be an effective technique at any grade level, providing opportunities for practice and benefiting both tutors and tutees in achievement, self-concept, social relationships, and attitudes toward reading (Cohen, Kulik, & Kulik, 1982; Topping, 1989). As in any strategy, however, moderation is the key. The above-average reader should not be "used" in constant tutoring.

### Cooperative Learning
Like peer tutoring, cooperative learning can be beneficial for all learners. However, tasks must be carefully structured (Johnson, Johnson, & Holubec, 1990). Above-average readers will resent cooperative learning if they feel that their peers are not cooperating and if their grades suffer as a result (Matthews, 1992).

### Homogeneous Groups
Above-average readers need some time to work in homogeneous groups (Johnson & Johnson, 1992). While these students benefit from heterogeneous instruction, they also benefit from working with each other.

### Reading Rate
Once students read with some fluency, they should be taught that good readers use a variety of different reading rates (Beers, 1986a). Students must learn to read with flexibility depending on the purpose for reading, the type of material being read, the level of difficulty, and their familiarity with the subject matter. Students should

practice finding appropriate reading rates by reading diverse materials at various speeds.

### Study Techniques

Although students who read above grade level usually have less trouble than poorer readers in understanding their textbooks, above-average readers can still benefit from specific instruction in study techniques (Beers, 1986a). Some recent research evidence on middle and high school students' perceptions of textbook adaptations suggests that higher achieving students are not receiving the instruction in reading and study strategies they think they need (Schumm, Vaughn, & Saumell, in press).

Most students develop their study skills by osmosis or by luck. Some of the study skills that may prove most useful to above-average readers at all grade levels beyond the very early grades include Cornell Notetaking (Pauk, 1983), mnemonic techniques for memory (Bragstadt & Stumpf, 1982), semantic mapping and other visual organizers, time management, and analytic reading strategies (Whimbey, 1983). All students should be taught to use efficient, effective study strategies.

If an advanced reading class is not included in the secondary curriculum, you may be able to help above-average students by visiting classes to present test-taking strategies, especially those required for college entrance. If your school does have a course geared specifically to test-taking skills, you may wish to offer your assistance to the instructor by developing expertise in one specific area.

One RRS we know developed an entire unit of study on analogies and then worked with the teacher to present the material to the students. Another RRS developed several lessons on strategies for completing different types of standardized tests—PSAT, SAT, and ACT—and then coached the students on the strategies most appropriate for each test.

### Research Papers

Another area in which above-average readers may need some assistance is in writing research papers. You may want to work with teachers to present the most appropriate form for footnotes and bibliography entries. In addition, you might suggest presenting information on notetaking, paraphrasing, outlining, and plagiarizing.

Don't overlook above-average readers! These students will often use and retain the information you share with them to a greater degree than do other students. Your efforts with these students may be highly rewarding.

## Conclusion

Sharing teaching and learning strategies can be one of the most exciting aspects of the RRS role. Before long, teachers will begin telling you about their successes and informing you about additional ways they have discovered to help all students learn how to learn.

# 8

# Analyzing Instructional Materials

```
                    ┌──────────────┬──────────────┬──────────────┐
              ┌───────────┐  ┌───────────┐  ┌───────┐  ┌──────────────────┐
              │ Textbooks │  │ Workbooks │  │ Kits  │  │ Computer Software │
              └───────────┘  └───────────┘  └───────┘  └──────────────────┘
```

**S**ELECTING INSTRUCTIONAL MATERIALS is a critical task because virtually all instruction winds up being based on these selections. There is a lot more to the process of selecting materials than meets the eye. The selection process can be a prime staff development opportunity for your faculty. Refer to the list of publishers in Appendix C as necessary.

## Textbooks

- "This series has too many workbook pages. I won't vote for it."

- "I loved X series before. I want it again."

- "I hated X series. No way will I vote for their new book."

- "Look at the videos that come with this series! This is the series for me!"

Comments like these reflect narrow views that can impede faculties from getting a broad picture. Textbook selection today is complex, but it wasn't always that way. As Nila Banton Smith (1986) reminds us, choices in colonial America were limited to the *New England Primer* and a Holy Bible. Throw in a slate and a lunch pail, and children were fully equipped for the school year!

Today, however, educators charged with the responsibility of text selection are barraged with a bewildering array of textbooks. And the consequences of their choices are monumental. First, the outlay of dollars does not leave any margin for error. Once a decision is made, it may well be set for five years or more as a result of the economic infeasibility of reordering. Second, the texts can and in many cases *will* dictate the curriculum. Studies suggest that up to 95 percent of teacher decision making is governed by textbooks (Muther, 1985c) and that this reliance on textbooks is the expectation of administrators (Shannon, 1987). Therefore, a simple "flip test" (i.e., a cursory examination of sample texts) is totally unacceptable.

Following is a smorgasbord of strategies from which schools can select during their text adoption process.

## Form a Textbook Committee

Textbook selection is best done by a committee. The more broad based the committee, the more the ownership in the selection. This is critical. The best text in the world will do no good if it sits on a shelf. At some level, textbook adoption committees should include administrators, curriculum supervisors, teachers, parents, and students.

*Outline a selection procedure.* Delineate an overall selection procedure at the first committee meeting. A proposed sequence of objectives and corresponding tasks can be presented at this first meeting, then discussed and amended until consensus is achieved. Communicate the procedure (including deadline dates) to parents, and develop a plan for keeping parents up to date with the procedure as it unfolds. Also, determine a mechanism for soliciting input from and otherwise communicating with the administrators, teachers, parents, and others who are not included on the selection committee.

An important component of the selection procedure is to determine the role of publishers' sales representatives. Decide if, how, and when they are to be involved. They can be helpful, but their flashy and biased presentations can sway committee members. Barnard and Hetzel (1986) call this glitz "the wine and cheese phenomenon." What's more, the last presenter always has the advantage.

If sales representatives are to be invited to make presentations, establish a set of guidelines. Ask for specific evidence to support publishers' claims. Consider timing. How many minutes will each publisher be allowed for presentation? Should publisher representatives be present before, during, or after the time when the committee looks at materials? Would you prefer, for example, that committee members start making up their own minds before seeing sales representatives? Consider how gifts from representatives will be handled to prevent any undue influence.

*Conduct a needs assessment.* Consider several areas of need, including subject matter content (what content do we wish to teach?), social content (what values do we wish to impart?), difficulty level and user friendliness (are levels of difficulty and text features appropriate for the intended group of students?), and instructional design (how do we wish to teach the content?) (Young & Riegeluth, 1988).

A variety of methods can be used to conduct a needs assessment (Johnson, Meiller, Miller, & Summers, 1987). A survey (open- or closed-ended) of administrators, teachers, and parents can gauge their perception of needs. Focused discussion at meetings can clarify priorities and concerns.

Muther (1988) provides a Forced Choice Analysis form that enables faculties to prioritize the issues that are most important to them in text selection. This tool can be invaluable in diluting controversy. When a school has decided on its three most crucial issues, it becomes harder for any one person or clique to focus on a single pet issue. Otherwise, we may have one teacher voting because of the phonics component, another because of the literature component, and so on.—Not surprisingly, we may thus have divisiveness that could have been avoided.

*Plan for a research update.* Because the textbook selection committee is likely to be composed of members with varying levels of familiarity with current research, planning for a research update is critical. Muther (1985b) suggests limiting the research update to results only. Committees do not need to be encumbered with statistically significant differences and the like. Muther suggests using consultants or providing short written research tips. The Florida Reading Association followed her advice and produced an attractive packet of "Teachers on the Cutting Edge" (1990) half sheets that could each be put in teachers' mailboxes once a week as basal adoption time neared. These contained a research tidbit, the reference, and a classroom implication.

*Define the ideal.* Information gathered from the needs assessment and research update can then be used to define and describe the ideal textbook. This vision of the ideal is particularly useful in guiding the committee as it sets up initial screening, in-depth screening, and final selection criteria (Young & Riegeluth, 1988).

*Conduct initial screening.* Only now do you proceed with an initial screening—that is, targeting three to five series to scrutinize thoroughly. A checklist based on the "vision of the ideal" can be helpful in this process. Bailey (1988) suggests that a checklist should be relatively easy to complete and should include items relevant to each of the assessed needs.

*Don't be swayed by labels!* No matter how often we make this point in our districts, it never really seems to sink in. In 1990 the state of Florida asked basal publishers to categorize basal series as "traditional" or "integrated." From our perspective, series that would up in *different* categories were sometimes more similar than series *within* a category, but they were perceived quite differently by educators who allowed themselves to be taken in by the label. Don't trust the correlation or the table of contents. You have to get inside the books.

*Conduct an in-depth review.* Conduct an in-depth examination of each series identified during the initial screening phase. As with the needs assessment, inspect four major elements of text: subject matter content, social content, difficulty level, and instructional design.

Because the in-depth examination is time-consuming, it may be prudent to appoint subcommittees to complete various examination tasks (Barnard & Hetzel, 1986). For example, one subcommittee can evaluate only the social content of all targeted series. Or each subcommittee might focus on one aspect of the subject matter content. An example of the latter would be a subcommittee to do a horizontal trace (Muther, 1988) of main idea instruction in the fourth-grade basals of each series, as is explained in the section on instructional design. You will learn through this kind of focus much that you would never learn with a flip test.

• *Subject matter content:* Young and Riegeluth (1988) recommend that content analysis include, among other things, an examination of the depth and comprehensiveness of content coverage and the currency and accuracy of information. The guiding questions are, "What is being taught?" and "Is the content consistent with our curriculum requirements?"

One technique for comparing content coverage is a story sort for basal or literature textbooks (Muther, 1987), or a topic comparison for content area texts (Muther, 1988). With these procedures, a search is made for (1) a story that occurs—if possible—at the same level in three narrative texts (story sort), or (2) the same topic in three content area texts (topic comparison). These are then photocopied and compared. These procedures allow for a direct examination (without the distraction of color) of how different textbooks cover the same material. Muther (1988) also recommends doing a "kid rating" whereby the potential users of the book do the comparisons and provide their evaluations.

• *Social content:* Social content evaluation is guided by the quesiton, "What values are being imparted—overtly and implicitly?" Certainly the social content analysis of texts must reflect designated local needs and values as determined in the needs assessment. Seek texts that offer equitable representation of races, ethnic groups, genders, age groups, and the handicapped. Equitable representation cannot simply be ascertained by frequency of appearance. It is necessary to examine materials closely and systematically to detect subtle biases (Young & Riegeluth, 1988).

• *Difficulty level:* Students appreciate textbooks that facilitate learning. Following are some criteria you can use to help determine text difficulty.

—Traditional readability formulas can serve as rough gauges of text difficulty. Readability levels are often reported as grade levels. Two commonly used scales are the Fry Readability Graph (Fry, 1977) and the Raygor Readability Estimate (Raygor, 1977). Users must be cautious, however, and remember the following:

1. Typically, only two of the many factors that affect readability are measured by readability formulas.

2. The exactness of a grade indicates a level of precision that we simply don't have. Indeed, different formulas may yield very different figures.

3. Materials artificially written to fit a formula are often more difficult than the level would indicate (e.g., deleting a *because* and chopping a sentence into two parts will force the student to make the causal inference).

—Textbooks should also be examined to determine the degree to which they include features that enhance comprehension. Textbooks that include such features as headings and subheadings, vocabulary in boldface type, well-placed graphics, introductions, summaries, and glossaries are considered to be "friendly" or "considerate" to the reader. Several checklists for evaluating the friendliness of text have been devised (Irwin & Davis, 1980; Readence, Bean, & Baldwin, 1992; Singer, 1986):

—The cloze procedure can help determine how well a textbook matches the reading level of students. A cloze test consists of a passage extracted verbatim from a target textbook from which words have been systematically deleted. Students' ability to construct meaning from the textbooks is gauged by how well they can supply the missing words. Reading methods and content area reading textbooks provide descriptions of how to construct and administer a cloze text (see, e.g., Readence, Bean, & Baldwin, 1992). Note, however, that cloze tests are more a measure of language production than of comprehension per se. See the description of the Degrees of Reading Power (DRP) test (1984) in Chapter 9 for an alternative in which choices for each deleted word are provided to students.

Note also that readability data (in DRP units) are available for many textbooks to help gauge the student–textbook match. Even if you are not using the test and are thus not able to obtain student scores, you can use DRP readability values as one gauge in ranking texts by difficulty level. If DRP scores are not reported with new textbooks, you can usually get this information from the publisher. Once you have DRP values for the text, it will be helpful to know the following approximate equivalents from the DRP Readability Report: 40—Grade 1; 44—Grade 2;

49—Grade 3; 51—Grade 4; 53—Grade 5; 56—Grade 6; 57—Grade 7; 58—Grade 8; 59—Grade 9; 60—Grade 10; 61—Grade 11; 64—Grade 12.

—The ultimate judge of whether or not a text is readable is the reader. A strategy has been developed to help students (middle grades and up) to conduct an independent informal evaluation of the level of text difficulty (Schumm & Mangrum, 1991). The strategy, known by the acronym FLIP, helps students evaluate text by taking text Friendliness, Language, and their own Interest and Prior knowledge into consideration.

• *Instructional design:* An evaluation of instructional design is guided by the question, "How is content taught?" Young and Riegeluth (1988) suggest that the instructional design of texts be evaluated on three levels: the macro level, the micro level, and message design.

A *macro-level* evaluation provides an overall picture of the instructional design of the textbook, generally through the scope and sequence chart.

A *micro-level* evaluation determines how a particular skill is presented. A skills trace (Muther, 1985a; Cotton, Casem, Kroll, Langas, Rhodes, & Sisson, 1988) is one way of doing this. With a skills trace the evaluator isolates a particular skill and traces it through the series of books across a sample of perhaps three grade levels. This helps evaluate systematically how a skill is introduced, developed, and reinforced. Muther (1988) sees skills traces as being both horizontal (three series at a designated grade level) and vertical (three grade levels in one series). At the micro level it is also important to assess if adaptations for learners with special needs are incorporated in skill and concept instruction. The absence of suggestions for adaptation will put an unnecessary burden on teachers if instructional modifications are to be developed to meet individual needs. See Chapter 7 (the section on "Serving Special-Needs Students") for suggested textbook adaptations.

As skill presentation is scrutinized, it is imperative to keep in mind the implications of Durkin's classic study (1981). Does the text teach and not just test skills? In other words, are specific instructional strategies provided: what to do, how to do it, when to use the strategy, and why it will help.

*Message design* evaluation deals with an appraisal of page layout. Conn (1988) proposes an examination of headings and subheadings to determine the flow of presentation, and individual units to see if they are focused and manageable from an instructional standpoint. Other questions are: Does the page format facilitate learning? Are graphics in close proximity to corresponding text?

Examine the message design of all major components of the text, including the text itself, the teacher's edition, and "core" supplementary materials (those that have direct impact on the quality of daily instruction—perhaps the tests that go with the series and/or the workbooks). Don't worry about supplementary materials that are not part of the core. If your school cannot afford all these supplementary materials, it's best not to get swayed by them. Instead, spend your energy looking at the text itself and the supplementary materials that probably will be used.

Worksheets and related supplementary activities should be evaluated for task content, task design, opportunities for sufficient and appropriate review, clarity and consistency of instructional language, and opportunities for open-ended responses (Center for the Study of Reading, 1990). See the next section, on "Workbooks," for further detail. Tests should include clear guidelines for administration, scoring, and interpretation; unambiguous directions and item content for students; and a distinct match between what is being taught and what is tested (Center for the Study of Reading, 1990). See Chapter 9 for a global view of assessment.

—Finally, when considering message design, also scrutinize teachers' manuals. Is information presented in a "considerate," usable manner? Does the manual include creative supplementary activities?

*Make the final decision:* One of the best ways to obtain information about the worth of a textbook is to communicate with professionals currently using the text through structured telephone interviews or through site visits (Muther, 1988). In either case, include at least three districts to visit (the best route) or to interview. The use of pilots is another possibility but is not recommended. Unless one teacher pilots all texts being considered, each teacher typically prefers whichever text she or he piloted. And teachers can seldom afford to interrupt their teaching to pilot several texts.

Before the final decision is made, summarize and evaluate all data collected. Finally, reflect back on the initial designation of an ideal text, and then *make a selection.*

### Implement Program and Monitor

You're not through yet. Help to develop an overall model for implementation that includes inservice training for teachers and orientation for parents *before* as well as *during* implementation. Make arrangements for using ongoing support services available from publishers. Then monitor program implementation so that adaptations can be made as soon as possible.

Is this smorgasbord too heavily laden? You'll have to select among the strategies we've provided. But the more thorough your review, the more learning your faculty can engage in during the process and the more satisfied they will be with their choice.

### Workbooks

In *Becoming a Nation of Readers,* the Report of the Commission on Reading (Anderson, Hiebert, Scott, & Wilkinson, 1985), one strong recommendation was that children should spend less time completing workbooks and skill sheets and more time engaged in genuine literacy tasks. Jachym, Allington, and Broikou (1989) actually computed the cost of seatwork in terms of personnel time for duplicating, paper, and the like, and found that these materials added up to an extraordinary expense. The role of the RRS should include providing teachers with suggestions for seatwork alternatives. If teachers insist on workbooks, however, the following guidelines (Osborn, 1984, pp. 110–111) can be used:

---

### SOME GUIDELINES FOR WORKBOOK TASKS

1. Workbook activities should match the instruction and learning occurring in the lesson.

---

2. Workbook activities should provide a systematic, cumulative, and meaningful review of instruction.

3. Workbook activities should match the most important learning occurring in the reading program.

4. Workbooks should provide relevant tasks for students needing extra practice.

5. The vocabulary and concepts of workbook activities should correlate with the experiential and conceptual background of the students and the basal series itself.

6. Language used in the workbook should be consistent with that of the instructional process.

7. Instructions for completing workbook activities should be clear and easy to understand. You should help students with practice examples to ensure that they understand the tasks.

8. The layout of the pages should be attractive and useful.

9. There should be enough content to ensure learning.

10. Workbook content should be accurate and precise.

11. Some workbook activities should be recreational in nature.

12. Students should respond in a consistent manner from one workbook activity to another.

13. There should be a close correlation between reading and writing response modes.

14. Discussions and illustrations of how the various tasks relate to reading should accompany workbook activities.

## Kits

For those of us who started teaching in the 1970s, reading kits (the SRA materials come to mind most quickly) seem to have gone the way of bell-bottom pants. Yet some reading clinics and classrooms around the country are still using reading kits. Indeed, some students make progress in reading while using carefully paced programs. Some students and teachers actually enjoy such structure. If reading kits are to be used as part of the reading program, the following considerations should be made:

1. The pacing and reading level should be appropriate for target students.

2. The program should be flexible so that students can work on only the skills they need and not on unnecessary skills.

3. The interest level of passages should be high and the writing compelling.

4. The program should be consistent with the ongoing program of reading instruction.

## Computer Software

Selecting computer software can be confusing for the novice. Often teachers are reduced to using catalog descriptions or questionable advice to make decisions. If teachers are dissatisfied with the software, precious educational dollars are wasted. Although reviews of specific computer software in publications like *The Reading Teacher* and *Journal of Reading* can be helpful, the following guidelines from the International Reading Association provide some valuable general suggestions for selecting nonprint media:

### International Reading Association Criteria for Selecting Nonprint Media for the Reading Curriculum

Print media include printed materials in books, pamphlets, magazines, or newspapers. Nonprint media include any other means of conveying information, including television, radio, computer, music, games, audio tape, film, video disk, video tape, and cable television.

1. Materials shall support and be consistent with the general educational goals of the school district.

2. Materials shall contribute to the objectives of the instructional program.

3. Materials shall be appropriate for the age, level of social and emotional development, and interests of the students for whom the materials are selected.

4. Materials shall present a reasonable balance of opposing sides of controversial issues so that students may develop the practice of critical reading and thinking. When only one side of an issue is currently available, the nature of the bias will be explicitly discussed and explained to the students.

5. Materials shall provide a background of information that will enable pupils to make intelligent judgments in their daily lives.

6. Materials shall provide a stimulus for creative reading, writing, listening, and thinking.

7. Material shall reflect the pluralistic character and culture of society and shall foster respect for women and for racial and ethnic minority groups.

8. Materials shall be of acceptable technical quality, with clear narration and synchronized picture and sound.

9. Materials should be selected on the basis of their aesthetic quality and should provide students with an increasing appreciation of the world around them.

10. Materials should encourage affective responses and further humanistic concerns.

In addition to these generic suggestions for selecting nonprint media, more specific considerations should be made when selecting computer software. Radencich

These criteria were approved by the International Reading Association Board of Directors, May 1984. Reprinted with the permission of the International Reading Association.

(1991) compiled suggestions for developers of computer software from a variety of sources. These suggestions can serve as a guide for consumers as well. Her suggestions are organized into four categories: educational content, presentation, interaction, and teacher use.

---

## SOFTWARE EVALUATION SUGGESTIONS

*Educational Content*
- _____ Content is planned, sequential, and original.
- _____ Concepts and vocabulary are of consistent level of difficulty.
- _____ Recall of prior learning is encouraged.
- _____ Remediation is differentiated from review.
- _____ Pretests are included.
- _____ Evaluation components are included.

*Presentation*
- _____ Presentation is logical and well organized.
- _____ Facts are accurately presented.
- _____ Grammar, spelling, and usage are correct.
- _____ Response and loading time are quick.
- _____ Sound enhances but does not distract.
- _____ Graphics and color enhance.
- _____ Screen display is clear.
- _____ Menus are descriptive.
- _____ Score is displayed.
- _____ A "help" option is provided.
- _____ "Crashing" safeguards are included.
- _____ Exiting and reentering are easy.
- _____ Sufficient component parts are included.
- _____ Violence and sarcasm are avoided.
- _____ The presentation is motivating and challenging.

*Interaction*
- _____ The difficulty level can be controlled.
- _____ Entries can be corrected.
- _____ Waiting signals are clear.
- _____ Cues and prompts fade to help the user answer questions.
- _____ There is a range of appropriate responses.
- _____ Intermittent reinforcement is provided.
- _____ Specific feedback is provided for errors.
- _____ Personalized responses are provided.

*Teacher Use*
- _____ Minimal teacher monitoring is needed.
- _____ Software can be modified to meet individual needs.
- _____ Alternative learning opportunities are suggested.
- _____ A data trail is provided.

*Source:* Adapted from M. C. Radencich, "Publishing Computer Software," in James F. Baumann & Dale D. Johnson (Eds.), *Writing for Publication* (pp. 176–178). Newark, DE: International Reading Association, 1991. Reprinted with permission of Marguerite Radencich and the International Reading Association.

## Conclusion

The quest for instructional materials can become a team effort for members of a school community. When teachers or RRSs attend conferences, all can bring back tales and treasures from publishers' displays. When they are deciding how to spend precious education dollars, teachers and the RRS can work collaboratively to establish guidelines. If sufficient time is allocated for this process, shopping together for instructional materials can be fun!

# 9

# Assessing Student Performance: An Ongoing Decision-Making Process

**R**EMEMBER WHEN YOU RECEIVED your Scholastic Aptitude Test or Graduate Record Examination scores in the mail? Only a confident few were able to open that letter without trembling hands. Those scores had an influence on our future. Assessment is much more than test taking; assessment—particularly in the area of literacy education—has an enormous impact on instruction and on individual lives. In this chapter assessment will be approached as a decision-making process with the questions in the graphic organizer at the beginning of this chapter serving as the framework for decision making.

## What Is the RRS Role?

Assessment is an integral part of instruction and occurs every single school day (Teale, Hiebert, & Chittendon, 1987). Valencia and Pearson (1987) describe optimal assessment as follows:

> . . . the best possible assessment of reading would seem to occur when teachers observe and interact with students as they read authentic texts for genuine purposes. As teachers interact with students, they evaluate the way(s) in which the students construct meaning, intervening to provide support or suggestions when the students appear to have difficulty. (p. 728)

Duffy and Roehler (1989, p. 61) define assessment as "collection of the data used to make decisions." Henk (1985, p. 284) comments, "An assessment is only as good as the individual who interprets the data."

The notion of literacy assessment as a decision-making process can be used to guide the planning of a schoolwide assessment program. As with any major program decision, representatives from subgroups in the school community (administrators, classroom teachers, parents, school district personnel, and students) need to be consulted. A Reading Committee (see Chapter 5) can be instrumental in structuring an assessment plan for the school.

As the RRS you will play a role in the school's literacy assessment program and in assisting individual teachers in their in-class assessment efforts. In some unfortunate instances the RRS role is limited to management of standardized and basal tests. We see the role of an RRS in schoolwide assessment as being more substantive. We see the RRS as a coparticipant in structuring a schoolwide assessment program that is consistent with the school's philosophy of literacy education.

You may also inform teachers about current assessment procedures and tools. Individual teachers can and should have some autonomy in the form and content of assessment in their own classrooms. Certainly, the assessment should be compatible with the school's overall assessment plan. But if assessment is going to be ongoing, informal, and curriculum-based, some decision making must rest in the hands of individual teachers. The RRS can help empower teachers in building their repertoire of assessment tools. Assessment procedures can be shared through inservice sessions, newsletters, and simply passing around copies of articles of new developments in assessment. It is also important that teachers have the opportunity to share their assessment innovations with each other. These innovations can include assessment tools, procedures, record keeping, and reporting to parents.

From time to time some RRSs are asked to serve as diagnosticians. Indeed, in many schools diagnosis is an integral part of the RRS role. Elementary teachers who lack the time to administer an informal reading inventory to an individual child may call on the RRS. Content area teachers who do not have skills in using formal and informal assessment tools may ask the RRS to determine the reading level of a secondary student. Although this role is certainly important, be judicious in allocating your time to diagnostic tasks. They can eat away at the time and energy you need for other responsibilities.

Another role that you can play is working with teachers to explore ways for students to become involved in the assessment process. Students are typically viewed as the object of assessment, but students can also be collaborators in both data collection and data analysis. Students' responsibility for their own learning, though traditionally overlooked (Goodlad, 1984; Gutmann, 1987), is receiving increased attention (Ericson & Ellett, 1990). Students can be involved in identifying components of assessment portfolios. They can be interviewed to help the teacher determine student-identified goals for literacy improvement and the degree to which those goals were met. Finally, students can be taught how to conduct a self-analysis of their own work. Indeed, teachers exploring portfolio assessment are finding that they cannot manage without using students to help with data management. Not only does this save time for the teacher, but it also results in a richer program for the students. Paper-and-pencil assessments are insufficient to identify student needs. The voice of students must be heard.

## What Are We Assessing?

The content of literacy assessment can be narrowly viewed as those reading and writing subskills included on standardized tests. However, this view represents an outmoded definition of literacy (Hinson & Radencich, 1990). The definition of literacy that sufficed for an earlier generation and a different economy has been replaced by a host of higher literacies: computer, scientific, civic, and cultural. These higher literacies call for students to analyze, think critically, evaluate, synthesize information, communicate effectively, solve problems, learn how to learn—in general, to learn far more actively than traditionally (Brown, 1989).

To clarify the goals for assessment, you should first clarify the goals for instruction (Winograd, Paris, & Bridge, 1991). Paris et al. (1992a) list seven critical dimensions and attributes of literacy that should be considered in assessment plans: (1) engagement with text through reading, (2) engagement with text through writing, (3) knowledge about literacy, (4) orientation to literacy, (5) ownership of literacy, (6) collaboration, and (7) interconnectedness of the curriculum. Duffy and Roehler (1989) have proposed three primary goals that can be used to guide the content of literacy assessment: attitude goals, process goals, and content goals. A comprehensive literacy assessment program should include all of these goals, and specific assessment tools for each goal will be offered in this chapter.

- *Attitude goals* can include not only students' attitudes about reading and writing in general and about themselves as readers and writers, but also attitudes about specific pieces of writing.

- *Process goals* in the Duffy and Roehler model incorporate the traditional skills we tap in reading and writing tests, as well as metacognitive strategies that empower students to reflect on their own understanding before, during, and after reading.

- *Content goals* relate to reconstructing the author's intended meaning in textbook, functional, and personal reading. Process goals must be placed within a genuine context or they become isolated subskills that students cannot transfer to similar tasks. Content goals provide this meaningful context.

## Why Are We Assessing?

Two of us are district reading supervisors. We get calls from schools asking us what test to order. Our first question is always, "Why are you assessing?" Sometimes the answer to this question hasn't been thought out. Yet, your choice of an assessment tool will be contingent on your purpose for testing. Stoodt (1981) suggests five purposes for reading assessment:

1. To assure the teacher that students are grouped appropriately

2. To allow the teacher to meet specific learning needs

3. To evaluate the strengths and weaknesses of the instructional program

4. To assess individual growth and development

5. To account to the community

Your state, school, district, or local administrator may establish your purposes for assessment. If your assessment program is well defined, you will not wind up with test scores that are merely filed away and are not an integral part of ongoing instruction.

## How Will We Manage Assessment Results?

At one level, managing assessment results means making the best use of them. When disseminating results of standardized tests to parents, management might mean educating parents in areas such as the limitations of standardized tests and the lack of significance in minor score changes from year to year.

When making school use of standardized test results, management will begin not only by studying scores from each class and each grade, but also by comparing scores from year to year. Comparisons between years should involve not only examinations of the grade levels themselves (e.g., grade 1 in each compared), but also tracking of classes of students (e.g., grade 1 in year 1 becoming grade 2 in year 2). Management of standardized test results might also mean looking closely at scores that seem questionable based on everyday performance. Wide discrepancies between standardized test scores and everyday performance can be due to any number of factors, such as illness on the day of the test, students not motivated to perform up to capacity on a daily basis, "doctored" test scores, error in test administration, test anxiety, or lack of congruence between test and curriculum.

A further dimension of management is that helping teachers use test results wisely. At the elementary level, because teachers typically have self-contained classes and teach reading and writing, most teachers are aware of students' standardized test scores. In departmentalized secondary settings, however, many teachers would like information about students' strengths and weaknesses in order to meet individual needs. For the secondary RRS, a plan for dissemination of data on student reading to those teachers who want the information is essential.

On a broader scale, the issue of managing assessment deals not only with standardized test scores, but with the wealth of assessment data that the teacher makes use of on an ongoing basis: student self-evaluation, observation, questioning of students, and the like. Will any of this type of data go with the student when he or she is promoted or transferred? The contents of students' cumulative records may be determined by your state department of education or local school board. As RRS, however, you may have input in determining the nature of the more informal accumulation of student work that is presented to parents and administrators. For example, your school may wish to keep student portfolios with samples of work from every year the students are in attendance. Again, a reading committee can be helpful in determining what common information can be kept by all teachers in the school, how it will be recorded, and who has access to this information.

## How Will We Cope With High-Stakes Tests?

It is probably fair to operationally define high-stakes tests as those that are generally reported in the newspaper. We are all concerned with the way high-stakes tests such as minimum competency tests and standardized tests can destroy the very learning they are supposed to facilitate. For students, high-stakes tests determine tracking, special programs, promotion, diplomas, and self-concept. For schools, high-stakes tests determine good or bad publicity, administrative jobs, merit school money, and community respect. When test scores are plastered over headlines, the result is virtual elimination from the curriculum of any learning that is not measured on the test.

When students are consulted, the picture becomes even more grim. Paris, Lawton, and Turner (1992) found disturbing trends among students in grades 2 to 11 as they get older:

- A growing suspicion about the validity of test scores

- A growing realization that students are not well informed about the purposes and uses of achievement tests

- Increasing apprehension that test scores may become the basis for comparative social judgments

- Decreasing motivation to excel on standardized tests

- The surprising admission among older students that they felt less well prepared to take the tests

Leaders in the field of reading and writing have called for change in reading assessment. Valencia and Pearson (1987, p. 726) wrote: "The tests used to measure reading achievement do not reflect recent advances in our understanding of the reading process. If we are to foster effective instruction, the discrepancy between what we know and what we measure must be resolved." Both the Association for Supervision and Curriculum Development (ASCD) and the International Reading Association (IRA) have issued position statements in response to problems with high-stakes tests. In *Becoming a Nation of Readers* (Anderson, Hiebert, Scott, & Wilkinson, 1985, p. 100), the authors state, "If schools are to be held accountable for reading test scores, the tests must be broad-gauged measures that reflect the ultimate goals of instruction as closely as possible. Otherwise, the energies of teachers and students may be misdirected."

Alternatives to traditional testing that emphasize informal, ongoing assessment are being promoted. Some new basal readers take into account this need for informal assessment. Some movement in this direction is also apparent from individual psychological testing, where input regarding day-to-day performance is being given an increasing level of importance (Ysseldyke & Christenson, 1987). However, such informal assessment is generally viewed as a supplement to, not a substitute for, more conventional standardized reading tests. Despite the many limitations of such tests, tests for accountability are likely to be with us for some time. As we all try to cope, here are some suggestions for surviving high-stakes tests:

## TIPS · COPING WITH HIGH-STAKES TESTS

- Follow a plan that is agreed on by the district, or at least the school. Although everyone wants to "raise test scores," the means that will be acceptable will vary among districts and schools. For example, use of commercial materials that practically duplicate the most common standardized tests on the market may or may not be considered to be ethical in your school or district.

- Keep in mind that any one test is just a fragment of the complete picture of a student's reading/writing profile or of a school's total reading/writing program.

*(continued)*

### TIPS (continued)

- Decide at the beginning of the school year how results from a variety of tests will be communicated to parents and to the community. Make a plan for disseminating this information.

- Hold an inservice session for teachers so that they are prepared to orient students to the format of the high-stakes test and to general test-taking skills.

- Encourage teachers to prepare for standardized tests all year long in informal, contextually appropriate ways that are consistent with the regular instructional program. For example, when reading content area passages in class, have students write and answer questions that are similar to those frequently found on standardized tests (e.g., central thought, detail question, context clue).

- Avoid the temptation to squander valuable instructional time in teaching to the precise content of tests rather than teaching underlying concepts.

- Provide teachers with practice materials so that students can become familiar with the test format. In the weeks before the test, orient students to test-taking skills. Many students do not know how to keep their place on an answer sheet, mark answers on a separate answer form, or pace themselves during timed tests.

- Provide teachers with materials to practice reading passages and answering questions under timed conditions. Jamestown Publishers offers *Timed Readings* for grades 4–12, and Teachers College Press publishes the *McCall Crabbs Standard Test Lessons in Reading* for grades 2–12. Note that it is flexible reading more than uniformly fast reading that is really helpful, so that the use of timed readings helps only one aspect of reading efficiency.

- For elementary school, prepare a letter to send to parents before the test with traditional reminders about putting children to bed early, feeding them a good breakfast, and so on. We know of one parent who took her child out to breakfast on the first day of testing so that her child would have positive associations with testing! Remind parents that the standardized test is just one facet of a total assessment program.

- Remind parents of other assessment results that will be made available to them, and tell them when and how they can expect to see those results. Orange County, Florida, sends report cards home in a pocket in the last page of a student-made book. The book starts with a letter explaining that each page shows a different picture of the child's accomplishments. Pages include such samples as a piece of art, a summary of a scientific experiment, and an "I can do" list.

- Prepare a student flyer containing a variety of test-taking tips (see Appendix B).

- Hold an inservice session for teachers so that they know how to interpret the results of the standardized test. (See the section on norm-referenced tests in this chapter.)

## What Tools Will We Use for Assessment?

There are no perfect assessment tools. Pearson (1992), in a presentation to the International Reading Association, outlined the advantages and disadvantages of each major form of assessment. He concluded that assessment had to be "messy" to be at all valid. Formal techniques are constraining and often miss some aspects of the human element. More informal techniques often do not offer the comfort of "measurable" gains. Valencia, McGinley, and Pearson (1990) contend that assessment should be multidimensional and that a variety of formal and informal tools should be used in a schoolwide program.

---

### QUESTIONS FOR SELECTING ASSESSMENT TOOLS: A BAKER'S DOZEN

1. What is my purpose in using this measure?

2. What attitude, process, or content goals does this measure address?

3. Are the format and content of the measure consistent with our purposes and goals?

4. Is the type of measure (formal or informal) consistent with our purposes and goals?

5. Is a commercially prepared assessment or local/teacher-prepared assessment tool most appropriate for our goals and purposes?

6. Are the administration and scoring time reasonable in terms of what we hope to learn?

7. Is the measure biased in any way against any linguistic or cultural group?

8. Does the measure assume prior knowledge that the target student(s) may not possess?

9. In the case of standardized tests, are adequate reliability and validity data available?

10. Are directions for administration, scoring, and interpretation of the measure clear and easy to follow?

11. Is an individual measure necessary, or will a group assessment tool suffice?

12. Are multiple forms and levels of the measure available?

13. Can the results of this measure be communicated easily to parents, administrators, and the community at large (depending on the assessment purpose)?

---

Literally hundreds of commercially produced assessment tools are available to educators. Any listing of such tests that we might offer would certainly not be exhaustive and, at the rate that new measures are being introduced, would immediately become outdated. For those wishing to keep up to date with newly developed instruments, see test reviews in *The Reading Teacher* and the *Journal of Reading*. For a detailed listing of reading tests in print up to 1990, see in the most recent edition of the classic *How to Increase Reading Ability* (Harris & Sipay, 1990, pp. 697–727). In general, a comprehensive assessment program will include norm- and criterion-referenced tests as well as informal assessment devices.

## Norm-Referenced Tests

Norm-referenced tests compare an individual student's performance with that of his or her peers. The emphasis of norm-referenced tests is not on the mastery of content but, rather, on the relative standing of an individual among students of a "norm" group of the same age or grade level. Norm-referenced tests can be group or individually administered. They are typically recommended as program evaluation tools and as screening tools (to be followed with measures more appropriate for individual assessment). Norm-referenced tests are also used, sometimes inappropriately, in grouping students. Regardless of the proposed use, we recommend that they serve as one tool in a multidimensional assessment program, although not necessarily on an annual basis.

The Stanford Achievement Test (1989) and the Iowa Tests of Basic Skills (1990) are typical norm-referenced tests. Although test formats vary, most offer standard, percentile, stanine, and sometimes grade equivalent scores. One instrument, Degrees of Reading Power (DRP) (1984), is a modified cloze test that yields scores in DRP units that can be translated to independent, instructional, and frustration reading levels. Readability data (in DRP units) are available for many textbooks so that teachers can gauge the student–textbook match.

One problematic area in the understanding of norm-referenced tests is the understanding of the median. The percentile score that is typically reported for a group is the median or the middle score. Educators wishing to boost median scores must realize that the median is not an average. Picture all the students in a group lined up, from the lowest score to the highest. The student in the middle of the line has the median score. If schools move the scores of the lowest students closer to the middle, but do not have any students crossing over the midpoint, they have not changed the median. The same applies to raising the scores of students who started out slightly higher than this midpoint. Median scores are raised only by moving students who are just below the midpoint and getting them to cross this point.

Educators who do not fully understand scores from norm-referenced tests not only have difficulty interpreting scores to parents, they quite often rely on grade-equivalent scores, a practice that has been discouraged by the International Reading Association (1981). A grade equivalent is an average point. Thus, in an average fourth grade, half the students will be above the fourth-grade level and half will be below it. Suppose that the test is a measure of knowledge of the alphabet. Virtually all fourth-graders will score 100 percent. So will all twelfth-graders. Thus, a score that places the child at the twelfth-grade level on this test does not mean that the child can identify the alphabet at a twelfth-grade level, only that he or she can do so as well as the average twelfth-grader can, which is also true for the average fourth-grader. Many publishing companies have discontinued the use of grade equivalents in recent years. The Baumann and Stevenson (1982) article in *The Reading Teacher* is beneficial in helping teachers interpret standardized test scores.

Also norm-referenced are writing production tests in which students respond to a prompt. Norms for these tests are often local ones created on the spot when a team scans through a set of papers to establish "anchor" or typical papers at each scoring level, say 1–4. Once this norming takes place, other papers are scored to determine where they fall in relation to the anchors.

## Criterion-Referenced Tests

Criterion-referenced tests assess student mastery of a specific goal. They are less global than norm-referenced tests and are typically more closely linked to a particular curriculum or set of competencies. A student's score on a criterion-referenced test is not compared to a norming population; instead, it is compared to a predetermined criterion. Criteria need not be traditional ones such as correctly completing 7 out of 10 items on a test. For example, a criterion could be using correct punctuation "most of the time" or including at least three types of writing in one's portfolio.

Criterion-referenced tests typically serve as tools to aid in individualizing instruction, grouping for instruction, and assessing individual progress. They can be developed by a teacher, school system, or state. Criterion-referenced tests accompany many basal reading programs. More generic criterion-referenced tests are also available from publishers.

## Informal Assessment Devices

> If we wanted to study the architecture of a building, we would not knock it down and study each brick and board. Something would definitely be missing from such an analysis! Likewise, our aim is to study aspects of reading within the context of real reading, not as isolated components of a complex process. Therefore, we need assessment devices that will have students read the kind of text they must read in school and at home. Only then can we draw meaningful conclusions about various important reading skills. (Gillet & Temple, 1982, p. 82)

Informal assessment devices are the heart of a comprehensive assessment program. They are informal in that administration and interpretation of results are more flexible than with commerically prepared norm- and criterion-referenced materials. Both teacher and student reports of evaluation of student reading and writing are incorporated. It seems that each new issue of professional journals includes a new suggestion for informal assessment. The choices are vast, but, "We must pick, choose, adapt, and adopt the measures that provide us with the information that fits our vision of reading and writing" (Winograd, Paris, & Bridge, 1991, p. 110).

To assist you in helping teachers select informal, multidimensional, authentic assessment, we have compiled an annotated listing of informal assessment tools for meeting attitude, process, and content goals, It is not within the scope of this book to provide you with specific details for all assessment tools, but we can briefly describe various instruments (primarily teacher-constructed) and give you references so you can "read more about it." Most of the assessment tools listed here are appropriate for a variety of grade levels and can be used in reading/writing and content area classrooms. Because some are designed to meet more than one goal, there is some overlap.

## Tools for Assessing Attitude Goals

• *Attitude inventories:* Attitude inventories can be helpful in determining student attitudes about reading/writing and about themselves as readers/writers. Some teachers use these inventories at the beginning and end of the year (pretest/posttest) to gauge the impact of personal reading programs. Inventories are available in the form of rating scales and open-ended sentences. A sample Student Interest Attitude Inventory for upper elementary and secondary students is presented in Appendix D. Other published attitude inventories can be found in the following sources:

Alexander, J. E., & Filler, R. C. (1976). *Attitudes and reading.* Newark, DE: International Reading Association.

Kennedy, L. D., & Halenski, R. S. (1975). Measuring attitudes: An extra dimension. *Journal of Reading, 18,* 518–522.

McKenna, M. C., & Kear, D. J. (1990). Measuring attitude toward reading: A new tool for teachers. *The Reading Teacher, 43,* 626–639.

• *Interest inventories:* At the beginning of the school year, interest inventories are invaluable in helping teachers get to know students' likes and dislikes quickly. Sentence completion inventories are probably the most useful (see the Interest and Attitude Inventory in Appendix D), but checklists and questionnaires are also available in print and, in the case of BookWhiz, on diskette:

Dulin, K. L. (1984). Assessing reading interests of elementary and middle school students. In A. J. Harris & E. Sipay (Eds.), *Readings on reading instruction* (pp. 344–357). New York: Longman.

Eberwein, L. (1973). What do book choices indicate? *Journal of Reading, 17,* 186–191.

Heathington, B. S. (1979). What to do about reading motivation in the middle school? *Journal of Reading, 22,* 709–713.

Norris, L., & Shatkin, L. (1987). *BookWhiz* (grades 6 to 9). Princeton, NJ: Educational Testing Service.

Norris, L., & Shatkin, L. (1989). *BookWhiz, Jr.* (grades 3 to 6). Princeton, NJ: Educational Testing Service.

Norris, L., & Shatkin, L. (1989). *BookWhiz Teen* (grades 9 to 12). Princeton, NJ: Educational Testing Service.

• *Dialogue journals:* A dialogue journal is a written conversation between two people—between individual students and the teacher or between pairs of students. After reading a book or story, a student can write a brief reflection about his or her interest in and attitude toward the material. Then the dialogue journal is passed on to the "journal partner," who writes a response to the student's entry and adds a reflection about his or her own reading. The dialogue journal format encourages communication about reading and is an ongoing record of students' interests and attitudes.

Atwell, N. (1984). Writing and reading literature from the inside out. *Language Arts, 61,* 240–252.

Bode, B. A. (1989). Dialogue journal writing. *The Reading Teacher, 42,* 568–571.

Bromley, K. D. (1989). Buddy journals make the reading–writing connection. *The Reading Teacher, 43,* 122–129.

Gambrell, L. B. (1985). Dialogue journals: Reading–writing interaction. *The Reading Teacher, 38,* 512–515.

• *Reading logs:* A reading log is one window to student reactions to their reading. A reading log is a notebook in which students can write their reflections about what they read. A format for entering log entries should be determined. This format might include the date, number of pages read, and title of the passage read. Students then can record their personal feelings.

• *Teacher-completed checklists:* One way of recording literacy attitudes and habits is through checklists. Au et al. (1990) provided an example of this with their "Checklist for Ownership of Reading." The authors defined *ownership* as literacy attitudes and habits. This recording device for informal observations can be used at regular intervals to gauge student change.

Au, K. H., Scheu, J. A., Kawakami, A. J., & Herman, P. A. (1990). Assessment of students' ownership of literacy. *The Reading Teacher, 44,* 154–156.

• *Student interviews:* We would never go to a physician's office and expect a diagnosis before we open our mouths. Yet we do this with students in school. We forget to consult the experts—the students themselves. Probably the best way to determine student interests and attitudes is through personal conversations and interviews. During such sessions it is important to *listen* to what the student has to say and to probe for reasons for negative attitudes and for possible areas of interest that may not have been detected with paper-and-pencil instruments. Although such interviews are difficult to arrange, they are imperative in establishing a positive relationship in a community of literacy learners. Take notes on the interview and keep it as brief as possible. The following are some types of questions that can be asked:

What is the best book you ever read? (interest)

What is your favorite kind of book? (interest)

Do you like to read? (attitude)

Do you have a library card? (habits)

What would make you a better writer? (knowledge)

A comprehensive description of various types of semistructured and open-ended interviews is presented in:

Seda, I., & Pearson, P. D. (1991). Interviews to assess learners' outcomes. *Reading Research and Instruction, 31,* 22–32.

• *Learning biographies:* Students can tell (in a personal conversation with the teacher) or write their own "reading and writing history." Histories can include how the students learned to read and write; successes and challenges along the way; and reading and writing habits, interests, and attitudes. These biographies can form the core of a "who I am as a person, as a reader, and a writer" type of portfolio. For a description of this type of portfolio, see:

Hansen, J. (1992). The language of challenge: Readers and writers speak their minds. *Language Arts, 69,* 100–105.

## Tools for Assessing Process Goals

• *Metacognitive inventory: Metacognition* refers to a reader's ability to monitor his or her comprehension and to activate appropriate corrective strategies when comprehension hits a "clunk." To gauge students' use of metacognitive strategies, a multiple-choice questionnaire has been developed. This measure presents students with reading situations (i.e., "Before I begin reading, it's a good idea to:") and then provides choices about actions that can be taken in order to understand a selection.

Schmitt, M. C. (1990). A questionnaire to measure children's awareness. *The Reading Teacher, 43,* 459–460.

• *Comprehension rating:* Students can be encouraged to monitor their own comprehension by using comprehension rating systems.

Davey, B., & Porter, S. M. (1982). Comprehension rating: A procedure to assist poor comprehenders. *Journal of Reading, 26,* 197–201.

• *Think-alouds:* A think-aloud is a structure for promoting students' reflection about their own reading. With a think-aloud, students read a passage orally or silently, ask themselves questions while doing so, reread to clarify, hypothesize, insert bits of prior knowledge, express puzzlement, and engage in other such metacognitive processes. Whenever readers come to a difficult part, they stop, describe the "clunk," and then try to problem-solve about ways to "fix up" the problem. Typically, think-alouds do not come naturally to many students, so the teacher needs to model the process. Think-alouds can provide the teacher and individual students with insight about how students process text. An example: The candidates were both lying. (*Hmm. That sounds familiar.*) Had lying become a necessary part of running for office? (*What does "running for office" mean? Maybe if I keep reading I'll get a clue.*) Had candidates always lied? If so, could the lying be excused if it was for a greater purpose than simply getting elected? (*Oh, I see. Getting elected. Running for office means trying to get elected.*) These questions needed to be answered.

Davey, B. (1983). Think-aloud—modeling the cognitive processes of reading comprehension. *Journal of Reading, 27,* 44–47.

• *Writing process checklists:* Checklists can be used to assess students' progress in the various stages of the writing process (i.e., prewriting, drafting, revising, editing, and publishing).

McKenzie, L., & Tompkins, G. E. (1984). Evaluating students' writing: A process approach. *Journal of Teaching Writing, 3,* 201–212.

## Tools for Assessing Content Goals

• *Informal reading inventories:* Informal reading inventories (IRIs) have been recognized as an efficient way to discover a great deal of information about a student's strengths and weaknesses in reading. If the information used is limited to quantitative data (independent, instructional, and frustration reading levels), then the potential contribution of the IRI is squandered. Growing numbers of teachers are becoming familiar with the variety of information that an IRI can yield, and are familiar with the implications of the type of diagnostic thinking that users of IRIs can carry over to ongoing, informal assessment. For example, teachers may (1) take the suggestions of some IRIs for analysis of graphophonic, syntactic, and semantic miscues, or analysis of retellings, and (2) mentally conduct such analyses during routine reading sessions. Many basal readers now include IRIs in their supplementary materials. Commercial inventories other than those included with basals are also available. Here are some examples:

Ekwall, E. (1986). *Ekwall reading inventory,* (2nd ed.). Boston: Allyn and Bacon.

Johns, J. (1988). *Basic reading inventory: Pre-primer—Grade eight,* 4th ed. Dubuque, IA: Kendall/Hunt.

Johns, J. (1982). *Advanced reading inventory.* Dubuque, IA: Kendall/Hunt.

Leslie, L., & Caldwell, J. (1990). *Qualitative reading inventory.* Glenview, IL: Scott, Foresman.

• *Interactive teaching/testing assessments:* In recognition of the close relationship between assessment and instruction, a number of commercial tools have been developed to link teaching and testing. The focus is on identification of student needs within genuine reading and writing tasks and then providing instructional suggestions for meeting those needs.

*Integrated assessment system.* (1990). San Antonio, TX: Psychological Corporation.

Raju, N. (1991). *Integrated literature and language arts portfolio program.* Chicago: Riverside.

*The Riverside curriculum assessment system.* (1991). Chicago: Riverside.

Roswell, F. G., & Chall, J. S. (1991). *Diagnostic assessment of reading with trial teaching strategies (DARTTS).* Chicago: Riverside.

• *Retellings:* Story retelling is a postreading or postlistening activity in which students tell what they remember orally or in writing. Retelling helps the teacher to assess students' general comprehension of a story, their knowledge of story structure, and their ability to organize their thoughts. Retellings can be guided (with the teacher asking directed questions) or unguided. One evaluation checklist which has been devised to assess students' retellings is included in:

Mitchell, J. N., & Irwin, P. A. (1990). The reading retelling profile. In G. G. Duffy (Ed.), *Reading in the middle school* (p. 147). Newark, DE: International Reading Association.

• *Summary writing:* Summaries are a way to assess students' understanding of text. One way to diagnose understanding of summarization is to have students read a passage and then provide them with good and poor summaries of the passage. Another way is to have them write summaries and then conduct a self-, peer, or teacher evaluation of the summary.

• *Sentence verification technique:* The Sentence Verification Technique (SVT) is a procedure for assessing reading comprehension of either narrative or expository passages. After reading a passage, students read a list of test sentences and decide if each sentence is an "old" sentence (a quote or paraphrase of a sentence in the passage) or a "new" sentence (a meaning change of a sentence in the passage or an unrelated sentence). Details for constructing a SVT test are provided in:

Royer, J. M., Greene, B. A., & Sinatra, G. M. (1987). The sentence verification technique: A practical procedure for testing comprehension. *Journal of Reading, 30*, 414–422.

• *Title recognition tasks:* A title recognition task is a quick gauge of the breadth of students' reading and exposure to print. Title recognition scales for primary grades (Schumm, Vaughn, & McDowell, 1992) and intermediate grades (Cunningham & Stanovich, 1991) are now available. A title recognition task is a listing of book titles including obscure books, moderately familiar books, books that children are likely to encounter, and fake book titles. Each title is followed by spaces for students to check whether they have heard of the book or not. Students are informed that some of the book titles are fake, so any guessing will be detected.

Cunningham, A. E., & Stanovich, K. E. (1991). Tracking the unique effects of print exposure in children: Associations with vocabulary, general knowledge, and spelling. *Journal of Educational Psychology, 83*, 264–274.
Schumm, J. S., Vaughn, S., & McDowell, J. (1992). *Assessing exposure to print: Its relationship to cognitive ability and literacy skills in early elementary children.* Paper presented at the National Reading Conference, San Antonio, TX.

• *Anecdotal records:* An anecdotal record is a listing of ongoing observations. Anecdotal records help to see patterns in achievement or behavior. Anecdotal records can take several forms: a sheet in a binder for each student, labels pasted on a folder for each student, a card file, and so on.

Rhodes, L. K., & Nathenson-Mejia, S. (1992). Anecdotal records: A powerful tool for ongoing literacy assessment. *The Reading Teacher, 45*, 502–509.

## Portfolio Assessment: Putting It All Together

In recent years, educators have rebelled against the overuse of standardized tests and have advocated individualized, ongoing, dynamic assessment based on a variety of formal and informal tools (Calfee & Hiebert, 1991; Johnston, 1984). Such tools are sometimes gathered in assessment portfolios. Artists, photographers, and models have portfolios to provide representative samples of their work. Student assessment portfolios are similar in that they are compilations of a variety of data about individual student progress in reading and writing, kept in a special (usually expandable) folder or other personalized container. Teachers can use portfolios to guide further instruction and to provide tangible evidence of literacy development to parents, administrators, and students themselves. Indeed, the National Assessment for Educational Progress (NAEP) and several states, notably California and Vermont, are exploring ways to use student work samples for achievement documentation on a statewide basis.

Assessment portfolios are living documents. They are constantly growing, reshaping, and contributing to ongoing decision making about instruction. They are not meant to be secretive and teacher-centered (like a grade book). Rather, they are meant to be a teacher–student collaborative effort to provide evidence of student progress. Parents can also be encouraged to make contributions. This helps them learn more about their child's development as a reader and a writer.

Thinking on portfolios is constantly evolving. There is no one right way to do portfolios. They can include a variety of entries. Some teachers keep standardized tests and basal reader assessments in the portfolios; others keep such information in a separate "teacher" folder. Still others see portfolios more as scrapbooks (Hansen, 1992). Peters (1991) has suggested, "You can't have authentic assessment without authentic content." He recommends that teachers select material for assessment that reflects themes that are critical to content learning, that is grounded in real-life experiences, and that is reflective of students' development as literacy learners.

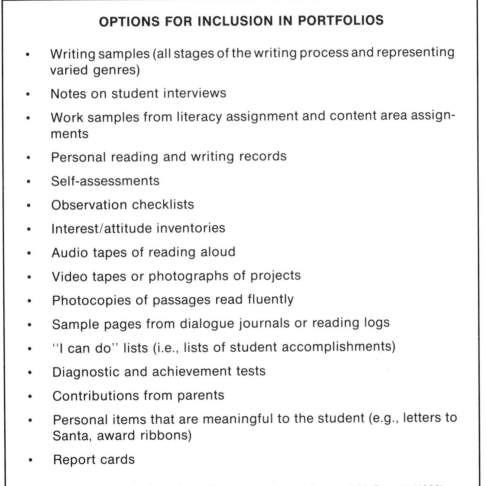

**OPTIONS FOR INCLUSION IN PORTFOLIOS**

- Writing samples (all stages of the writing process and representing varied genres)

- Notes on student interviews

- Work samples from literacy assignment and content area assignments

- Personal reading and writing records

- Self-assessments

- Observation checklists

- Interest/attitude inventories

- Audio tapes of reading aloud

- Video tapes or photographs of projects

- Photocopies of passages read fluently

- Sample pages from dialogue journals or reading logs

- "I can do" lists (i.e., lists of student accomplishments)

- Diagnostic and achievement tests

- Contributions from parents

- Personal items that are meaningful to the student (e.g., letters to Santa, award ribbons)

- Report cards

Adapted from M. C. Radencich, R. Flash, D. Miller, N. Minges, & M. Starrett (1992).

Detailed guidelines for developing portfolios have been presented elsewhere (Au, Scheu, Kawakami, & Herman, 1990; Flood & Lapp, 1989; Harp, 1991; Tierney, Carter, & Desai, 1991; Valencia, McGinley, & Pearson, 1990; Wolf, 1989). The most immediate reaction from the uninitiated is, "This seems like a lot of work. How can I possibly do this with thirty students in my class?" The following tips may help:

## TIPS · DEVELOPING ASSESSMENT PORTFOLIOS

- Develop a portfolio plan that is consistent with your purposes for assessment.

- Clarify what types of entries will go into portfolios and what types of work will go into any other work folders that may be used.

- Start with only a couple of different kinds of entries. Expand as you are ready.

- Work with a buddy or a grade-level team of teachers as a support group as you experiment with portfolios.

- Have as a long-term goal the inclusion of a variety of assessments that address content, process, and attitude goals across the curriculum.

- Place the portfolios in the classroom in a highly accessible spot. Students and teachers should be able to add to the collection quickly and easily.

- Develop summary sheets or graphs that help to collapse a body of information (e.g., "I can do" lists, lists of books read or pieces of writing completed) and let students record these data when possible.

- Don't worry about keeping everything. Work with the student to choose a few representative measures that will demonstrate the student's literacy progress.

- Encourage students and teachers to review the portfolio periodically (at least four times during the school year). This review should be a time to celebrate progress made and a time to set future goals. Students can review the portfolio with a buddy before reviewing with the teacher. This will prepare them to help make decisions about what to keep. Student and teacher notes of this review can be kept in the portfolio.

- In preparing for a parent conference, have students develop a table of contents for the portfolio.

- At the end of the school year, evaluate your portfolio experience. Make a list of what you plan to include next year and what you found to be unnecessary.

## Models for Monitoring Student Progress

### Kamehameha Elementary Education Program (KEEP)

Hawaii, like most other states, has used standardized test scores as the basis of its assessment program. To develop an assessment program more compatible with their whole literacy curriculum, Kathryn Au and her colleagues at the Kamehameha Elementary Education Program (KEEP) have developed a portfolio assessment system (Au et al., 1990; Paris et al., 1992a). To guide their assessment portfolios, they determined grade-level benchmarks derived from the state language arts curriculum guide, a standardized achievement test, and their scope and sequence charts. Profile sheets were then used to compare students' progress (using data from a variety of assessment tools) with the grade-level benchmarks.

### Portfolio Assessment at Blackburn Elementary School

Blackburn School is a primary school in Manatee County, Florida. Blackburn's initiation into portfolio assessment was part of a two-year inservice program focusing on aligning assessment with whole language instruction (Lamme & Hysmith, 1991). Students and teachers collected three different types of information: student work, student reflection and self-evaluation, and teacher anecdotal records (observations, checklists, etc.). Of particular note are the writing, emergent reading, and response to literature developmental scales designed as part of this project. Also noteworthy is the amount of parental and student involvement generated. Teacher reaction to portfolio assessment was generally positive, particularly with teachers who were enthusiastic about whole language instruction in general. Blackburn's assessment devices became the basis for similar assessment throughout the district.

### Louisiana State University Laboratory School

A major challenge in high schools is monitoring individual literacy development. We have all heard horror stories of high school graduates who cannot read at a third-grade level. Parents, politicians, and the media ask: "How are these students permitted to graduate from high school?" and "Who is keeping track of whether or not kids can read and write?"

At Louisiana State University Laboratory School, students with low achievement test scores are discussed during an annual grade-level teachers' meeting (Schumm, 1988) where teachers decide whether or not the test score is reflective of the students' ongoing performance in textbook reading assignments. If there seems to be a problem, parents are invited to the school to discuss the possibility of enrolling their child in a credit-bearing reading course. The focus of the course is determined by individual student needs, with a strong emphasis on content area reading and writing competencies. An alternative to the course is an after-school program to assist students with content area reading and writing. Of course, the parent may choose to hire a private tutor or to ignore the options provided by the school. The important point is that students' literacy needs are attended to on a systematic basis and a choice of services is provided.

## Conclusion

At the outset of this chapter we said that assessment is much more than test taking. The advent of assessment that emphasizes ongoing, informal, and authentic student observation has begun to transform traditional psychometric practices. It is imperative that, as an RRS, you keep abreast of developments in this area and communicate innovations described in the professional literature as well as state and local policy changes to members of the faculty. Because assessment is a decision-making process that has high impact on student lives, it is necessary that we base our decisions on the best information available.

# 10

# Implementing Motivational Reading/Writing Programs

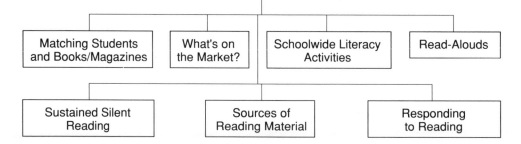

| Matching Students and Books/Magazines | What's on the Market? | Schoolwide Literacy Activities | Read-Alouds |

| Sustained Silent Reading | Sources of Reading Material | Responding to Reading |

**I**T HAS BEEN SAID you can lead a horse to water but you cannot make him drink. It has also been said you *can* make him drink—if you use a little salt. This chapter provides literacy salt. Students will read if they are motivated to do so. As the RRS, you can provide the "salt" and urge other teachers to do the same. In this chapter we offer a collection of suggestions for implementing a motivational reading program in your school. Choose what seems best for you and *get shaking!*

## Matching Students and Books/Magazines

Facilitating the student–selection match is crucial to a successful motivational reading program. As the school year progresses, most teachers learn about students' interests in various types of reading material and their attitudes toward reading. But to maximize the opportunity to match students and books early in the school year, it helps to ascertain students' interests and attitudes fairly quickly. Chapter 9 includes references to a variety of ways to determine such information: personal interviews, rating scales, open-ended sentence forms, reading reflection logs, and reading dialogue journals.

Initially, direct assistance from teachers is needed to help many students select books and magazines. Ultimately, however, it is important that students learn to choose reading material independently. As you have probably observed, during school library periods, many reluctant readers roam around aimlessly and then finally grab a book near the end of the period. Unfortunately, the book rarely if ever is opened. Many students simply do not know how to select reading material. The RRS and the media specialist can provide a joint inservice session to bring new books to the attention of teachers and help them problem-solve about making student–selection match and finding ways to promote student independence in textbook selection.

For elementary students, we have found the so-called five-finger rule of thumb quite helpful in fostering independence in selecting books. The child is directed to select a book that looks interesting and then start reading the first page. While reading, the child puts one finger up for each word he or she does not know. If the child runs out of fingers before the end of the page, then the book may be too difficult. This is not exactly the Fry Readability Chart, but it does provide a quick index of reading difficulty for the child.

You can help students find interesting and appropriate reading material by using the "Strategy for Helping Students Find the 'Right' Book" in Appendix B. This sequence was written for middle school students but can be adapted to other levels. It can be given to teachers for classroom use, to the student body as a whole (perhaps on closed-circuit television, or in a newsletter), or to individual students as needed.

## What's on the Market?

Helping teachers and students find engaging and appropriate books has traditionally been the task of the school media specialist. With the thrust in recreational reading and literature-based curricula, however, the RRS is also asked to recommend books. Any systematic effort should begin with communication between the school media specialist and you. This professional collaboration can help keep you up to date and can foster cooperative efforts to serve the school as a whole.

One suggestion for such a collaborative effort would be monthly book talks between library personnel and you. These book talks (perhaps over a brown bag lunch) can be used to develop awareness of what's on the market, students' favorites within the school, and the needs of teachers and individual students. A variation is to start a Teachers as Readers book-sharing club that gathers and discusses books, perhaps in each other's homes or in restaurants, on a monthly basis (Cardarelli, 1992).

An enjoyable way to keep up with what's new is to spend time in bookstores and libraries regularly. Take a pal and try this on a Saturday morning, perhaps. Print resources that can also help you (usually available at your public or university library) are as follows. One caution, however. If the lists that follow are shared with parents, they need to understand that no book list is etched into stone. Book lists are merely starting points from which readers should feel free to wander.

1. *Children's Choices:* Since 1975, *The Reading Teacher* (a monthly publication of the International Reading Association) has published an annual listing of children's book choices in the October issue. Books that a sample of 10,000 students like best are presented as an annotated bibliography and are categorized as follows: all ages, younger readers, middle grades, older readers. Children's choices from 1989 to 1991 are now available in monograph form (International Reading Association/ Children's Book Council, 1991). If you would like to distribute the annual listing to teachers, reprints are available from IRA in bulk:

> International Reading Association
> P.O. Box 8139
> Newark, DE 19714-8139

2. *Young Adult Choices:* Since 1987, *The Journal of Reading* (a monthly publication of the International Reading Association) has published a list of books preferred by middle school and high school readers in the November issue. As with "Children's Choices," reprints of the annotated list are available from IRA.

3. Updates on Newbery and Caldecott Medal books.

4. Updates on other awards (e.g., Coretta Scott King Award, Children's Book Council, American Institute of Graphic Arts):

Children's Books: Awards and Prizes
Children's Book Council
67 Irving Place
New York, NY 10003

5. *Newspaper reviews:* The *New York Times* and the *Christian Science Monitor* both publish reviews of books for children and adolescents. The *Book Review Index* (Gale Research Company) also provides information about where a book has been reviewed.

6. *Magazine reviews:* Regular book reviews appear in the following professional journals:

Booklist
American Library Association
50 East Huron
Chicago, IL 60611

The Horn Book
14 Beacon Street
Boston, MA 02108

Language Arts
National Council of Teachers of English
1111 Kenyon Road
Urbana, IL 61801

The Reading Teacher
International Reading Association
P.O. Box 8139
Newark, DE 19714-8139

The Journal of Reading
International Reading Association
P.O. Box 8139
Newark, DE 19714-8139

School Library Journal
R. R. Bowker Company
121 Chanlon Road
New Providence, NJ 07974

## Schoolwide Literacy Activities

To establish a school culture that includes a community of readers and writers, it is helpful to organize schoolwide activities that highlight the importance of literacy.

You can serve as the catalyst to make sure some schoolwide activity is always in progress. Schoolwide reading programs can be innovative ideas that emerge from your local community, or they can involve participating in existing programs stemming from local, state, or national businesses or nonprofit organizations.

Focus on programs that provide intrinsic motivation. Keep any extrinsic motivators small (buttons, stickers, etc.) so that the reward does not become the reason for the reading. Kohn (1991) warns that intrinsically appealing activities lose their appeal if they are nevertheless extrinsically rewarded and the extrinsic reward is then removed.

Kerri Post, a parent from Miami, Florida, provided a powerful incentive for her two elementary children, Shannon and Devin, to read. She had the girls solicit donations for a family read-a-thon. Friends and family donated money for each book the girls read. Shannon and Devin then gave the money to the University of Miami Student Literacy Corps to buy books for children who could not afford them. With some imagination, similar programs that promote reading and teach children important lessons about citizenship can be implemented at the school level.

There are three keys to a successful schoolwide literacy program. The first is *opportunity* for all students. A competitive program (such as a writing contest that appeals only to the most academically adept students is limited at best. The second key is *organization*. And the third is keeping *enthusiasm* sky-high.

---

## TWENTY SUGGESTIONS FOR SCHOOLWIDE LITERACY ACTIVITIES THAT GIVE EVERYONE A CHANCE TO PLUG IN

1. Reading sleepovers

2. Read-alouds by high-profile community members

3. Peer or cross-age reading programs

4. "Write to Your Favorite Author"

5. Character dress-up days

6. Used book sales or exchange programs

7. Student book reviews in school newsletter or pockets in school library books

8. Audiotaping of books for younger children

9. Reading of student-authored pieces on school television

10. Bilingual presentations of favorite stories (e.g., "The Three Pigs"/"Los Tres Cerditos")

11. Book fairs

12. Family folktale storytelling "bees"

13. Storybook/author door decorating activities

14. Special days—Comic Book Day, Celebrate a Book Day

15. "Literary clubs" that meet before or after school or at lunch

---

16. Monthly contests (e.g., designing a bookmark, slogan, T-shirt, etc.)

17. Lotteries in which faculty and students earn entries for every book read (Lubell, 1991)

18. Children's or young adult author of the month

19. Student-authored section in the school media center

20. "I Read to the Principal Today" programs in which the children whose names are drawn at random read to the principal and are rewarded with a button or a snapshot on a bulletin board

---

**BUSINESSES AND NONPROFIT GROUPS THAT SPONSOR LITERACY PROGRAMS**

MS Read-a-Thon
(305) 599-0299

Pizza Hut Book-It!
800-4-BOOKIT

Reading Is Fundamental, Inc.
202-287-3220

World Book
PIE (Partners in Excellence) Reading Program
800-621-8202

---

**TIPS · ORGANIZING SCHOOLWIDE LITERACY ACTIVITIES**

• Decide on a coordinator.

• Devise a rough plan.

• Enlist administration and faculty support.

• Organize a committee. Involve parents, students, and teachers and other staff.

• Brainstorm a name for the program or, if linking with an existing program, personalize the name to fit your school. For example, Lubell's (1991) "Lotto Read" became "Cougar Challenge" at one school and "Reading Raffle" at another.

• Decide on logistics. Identify the tasks, personnel, and timeline.

• Identify ways to promote the program (flyers, school television, etc.).

- Execute your plan.

- Evaluate your plan and decide how to embellish it in the future.

## Book Fairs

Students who might never pick up a book under other circumstances can often be found buying books at a book fair. One secondary RRS we know has been able to keep the substantial proceeds she has made from book fairs for school-related expenses throughout the year. This has paid for professional resources, for extensive newspaper-in-education activities, and for special requests from teachers. The latter can really come in handy!

Book fairs can be held twice a year or even more often. You and/or the media specialist can make arrangements with one vendor. Parents should be advised of the dates so that they can support the effort.

## Newspaper-in-Education Activities

Newspaper-in-education (NIE) activities often focus on one month of the year, but they can be ongoing. Cheyney (1992) provides a wealth of NIE activities. Teacher idea guides are often available free of charge with orders from local newspapers, *USA Today,* or magazines such as *Newsweek* and *Sports Illustrated for Kids.* NIE activities are usually quite inexpensive. Depending on the activities that are planned, a class set of newspapers or magazines may be usable in more than one class.

# Read-Alouds

The importance of reading aloud to students in terms of vocabulary acquisition, attitudes toward reading, and reading achievement is well documented in professional literature (Morrow & Strickland, 1989; Teale, 1987) and is becoming more apparent in the popular literature (Trelease, 1989). The benefits of reading aloud have been heralded in the media. Teachers are persuaded to read aloud to students of all ages, parents are encouraged to read aloud to their children, and the general public is urged to participate in volunteer read-aloud efforts in the schools.

Teachers, faculty and staff, parents, and community volunteers can all read aloud to children. Regardless of the reader, the purposes of the read-alouds are the same:

1.  To model fluent reading

2.  To promote enjoyment and appreciation of children's literature

3.  To develop a bond between the reader and the listener

4.  To stimulate and motivate independent reading

A research base for parent and teacher read-aloud techniques is beginning to emerge (see Sulzby & Teale, 1991, for review). Similarly, read-aloud training materials for parents (Edwards, 1990; Idaho Literacy Project, 1992) and teachers (Rothlein & Meinbach, 1991) are now available. Some simplified suggestions for reading aloud are as follows (some are appropriate for younger children, others for readers of all ages):

1. *Before the session* (see the read-aloud lists for students of different ages in Appendix B)
   a. Choose a book that you enjoy and that you think will appeal to your listener(s): a story, a book of poems, perhaps even some nonfiction (Carter & Abrahamson, 1991).
   b. Choose a book that is at—but mostly beyond—the student's reading level.
   c. Choose a book with interesting language. If it is a story, it should have vivid characterization and good dialogue.
   d. Practice reading the book.

2. *Before reading the book*
   a. Set guidelines for listening.
   b. Relax and establish an atmosphere of enjoyment.
   c. Talk about the title of the book.
   d. Talk about the author and illustrator of the book, and perhaps the dedication.
   e. Initiate your reading with questions about the topic of the book, prior experiences about the topic, predictions of what the story might be about.

3. *While reading the book*
   a. Read slowly, but don't talk down to your listener(s).
   b. Create the mood with the pitch, tone, and pace of your voice.
   c. Act out visual images—use puppets, perhaps.
   d. Use your sense of humor—ham it up!
   e. Encourage discussion and questioning.
   f. Share thoughts about pictures as you read, but don't overdo it!
   g. Complete what you begin or find an appropriate stopping point.

4. *After reading the book*
   a. Encourage the listener(s) to retell the story.
   b. Ask questions about details, reactions to the content, and extensions of the content.
   c. Permit the listener(s) to ask you questions.
   d. Consider extending the reading with a motivational follow-up (see "Responding to Reading" later in this chapter).

In addition to adult readers, children can certainly read to one another. Peer or buddy reading can occur in the classroom on a daily basis. Peer reading events can range from spontaneous pairing of students in a reading nook to more structured pairing of mixed-ability students.

Cross-age reading in which older and younger students read to each other may be more challenging logistically, but it can be worth the effort (Juel, 1991; Labbo & Teale, 1990; Morrice & Simmons, 1991). One model of cross-age reading involves children from an older class (sixth grade, for example) visiting a younger class (kindergarten, perhaps) regularly to read aloud. In some cases middle school or high school students visit children in an elementary class. These students may be honors students, students in corrective/remedial programs, students from special education classes, members of a service organization, or students enrolled in a secondary reading course. Both older and younger partners benefit from the book-sharing experience.

## Sustained Silent Reading

Just as we get better at football or piano with practice, so too is the case for reading. Sustained Silent Reading (SSR) provides students with a needed opportunity for reading practice which, in turn, results in gains in reading achievement (Fielding, Wilson, & Anderson, 1986). With SSR, students and teacher individually read self-selected material. Students are not quizzed on this material—it is one time when they can read just for the fun of it.

First, however, your teachers will have to buy into it, particularly in terms of committing themselves to modeling SSR rather than using SSR time for paperwork. And then they will have to buy into the logistics. How often will SSR be held? For how long? When will it be scheduled? Will it be monitored?

Even with faculty support, SSR can get to be old if it's done every day. If it is dropped as a result, you're back to ground zero. Thus, you might be wise to schedule SSR only two or three times per week and, on alternate days, to have other activities such as read-alouds, sustained silent writing, or discussions of current events. SSR may be scheduled according to each teacher's convenience, or it may be a whole-school effort in which secretaries, custodians—*everyone*—reads simultaneously. In some schools SSR is scheduled first or last in the day in order to start or end the day right. At the very least, it is essential that teachers who share an open area schedule SSR at the same time.

### Elementary Issues

*Becoming a Nation of Readers* (Anderson et al., 1985) tells us that the average primary student reads only seven or eight *minutes* a day. For students in the low group, the figure is even lower. Thus, the need for approaches like SSR is paramount.

At the elementary level, SSR can be scheduled to last from five to twenty minutes. The length can reach the upper end once students have gotten used to the procedure, particularly in the case of older children. Although SSR might be scheduled at any point in the school day, there are two schedules that we've seen most often.

The first involves having SSR first thing in the morning. The only problem with this is that if teacher X is scheduled to have, say, the art teacher come first thing every Monday morning, then his or her students will miss part of art all year long. Thus, some schools choose a second schedule in which SSR is rotated. If it takes place at different times every month, for example, then the time "lost" from other subjects would be equalized.

Kindergarten and first-grade classes can use the SSR time for read-alouds, for children to look at picture books, or for "mumble reading"—when children mumble the words to themselves. The teacher can alternately model silent reading and confer with individual students.

### Secondary Issues

Scheduling of silent reading in secondary schools is accomplished in different ways: In some schools, periods one day a week are shortened to allow for an SSR period of perhaps twenty minutes. Other schools alternate the periods in which SSR takes place. In either of these models, the "burden" is evenly distributed among teachers.

One depressing issue at the secondary level is that of students who do not want to let on that they value reading—they don't want to be seen as deviating from the norm. There is no easy solution to this problem. The obvious strategy is to try to make reading so appealing that the norm changes. An alternative strategy, which is probably most feasible in small schools, is that of putting together for part of the day a group of students who are suspected of being closet readers, so that the readers are not seen as deviants.

### Achieving Administrator, Teacher, and Student Cooperation

A typical problem with SSR is that of ensuring that there is enough reading material. See the next section in this chapter ("Sources of Reading Material") for suggestions on how to tackle this issue. Another typical problem with SSR is that of selling the importance of role models. Just as offspring of football enthusiasts often grow up to appreciate football, offspring of book enthusiasts often grow up to savor reading. Many children are not surrounded by role models of readers these days—either at home or in society at large. Thus, it is particularly important that the teacher give the message that, "No matter how much is on my desk waiting to be done, reading is so important that I will stop and read, too." Use the following tips to help you engage teacher support.

### TIPS · COOPERATION FOR SSR— KEEPING THE MOMENTUM GOING!

- Explain to teachers the importance of their modeling reading for the students. Remind them that reading the newspaper, a magazine, a novel, or a journal can be fun.

- Try a candid camera routine. Post pictures of participating classes on a highly visible bulletin board. Student pressure on the teacher or peer pressure on students can work wonders.

- Announce—or, better still, have your principal remind classes—that SSR will soon start. Follow this up by another announcement when the designated time arrives.

- Announce SSR times on moving-letter displays, if available. This is particularly helpful in schools that have a rotating schedule.

- Have someone sit by the public address system while SSR is in progress so that no one forgets and interrupts with an announcement.

- Suggest that your administrator visit different classrooms to participate.

- Include teachers in your reward system. Some secondary schools do this quite successfully (Lubell, 1991). In these schools, teachers and students win the right to enter a lottery by completing books and "chatting" about their books with a "mad chatter." Neighboring businesses provide prizes. (Any interest in tickets for two at a nice restaurant?) Donors and top readers are specially recognized at the end of the year.

- If students are more motivated to look at the pictures than to read, let them. Looking at the pictures may lead to reading.

## Sources of Reading Material

Reading choices in the classroom should include more than discards from the school library and books the students have currently checked out. A good selection of newspapers and high–low books and magazines is always helpful. The International Reading Association's books on easy reading (Ryder, Graves, & Graves, 1989) and on magazines (Stoll, 1989) can be invaluable. See "What's on the Market?" and other sections earlier in this chapter for additional ideas. Once classroom libraries have been assembled, you can be instrumental in setting up a checkout system.

Following are ideas for expanding classroom choices.

### TIPS · SOURCES OF READING MATERIAL

- Class libraries can be kept in bins that you can rotate from class to class.

- Public libraries or school libraries will often lend teachers class sets of twenty-five or so books to be kept for some time. Take advantage of these opportunities! Drive to the public library yourself if need be!

- In the case of beginning readers or limited English proficient students, it may be difficult to find enough predictable language books or other appropriate material. Options can include student-made books, books in the student's native language, and books accompanied by recordings.

- Teachers can bring magazines from home. Secondary content area teachers or elementary special area (e.g., art or music) teachers can bring to class magazines or books related to their field. This can help teachers see SSR as a valuable use of class time.

- One secondary school rotated responsibility for reading material into four departments; each took a week during the month. Thus, at some point during the science week, the science teachers took the students to the library so that they could get their SSR books for the week. Not only did this ensure that all students would have books, it also helped all teachers (rather than just the language arts teachers) have a sense of ownership in the program. Some would not otherwise have taken their students to the library this frequently.

- Stacks of paperbacks can often be picked up at garage sales and flea markets for a few dollars. You can persuade used bookstores to offer an especially good deal for such a worthy cause. Book drives can yield large numbers of paperbacks that community members may be all too willing to discard. Older students can donate books that they have outgrown.

- Any books gathered through these means should be examined by you or the media specialist in light of any censorship guidelines that may be in place at the school.

## Responding to Reading

Help teachers think of creative ways of having students respond to reading. Book reports have a place but are often overused. How about response logs? The teacher can periodically write comments on students' responses. Or how about short book reviews that are taped into the inside cover of a book? Other options include retellings and writing assignments that stem from a book—a new ending, a sequel, another version of the story with a change in characters, or a story rewritten as a play. The following list shows that the possibilities are endless. It was written with an elementary audience in mind, but secondary teachers will find some good tips as well (e.g., items #7, 20, 22, and 35).

---

### FANTASTIC ACTIVITIES FOR BOOK SHARING!

*Sharing Characters*

1. List ten characters in the book. Place them in alphabetical order.

2. List five characters and, next to each name, write the character's occupation.

3. How old do you think the main character is? Why? Name three things the character does that match that age.

4. If you could meet one of the characters, who would it be? List five questions you would like to ask him or her. What answers do you think you would receive?

5. Choose a character who made an important decision and describe that incident.

6. Describe the foods and drinks that one character might have for lunch.

7. List five characters from the novel. Give each a nickname and tell why you chose each.

8. Find an example of stress or frustration. Tell about it. How did the character resolve it?

9. Do you think the main character would like a job at a local fast-food restaurant? Why or why not?

*Favorite Character*

10. Would you choose the main character as your best friend? Why or why not?

11. Pick your favorite character. Give at least three reasons that you chose this one.

12. Pick your favorite and least favorite characters in the book. Give reasons that these characters could or could not be your friends.

---

13. Write a letter of advice to one of the characters.

14. Dress up as one of the characters or make a mask of the character.

15. Bring in props mentioned in the book and put on a play.

16. Your favorite character has just been granted three wishes. (None of the wishes may be for more wishes.) Tell what those wishes would be.

17. It's your favorite character's birthday. What gifts would you bring to the party?

18. Your favorite character just bought a baseball cap. Draw a picture of it. Explain the picture.

19. One of the characters has a problem. Describe it and tell how it was solved.

20. Make a diary entry that your favorite character might write.

*Scenes/Plot*

21. Act out various scenes in the book.

22. Make a video about one of the scenes in the book. You may have friends and family help with this assignment.

23. Pick seven events that happen in the book and write them on a timeline.

24. List five events that happen in the book in chronological order.

25. Write a follow-up chapter in your novel.

26. In what season does this novel take place? Give supporting statements.

27. Would you like to live in the setting (time and place) of this novel? Why or why not?

28. List different kinds of transportation mentioned in the book.

29. Use a blank world map or a U.S. map to locate settings in the book.

30. Compare and contrast objects found in the book with similar things we have today.

31. Find examples of feelings in the book—love, guilt, honesty, trust, loneliness.

32. Find an example of humor in the book.

*Other Fantastic Ideas*

33. Survey ten students from your class. Ask them two opinion questions about the book. Record your results.

34. Write a poem about the book.

35. Write a rap about the book.

36. Write a song about the book.

37. Radio-read your favorite part for the class, as if you were a radio announcer. Your friends may help you prepare.

38. If your book were made into a movie, who would you choose to play the various roles? You may pick friends or famous people.

39. Read a selection of the book to two friends and one family member. Write their reactions.

40. Make up a dozen questions and answers pertaining to the book. Have a class game with those quiz questions.

41. Make up three essay questions that would be good for the end-of-the-book test.

42. Tell the book's publisher your comments about the book.

43. Make up ten interview questions you would like to ask the author.

44. Make up a new title for this book. Why did you choose it?

45. Make a title for each chapter.

46. Look up the author in a reference book. Tell five things you learned about this person.

47. Keep a Wonderful Word List. When you come to a new word or a nifty saying or phrase, write it down.

48. Find three examples of onomatopoeia (sound words like *moo, cluck, slam*).

49. Draw a T-shirt outline. Design it with themes from the book.

50. Draw a picture of the house or apartment where one of the main characters lives.

51. Pretend you are the teacher in our class. How would you teach the lesson to make it interesting and exciting?

52. Be creative! Make up your own activity. Tell about it in a couple of sentences. Complete that activity. If it's "fantastic," then *your* idea could be activity #53.

*Source:* Adapted with permission from L. A. Blanchfield, "Fantastic Ideas for Book Sharing!" *Florida Reading Quarterly*, December 1991, pp. 32–33.

## Conclusion

In this chapter we have provided some literacy salt to add zest to motivational reading programs. Now it's up to you to sprinkle it judiciously.

# 11

# Providing Staff Development and Renewal

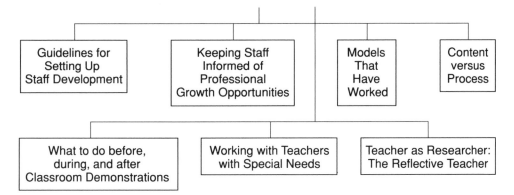

| Guidelines for Setting Up Staff Development | Keeping Staff Informed of Professional Growth Opportunities | Models That Have Worked | Content versus Process |

| What to do before, during, and after Classroom Demonstrations | Working with Teachers with Special Needs | Teacher as Researcher: The Reflective Teacher |

**S**TAFF DEVELOPMENT IS A fine art. It is not for a dilettante. As with any art, staff development has its frustrations, but the rewards can be tempting! This is a chapter that you will want to refer to again and again as you become a master. Because your own staff development is crucial in this process, share with your supervisor/director Appendix E's ideas for facilitating networking among RRSs.

## Guidelines for Setting Up Staff Development

Just as artists set out their materials with utmost care, so too must you prepare for staff development. Neilsen's quotes (1991, p. 676) paint a vivid picture of what can go wrong otherwise:

- Why is this article in my mailbox? Are you trying to tell me something about my teaching, or what?

- Who's got time to read this foolishness?

- This stuff is just common sense—I'm doing most of it already.

- So, what's this? Are we supposed to drop the latest trend and switch to this one?

Neilsen goes on to complain: "It's ironic. Isn't it? Our work as teachers is to foster a lifelong love for learning, to make learning contagious. But it seems, like the virus chicken pox, the virus is more acceptable in the young."

Barnard and Hetzel (1986, p. 65) do not mince words when they speak of the "dismal" history of inservice programs. Inservice has too often done something *to* people rather than *with* them. Much of it does not take into account the problems of teacher isolation, reluctance to change, and the needs of the adult learner. But even if your staff development is a class act, you will encounter resistance. There's often the feeling that if you need staff development, then you must be doing something wrong. This, of course, is unfortunate, since we can always profit from new twists in exercising the sophisticated art form of teaching. We find that for secondary staff development for content area teachers, the resistance can be particularly strong (see O'Brien & Stewart, 1990).

## TIPS · STAFF DEVELOPMENT AND RENEWAL

- Start with an open-ended needs assessment and/or with your school's philosophy of literacy education. A needs assessment might allow for options in terms of inservice delivery (would like literature on the topic, a brief explanation, a hands-on experience, or an ongoing training program). Ownership is essential! See Appendix A for a sample needs assessment.

- Consider establishing a professional growth committee. The mere existence of such a committee means the staff agrees that additional training is an inherent part of the profession of teaching (Barnard & Hetzel, 1986).

- Determine if inservice training is a logical answer to your need. Inservice training is appropriate when you are looking for an increase in knowledge or skill or an improvement in attitude. It is not likely to be helpful if the problem is, for example, a lack of materials or gross incompetence (Barnard & Hetzel, 1986).

- Make sure there is a match between the goals and the type of session presented. Is the session intended to give information? develop skills? change behaviors? (Korinek, Schmid, & McAdams, 1985).

- Know the prior knowledge of your teachers so that you can plan relevant sessions. Make sure you have a common vocabulary.

- Make sure that any guest presentations are done by a credible person who is both an adequate practitioner and an excellent presenter (Crandall, 1982).

- Think carefully about any consultants you suggest. Yvonne Freeman (Weaver, 1990, p. 281) offers some points to consider: "Outside consultants may make a big difference even though their message . . . may be the same as "what the school inservice people have been saying ('A prophet in his own land . . .')." "Consultants must be prepared to make theory *palatable*." "It is important that consultants give teachers lots of classroom examples of real teachers in real classrooms." Make sure that any invited speakers know your school's needs and are willing and able to meet them. Also, if possible, listen to consultants speak ahead of time to ensure that their message and delivery are not only appropriate but also interesting.

- Be careful also about suggesting staff members as presenters. This can be most effective. On the other hand, the "good old boy" or "the one who got to go to the last convention" just may *not* be the one to conduct the program. Mention the proposed presenter's name, and if you get groans, get someone else (Barnard & Hetzel, 1986).

- Send attractive agendas to teachers prior to meetings. Use borders or other clip art. Remember—"the medium is the message!" Jazz up titles. "Ring in the New Year!" is much more inviting than "January Meeting."

- Plan the schedule carefully. When it is possible to have meetings during the day rather than after school, do so. It is nice when education can resemble the business world in this regard. If there will be several sessions, space them out logically. For example, you may need time for teachers to apply something they have learned before they return for more information.

- Plan the location with care. Comfortable chairs are important. If tables are needed, find a place where they will be available. Avoid rooms with malfunctioning heating or air conditioning. In one elementary school that we know of, meetings are rotated around different classes. A couple of minutes of each meeting are spent with the teacher highlighting exciting happenings in that classroom. (This is a good way to motivate teachers to have something special to share.)

   We know of one middle school that held a staff retreat in a hotel on a Saturday. The relaxed atmosphere made it more of a social occasion than "work." No phone calls interrupted the meeting.

- Serve refreshments.

- *Listen!*—As Neilsen (1991, p. 667) points out, "Given an opportunity to air their frustrations, even the most bitter of comments in an open, nonthreatening atmosphere does wonders for the group and for the crusty cynics. If we don't take the comments personally, but instead empathize with the frustration and hear it out, we can move beyond confrontation to conversation."

- Keep to the agenda. Start and finish on time.

- Involve participants as soon as possible. Don't just have them sit passively! Music, laughter, metaphors are tools that help make brain-based learning (Caine & Caine, 1991).

- Move in close to the participants. One of us likes to stand by teachers (or administrators) who aren't paying attention. (Talk about nonverbal communication!)

- If you use transparencies, follow the "Transparency Do's and Don't's" found in Appendix C.

- If you provide handouts, make sure you have enough for everyone. Don't overdo it—there's only so much that people will read. Don't give them out any sooner than necessary—you don't want teachers to read them while a presenter is talking.

- Allow opportunities for follow-up, practice, feedback, and coaching. Plan for a long-term effort—three or four years minimum—for significant change (*Secondary Reading,* 1990). The Florida winner of the International Reading Association's 1990–1991 Exemplary Reading Program Award worked for two years with a regular consultant as they adopted a holistic approach to teaching. This allowed for ample opportunities for follow-up, practice, feedback, and coaching.

*(continued)*

### TIPS (continued)

- For a multisession activity, reassess the program as the sessions progress. If it is not serving its purpose, it may be better to end the training than to subject teachers to a waste of time and energy (Barnard & Hetzel, 1986).

- Model and encourage teachers to keep journals, writing before a meeting, as a problem is tackled, or before a meeting is ended to help with individual planning (Linda Henke, in Weaver, 1990).

- Provide teachers with an evaluation form and encourage them to comment on the most effective parts of the training.

- After an inservice activity, try to ascertain if it was effective for the purpose intended. The ultimate judgment is in observing whether what was provided in training is in fact, being incorporated in the classroom (Barnard & Hetzel, 1986).

## Keeping Staff Informed of Professional Growth Opportunities

When you try to "sell" professional journals or professional meetings, put yourself in the place of an advertiser. Think of what advertisers say, how they say it, and how often they say it. With a short and sweet message, advertisers tell you *why* you want their product. They tell you this over and over again. (Effective advertisers cleverly avoid antagonizing you with this repetition.)

This is easier said than done, however. Neilsen (1991) points out that teachers who bring new ideas and practices into the lounge conversation threaten to stir up a carefully cultivated atmosphere of boredom and faded ideals. She goes on to warn that these enthusiastic teachers can have the same effect on a staff as a new convert to long-distance running has on community of couch potatoes: It just makes everyone else look bad. So you've got to be judicious in how you spread your enthusiasm.

### TIPS · INFORMING STAFF OF PROFESSIONAL GROWTH OPPORTUNITIES

- "Remove the label" (Neilsen, 1991). Neilsen says that "using labels and trendy jargon" (e.g., "whole language") "can shut down a conversation as quickly as it began . . . . If we wear a role like the latest designer label, we may appear more like a copy than the real thing."

- Put highlighted articles in mailboxes of target teachers and administrators. One of us hooked a legislator into reading something lengthy by highlighting enticing points.

- Get others in the school to help you with the advertising so that teachers hear the same message from a variety of sources.

- Announce professional growth opportunities in a newsletter (see "Reading Newsletter" in Chapter 3), or, at the school site, on bulletin boards.

- Move journals that are a few months old from the school library to the teachers' lounge. Some teachers are not likely to go to the school library but may peruse these journals in the lounge.

- Copy the idea of one district specialist we know: Put blurbs about reading in "strategic" places in the restrooms.

- Use the idea of one elementary school that had a whole bulletin board dedicated to advertising an upcoming conference.

- Encourage administrators to provide release time and, if possible, expenses for teachers to attend conferences. Consider a fund-raising effort if necessary. We know of one principal who paid registration fees at a local conference for all teachers who had paid membership dues!

- Highlight teachers who are doing something special in newsletters or by encouraging them to present alone or with you at conferences.

- Get a group of teachers to start traveling conversation books (Neilsen, 1991, p. 676). These books serve "as forums for reading, writing, and talking with other teachers and administrators (parents and students, too!). The books—three-ring binders or sheaves with large clips—quickly grow fat and dog-eared as teachers exchange and respond to articles about literacy instruction, report on interesting professional news, and write about their classroom stories, challenges, joys, and frustrations."

*Professional Libraries*

You should keep a comprehensive personal and/or school professional library at school. You have to have information from journals and books at your fingertips. We know of one consultant who cut up her journals and filed articles by topic. An alternative is to duplicate key articles or file notes to yourself on where they can be found. Be free about lending out your material—just keep good track of who has what (see the section on "Professional Organizations" in Chapter 2).

## Models That Have Worked

Following is a breakdown of some models of staff development that may serve as starting points for your school.

### Gradual Release Model

Good teaching implies a gradual release of responsibility from teacher to student. It is as applicable to the RRS working with teachers as it is to any other teaching situation. Think of a teacher initially taking charge of all stages of learning, from modeling and guided practice to application, and gradually releasing responsibility in reverse order for application, then for guided practice, and finally for modeling (Gordon, 1985). This responsibility is released with the learner first explaining a line of reasoning, then answering questions and finding evidence, and finally actually asking the questions.

A variation of this model that we have seen work is that of the RRS starting and ending a series of inservice sessions with a whole group. In between, the RRS models lessons in individual teachers' classes, and these lessons are critiqued. The teachers use the same strategies at later dates, and these lessons, too, are critiqued. Teachers receive inservice credit for all their participation.

## Coaching

The athletic metaphor of coaching fits the role of the RRS to a tee. When a team of teachers works together to study new skills and polish old ones, coaches can lend support. Coaches provide companionship, give regular technical feedback, help determine appropriate use of the new skill, help to gauge student response to the new technique, and provide emotional support as teachers try new skills in front of students (Alvermann, Moore, & Conley, 1987; Joyce & Showers, 1982).

Coaching has reflective thinking at its core. A study in which two groups of teachers were taught reflective thinking and only one received follow-up coaching found significant differences in teacher behavior (see Sparks-Langer & Colton, 1991). The research of Joyce, Hersh, and McKibbon (1983) states that, with the *presentation* of theory, there is a maximum of 10 percent retention; adding *demonstration* yields another 10 percent retention; adding *practice* and *feedback* results in 20 percent retention or less; only when *coaching* for application is added does this figure rise to a maximum of 75 percent. These are powerful figures to support the need for coaching—that is, the need for an RRS.

Even with coaching, however, results are not guaranteed. Marzano (1987) found in one study that staff development does not result in high levels of implementation of the teaching of thinking processes "even when the staff development program is considered highly useful by participating teachers in a fashion suggested by Joyce and Showers." He states that effectiveness requires that staff development efforts often must "somehow engender a 'paradigm shift' among educators" (p. 9). The Michigan Reading Association (*Secondary Reading: A New Direction for the Future,* 1990, p. 40) lists three criteria essential to such a major restructuring:

- The effort must be *experiential* in that teachers do not simply learn how to teach strategies, but also experience these strategies as learners.

- The effort must be *reflective,* helping teachers analyze their own understandings.

- The effort must also *encompass the broader issues* in the present curriculum and in current assessment practices that constrain effective strategic instructional practices and inhibit the development of the most effective learning environment.

## Teaching Episode Model

The University of Miami School-Based Research Project uses a teaching episode model in which teachers first used dictaphones with think-alouds every time they thought about what they would do in the next week's lesson. Their lessons were then videotaped, after which teachers participated in *stimulated recalls,* which use videotapes to remind the person being taped of the sequence followed during taping, and allow this person to stop the videotape at any point to explain his or her thinking at that point in time.

You could adapt this by first modeling the entire process by planning, executing, and debriefing yourself. Then, with willing volunteer teachers, you could (1) listen with each teacher to his or her taped think-alouds, (2) help each teacher with the videotaping, and (3) go through the debriefing together.

## Model Classrooms

Some of the most effective staff development—and some of the least effective—can take place when teachers visit classrooms of their colleagues. Yvonne Freeman (Weaver, 1990, p. 281) advises us that "what teachers see when they visit may surprise or disappoint consultants and administrators, but teachers must be allowed to take away from their experiences what they are ready to notice." On the negative side, "the innovator who gives the appearance of 'having arrived' can quickly become the staff pariah unless he or she is willing to admit to growing pains, mistakes, and false starts" (Neilsen, 1991, p. 676). Thus, the host teacher must be chosen carefully. On the positive side, however, a visitor can walk away from a colleague's room with renewed ideas and zest. We have found that this is most likely to occur when:

- The visitor knows what to look for.

- The possibility of visiting is open to all teachers and not just to those "in trouble."

- The host teacher is one selected by the visitor.

- There is an opportunity for each visitor to observe more than one teacher so as to have a broader range of target behaviors to choose from in selecting ideas to incorporate in his or her own classroom.

- Host teachers are not necessarily exemplary but are comfortable with some target aspect of instruction and are glad to share this with others.

Visits could be systematized—for example, one grade level each month. As the RRS, you may be able to be a co-visitor. This will enable you to talk to visitors and host teachers about the visit before, during, and after visitations.

## Content versus Process

In your staff development, as in any teaching, you must find the right balance between content (*what* is taught) and process (*how* it is taught). It is easier for you, in a way, than for the classroom teacher, because much of your content *is* process. For example, you may be teaching a K-W-L (Ogle, 1986). In this strategy, you have three vertical columns. Two are filled in before a lesson, the K—what you *know,* and then the W—what you *want to know* or, in our adaptation, what you *wonder* about. Following the lesson, students fill in the L for what they *learned.* Say that you also want to teach cooperative learning. You can do the K-W-L *on* cooperative learning *and* you can have the teachers *do* cooperative learning in the process. Both K-W-L and cooperative learning are the content that you want to get across, but they are also processes that the teachers will use in delivering their own content of, say, science information. This use of strategies that you want teachers to use in their classrooms is called the Simultaneous Overlay Model (Kelly & Farnan, 1990).

You could start by pairing teachers and telling them how a Think-Pair-Share (McTighe & Lyman, 1988) works. Next, they can be given two minutes to *Think* about what they *know* of cooperative learning and what they *want to know* about it, and two minutes to *Pair* and discuss this with a partner. Participants then *Share* what they've brainstormed with the instructor, who fills this in in the first two sections of the K-W-L on the board. Finally, you go on to teach cooperative learning and then to work with the group to fill in the L (*Learned*) portion. Thus, you have taught both the content and the process of K-W-L, Think-Pair-Share, and cooperative learning.

Your willingness to spend time on process (e.g., taking the time to have participants evaluate their participation in a cooperative learning activity) will serve as a model for teachers. They do need sometimes to sacrifice content for the sake of process. We know of one teacher who had to spend an entire period having middle school students move into groups, out of groups, into groups, out of groups, and so on. Once the students had learned how to do this, the teacher was able to concentrate on content thereafter. Initial emphasis on process can pay off in greater learning of content in the long run.

## What to Do before, during, and after Classroom Demonstrations

Teachers often welcome classroom demonstrations. As Neilsen (1991, p. 677) says so well, "in literacy learning just as in marriage, parenting, or leadership, . . . demonstrations teach us more than words can ever say. And when we don't demonstrate what we advocate, our chances for a conversation based on trust go right out the window."

Classroom demonstrations must be handled with utmost tact. Sometimes you will be able to demonstrate for several teachers at a time. Arranging demonstrations might mean asking teachers if they will *let* you practice with their classes a strategy you just learned at a conference. It might mean asking grade chairs or department heads if you can do the strategy in their rooms first, so that no one will see this as something you are doing only for the "weak" teachers. Sometimes, when you start with the stronger teachers, others will come around and ask you why they're not getting the same service!

*Before* you go in,

- Think about the teacher's individual teaching style. If you introduce a strategy, be sure the teacher feels comfortable using it and be sure it complements the content area material being taught.

- Ascertain what the teacher would like you to teach. Suppose the teacher has problems getting children to predict. You might suggest modeling two prediction strategies so the teacher can evaluate each. After you have made arrangements with the teacher, say, to start with an anticipation–reaction guide (Readence, Bean, & Baldwin, 1992) with the social studies chapter under study, you should prepare the material and then check it out with the teacher to make sure that you understood correctly. We've learned this the hard way. Check with the teacher far enough in advance so that changes can be made before entering the classroom. This communication helps to avoid confusion and lets the teacher know that you are not trying to take over the class but are working in conjunction with him or her.

- Be sure the teacher understands that he or she should remain in the room during the lesson and that discipline in the classroom is his or her responsibility. You cannot be as conversant with the particulars of each teacher's discipline plan as the teacher him or herself. Even though you can handle minor difficulties without any problem, more serious problems will require teacher intervention. Any assistance you render in this arena generally should not take place in the presence of the students.

- Be prepared. Particularly when demonstrating in a secondary content area class, you may defer to the subject area teacher for certain answers, but you must be thoroughly prepared to teach your lesson. Be ready with answers to questions concerning whatever strategy you present. Make sure that your credibility as the reading specialist is not in jeopardy.

- Gather folded cards or pieces of cardboard on which students can put their names; this will help you communicate with students during your lesson.

*While* you demonstrate, the teacher should observe and prepare to discuss the lesson with you afterwards. If teachers see you as a "guest lecturer," tactfully make them aware that you are working with them and that you are modeling the strategies and lessons for them as well as for the students. This point must sometimes be made by the administration to ensure your success in the classroom. Here are some other tips:

- Make the lesson interesting and exciting. If students know that having you in their class will be fun, you will always be welcome.

- Be yourself. Students will appreciate your candor if you aren't sure about a particular aspect of the subject matter. Feel free to consult with the teacher to provide correct answers to students' questions. Let the pupils know that you are teaching them new strategies for working with the subject matter. You are not the subject matter specialist—that's the job of their regular teacher.

- Be sure to have closure at the end of the lesson. Prepare the students to shift attention to their teacher the way you would like to have the class readied for you during your next visit.

*After* your lesson, remember to follow up:

- You and the teacher should critique what went well and what didn't. A Teacher Lesson Evaluation form can be found in Appendix D. You might want to ask for student opinion as well!

- If you give students a follow-up assignment, offer to grade it and return it to the teacher. This sends home the message that you are lessening rather than increasing teachers' workloads.

- Consider having your lesson videotaped. This can be helpful not only to share with other teachers wishing to see it, but also for stimulated recalls in which you stop the video every time you wish to comment about your lesson.

- At a later time, you and the teacher can reverse roles.

## Working with Teachers with Special Needs

Some of the teachers you work with will, of course, have special needs. These could be based on any number of factors, including the stage of their careers or perhaps an unsatisfactory evaluation. If you are given the touchy assignment of working with a teacher who is perceived to be unsatisfactory, you should be especially careful not to take on the role of an administrator. On the positive side, teachers who have been found to be deficient will often welcome your help. Once you know what the administration has seen as unsatisfactory, and once you get a needs assessment from the teacher, you are ready to begin. Do basically what you would with any coaching. Discuss several options with the teacher. Model one of them. Discuss the session. Help the teacher plan a similar lesson. Watch the teacher teach it. Discuss. Show the teacher how to apply the strategy in other situations. Proceed as needed based on the results thus far.

## Teacher as Researcher: The Reflective Teacher

For many teachers, *research* is a four-letter word. The roots of this negative image are not hard to find. Researchers have communicated to teachers in subtle and not so subtle ways that it is the teacher's task to implement, not generate, research findings. Researchers have communicated to teachers that classroom teachers' research questions are not as well grounded as those of "experts" and that teachers' questions about their own classrooms are not particularly important. Those in academia present their research findings in a format that is technical and uninviting (Schumm, Konopak, Readence, & Baldwin, 1989). Finally, when teachers cooperate as subjects in research projects, they are often not provided with results.

In recent years, major strides have been taken in education to close the chasm between research and practice (Olson, 1990; Strickland, 1988). Indeed, the teacher-as-researcher movement has emerged to involve teachers in a more active role as members of the research community. Jerome Harste (1990) said that this movement has three major themes:

- *Voice:* Teachers have a voice, and this voice needs to be heard.

- *Conversation:* Teachers and university researchers must communicate with each other on an ongoing basis if research is ever to be reality-based.

- *Community:* A new vision of a community of learners consisting of children, parents, teachers, administrators, and university personnel must emerge.

The advantages of involving teachers as researchers are many:

- It creates among teachers and researchers a problem-solving mindset that helps teachers when they consider other classroom dilemmas.

- It improves teachers' decision-making processes.

- It elevates teachers in their professional status.

- It reduces teacher isolation.

- It empowers teachers to influence their own profession at classroom, district, state, and national levels.

- It offers the ultimate advantage of providing the potential for improving education for children.

Many of you may be thinking to yourself by this time, "This all sounds *great,* but you've got to be kidding! How can I convince already overtaxed teachers to become involved in research efforts?" Indeed, action research isn't for everybody. But for teachers who do raise questions, it helps to remind them that "most of the knowledge that defines the field (of English language arts) today has come from work that began with teachers asking questions in their own classrooms. . . . Some of the most valuable classroom research begins with small questions, with the wonderings of individual teachers as they engage in day-to-day work with their students" (Kutz, 1992, pp. 193–195).

Action-based research can occur in many different forms, ranging from informal to highly structured. It may begin simply with reflection through a journal, perhaps a dialogue journal, to organize thinking about one's teaching. Action-based research can involve a teacher working independently or a teacher collaborating with students, a fellow teacher, an administrator, or a university researcher. But the core of classroom action research is simply trying out something different in the classroom and reflecting about the results (as teachers do on a regular basis), and then taking it one step further by recording the results—in short, figuring out what works!

Judith Green (1987) suggested a seven-step plan for action-oriented research:

1. Identify an issue, interest, or concern.

2. Seek knowledge.

3. Plan an action.

4. Implement an action.

5. Observe the action.

6. Reflect on the observations.

7. Revise the plan.

No complicated statistical procedures are used unless the individual classroom teacher elects to do so. Action research is what many risk-taking teachers have done for years. Try it out and see how it works!

If you and/or your teachers are interested in initiating an action research program, what resources are available and how might you get started? Perhaps you can encourage a couple of teachers to network by conducting reciprocal observations of each other's classrooms. Or foster a collaboration in which a teacher and a student teacher record and share systematic classroom observations (Kutz, 1992). Or encourage teachers to work with their students to create collaborative research communities. Beyond these initial strategies, other possibilities can be tackled. Some school districts and local professional organizations are now offering mini-grants for classroom-based research (see "Grant Writing" in Appendix C). Many university professors are now structuring courses or course components to provide initial training in research procedures. Professional conference programs include collaborative presentations with university researchers and classroom teachers. There are university researchers who are anxious to meet other professionals willing to plunge into this exciting new world.

Professional publications are now available that outline basic tenets of the teacher-as-researcher movement, provide examples of existing efforts (Brandt, 1991; Olson, 1990; Samuels & Pearson, 1988; Santa, Isaacson, & Manning, 1987;

Pinnell & Matlin, 1989), and provide specific suggestions for how to put your thoughts into print (Baumann & Johnson, 1991; McDonnell, Frey, & Smith, 1991). The International Reading Association has organized a teacher-as-researcher special interest group and runs columns on action research in its newsletter, *Reading Today*. Following are some examples of action research projects:

• One example of an individual teacher's research effort is that of Marcia Truitt, an RRS at American Senior High School in Miami, Florida, who was the recipient of the Florida Reading Association's Action Research Award. She sought to find out whether reading comprehension could be improved if students had the opportunity to take a novel home and highlight main ideas and details. She reasoned that because high school students are not allowed to write in their texts, they do not develop the highlighting skills necessary for success in college. Although her results were inconclusive, Marcia had at least taken the first steps to answer a question that was of interest to her. With the help of her supervisor, she wrote up her results and then shared them at a conference.

• When Philip Balbi was a second-grade teacher in the Dade County (Florida) Public Schools, his class included three students who had experienced little success in reading, two of them limited English proficient. His findings revealed that using a language experience approach proved beneficial in improving the students' reading and spelling. Philip's research was eventually shared at conferences and was published (Balbi, 1986).

• Another example of the RRS effort is that of Rosalind Pomerance, an RRS at a junior high school in Palm Beach County, Florida. Rosalind actively taught reading strategies to *all* content area teachers by providing inservice workshops before and after school and by modeling strategies in their classrooms. This was an intensive mandated staff development program period. After two years of implementation, overall student grade point averages showed a rapid increase (growth from 4 percent to 25 percent of students with grade point averages of 3.0 or higher). This provided a strong, content area alternative to pull-out reading programs.

• The University of Miami School-Based Research Project is an example of a graduate course structured to empower classroom teachers to become action researchers. The intent is to improve teachers' knowledge, skills, and confidence in planning and making adaptations for students with special needs in their general education classrooms. This course is highly collaborative in nature. Each type of course participant, Dade County Public School (DCPS) researchers (the "students") and University of Miami researchers (the "faculty"), has a voice in course decision making.

Each DCPS researcher completes a case study of one special needs mainstreamed student. The DCPS researchers try out various interventions and adaptations with the target student and then draft weekly status reports of student progress for eventual compilation into a case study. Thus, class sessions become more like university research meetings. Initial findings are shared, problems are deliberated, and next steps are outlined. Each group member is considered to be both a learner and an authority. University personnel have expertise in special education and reading; DCPS personnel are content area specialists and authorities on the condition of the classroom. The product (the case study) is important; but the process (learning to communicate with each other as professionals and to develop reflective teaching practices) is paramount.

Teacher-as-researcher projects are not for everyone, but on every faculty there will be at least one teacher who is ready for this challenge. If necessary, serve as a spur!

## Conclusion

As you can see from this chapter, staff development is truly an art. Treat it with respect, but don't be daunted. The opportunity to teach and work with people is probably what got you into teaching in the first place. So get busy and enjoy!

# APPENDIX A

# Communication Tools

# ELEMENTARY TEACHER REQUEST FORM

TEACHER'S NAME                    GRADE                         ROOM #

_____         _____                      _____

PLANNING TIMES: _____

Dear faculty,

I am trying to determine how I can better serve the entire school as your Reading Resource Specialist. Please note that I am here for *all* faculty, including special area teachers.

Below is a list of services that I can offer you. Please check those that interest you and place the sheet in my mailbox when complete.

_____ Read to your class.

_____ Help bind books.

_____ Show you specific learning strategies. Please specify (vocabulary, test taking, questioning techniques, etc.).

_____

_____ Make presentations to your class on specific strategies.

        Please specify. _____

_____ Team-teach lessons.

_____ Evaluate new textbooks with you.

_____ Determine the reading ability of students.

_____ Arrange for taping selections for very poor readers.

_____ Help in grouping students.

_____ Locate relevant articles in professional journals.

_____ Arrange for visits from people outside the school.

_____ Help in the physical arrangement of your room.

_____ Help with theme development.

_____ Help with lesson plans.

_____ Help get books for classroom library.

_____ Provide inservice to assist you in recertification.

_____ Other: _____

Thank you for taking the time to read this. I look forward to hearing from you.

Sincerely,

Reading Resource Specialist

# SECONDARY TEACHER REQUEST FORM

TEACHER'S NAME                    SUBJECT                              ROOM #

_____          _____                            _____

PLANNING TIMES: _____

Dear faculty,

I am trying to determine how I can better serve the entire school as your Reading Resource Specialist. Please note that I am here for *all* content areas, including electives.

Below is a list of services that I can offer you. Please check those that interest you and place the sheet in my mailbox when complete.

_____ Read to classes.

_____ Show you specific strategies. Please specify (vocabulary, test taking, questioning techniques, study strategies, etc.)

_____

_____ Make presentations to your classes on specific strategies.

Please specify _____

_____ Team-teach lessons.

_____ Evaluate new textbooks with you.

_____ Arrange for taping chapters for very poor readers.

_____ Help with grouping students.

_____ Help construct study guides.

_____ Locate relevant articles in professional journals.

_____ Arrange for visits from people outside the school.

_____ Help get books for classroom library.

_____ Provide inservice opportunities to assist you in recertification.

_____ Other: _____

Thank you for taking the time to read this. I look forward to hearing from you.

Sincerely,

Reading Resource Specialist

# STAFF DEVELOPMENT NEEDS ASSESSMENT

Please check areas of staff development in which you would like to participate. Then rank those in priority order.

\_\_\_\_ \_\_\_\_ Classroom organization options

\_\_\_\_ \_\_\_\_ Meeting the needs of hard-to-teach students

\_\_\_\_ \_\_\_\_ Challenging accelerated students

\_\_\_\_ \_\_\_\_ Cooperative learning

\_\_\_\_ \_\_\_\_ Alternatives to seatwork

\_\_\_\_ \_\_\_\_ Computers and reading/writing

\_\_\_\_ \_\_\_\_ Word recognition strategies

\_\_\_\_ \_\_\_\_ Vocabulary strategies

\_\_\_\_ \_\_\_\_ Reading comprehension strategies

\_\_\_\_ \_\_\_\_ Thinking skills/strategies

\_\_\_\_ \_\_\_\_ Study skills/strategies

\_\_\_\_ \_\_\_\_ Teaching the limited English proficient

\_\_\_\_ \_\_\_\_ Teaching special education students

\_\_\_\_ \_\_\_\_ Newspaper-in-education activities

\_\_\_\_ \_\_\_\_ Children's/young adult literature

\_\_\_\_ \_\_\_\_ Multicultural teaching strategies

\_\_\_\_ \_\_\_\_ Integrating reading and writing

\_\_\_\_ \_\_\_\_ Spelling

\_\_\_\_ \_\_\_\_ Reading and writing across the curriculum

\_\_\_\_ \_\_\_\_ Writing process

\_\_\_\_ \_\_\_\_ Journal writing

\_\_\_\_ \_\_\_\_ Book reports

\_\_\_\_ \_\_\_\_ Alternative means of assessment

\_\_\_\_ \_\_\_\_ Update on research on reading/writing

\_\_\_\_ \_\_\_\_ Teacher as researcher

\_\_\_\_ \_\_\_\_ Increasing parental involvement

\_\_\_\_ \_\_\_\_ Grant writing

\_\_\_\_ \_\_\_\_ Other: _____

\_\_\_\_ \_\_\_\_ _____

## SAMPLE NEWSLETTER

# READING BETWEEN THE LINES

December 1987

### DEGREES OF READING POWER TEST

The Degrees of Reading Power, or DRP test, was implemented this fall in 17 middle/junior high schools and 10 senior high schools to compare students' reading levels with that of the text at the 7th and 9th grade levels. Reading teachers, administrators, and guidance counselors have attended workshops held since August concerning the administration and application of the test. In conjunction with the DRP, many reading teachers are now offering the Content Area Reading Strategies (CARS) Workshop to faculty members interested in learning techniques for reducing the "mismatch" which occurs when students' reading levels are lower than that of the textbooks.

### NEW IRA PUBLICATION

Stress and Reading Difficulties is a new book published by the International Reading Association. Written by Lance M. Gentile and Merna M. McMillan, this paperback book contains a 30-item "Stress Reaction Scale to Reading" on pages 14-16. To order a personal copy, IRA members may send $3.50 (or non-members send $5.00) to:

> IRA
> 800 Barksdale Road
> P.O. Box 8139
> Newark, Delaware 19714-8139

The book also includes information on research, assessment, and intervention of stress and reading difficulties.

### DROP EVERYTHING AND READ

Drop Everything and Read, or D.E.A.R., will again be held in conjunction with Celebrate Literacy Day on the third Thursday in February, or February 18, 1988. An idea from Billie Birney, University of Miami, is to ask students in all reading or language arts classes to pick one favorite book from the school library and to write the following on a piece of notebook paper:

> Title
> Author
> Rationale/Purpose
> One carefully chosen excerpt

Teachers can mount these pages on brightly colored sheets of construction paper and line their classrooms or even the halls of the school with interesting information about all the students' favorite books.

### STUDY SKILLS AND STRATEGIES

A new workbook from the College Skills Center, entitled Study Skills and Strategies, is available for preview at each secondary school. **One free copy** may be obtained by sending a written request to the following address:

> Pam Cummings
> 2936 Remington Avenue
> Baltimore, Maryland 21211

The author, Dr. Richard Santeusanio, visited the West Area of Palm Beach County last year to present effective strategies for studying. If this book seems valuable for your students, please let me know at PX 5117 for possible addition to the unified curriculum list for reading.

Penny Beers, Secondary Reading Specialist

### WAY TO GO, JO!

**Jo Tanner,** reading teacher at Jupiter Middle School, was nominated for the 1988 William Dwyer Award for Excellence in Education. Jo was chosen as a finalist for this prestigious award and will attend a banquet at the Royce Hotel on April 7, 1988, hosted by the Economic Council. Jo has served on several writing committees for reading curriculum, has helped develop a study skills curriculum, and has been an outstanding role model for her students. Congratulations are truly in order!

### DADE READING CONFERENCE

Mark your calendar now! The annual Dade Reading Conference will be held on Friday evening, February 19, 1988, and all day Saturday, February 20, 1988, featuring **Dr. Scott Paris,** a noted reading researcher at the University of Michigan and lecturer. Dr. Paris spoke eloquently on "Becoming Strategic Readers" at the recent Florida Reading Association (FRA) Conference at the Sheraton Bal Harbour. If you missed hearing him there, here's your chance to hear this interesting and dynamic speaker. Watch for a memo in early February for times and location.

### FLIP CHARTS

Free copies of "New Directions in Reading Instruction," the flip charts developed by the Secondary Reading Council of Florida (SRCF), are available by writing to the following address:

> Division of Public Schools –
> Resource Center
> Florida D.O.E.
> Knott Building
> Tallahassee, FL  32399

These colorful and informative booklets can be ordered for distribution to your faculty members. Included is a procedure entitled "Informed Strategies for Learning" (ISL), developed by **Dr. Scott Paris,** which helps students become aware of, understand, accept and use the comprehension and cognitive strategies.

The following books include chapters written by Dr. Paris:

> "Using Classroom Dialogues and Guided Practice to Teach Comprehension Strategies" in Reading, Thinking, and Concept Development, College Entrance Examination Board by T.L. Harris and E.J. Cooper (1985).

> "Teaching Children to Guide Their Reading and Learning" in The Contexts of School Based Literacy by Taffy Raphael (1984).

# APPENDIX B

## Instructional Aids

# SECONDARY STUDY HABITS INVENTORY

## I. Test Taking

1. Do you know how to manage test anxiety?     Y    N

2. Do you know how to prepare for multiple-choice, true–false, and matching tests?     Y    N

3. Do you know how to prepare for essay tests?     Y    N

4. Do you know how to take different kinds of tests?     Y    N

5. Do you review exams after they are returned to you?     Y    N

## II. Time Management

6. Do you know how to plan a study schedule?     Y    N

7. Do you have a system for keeping track of assignments?     Y    N

8. Do you know how to complete assignments on time?     Y    N

9. Do you know the times of day when you study best?     Y    N

10. Do you avoid starting new tasks before old tasks are started?     Y    N

## III. Textbook Reading

11. Are you satisfied with your reading ability and speed?     Y    N

12. Do you look over a chapter before reading it?     Y    N

13. Do you ask yourself questions about what the text will contain before reading?     Y    N

14. Do you use headings and subheadings of chapters to organize your reading?     Y    N

15. Do you relate what you already know about a topic to new information about that topic?     Y    N

16. Do you change your speed with different materials?     Y    N

17. Do you pay particular attention to words in italics or boldfaced type as you read?     Y    N

18. Do you know how to define an unknown word by using the words that surround it?     Y    N

19. Do you know how information is organized in textbooks?     Y    N

20. When you do not understand what you are reading, do you know how to fix up your misunderstanding?     Y    N

### IV. Lecture Learning

21. Do you avoid becoming distracted while the teacher is lecturing?    Y    N

22. Do you preread chapters before hearing a lecture?    Y    N

23. Do you know how to take notes from your textbook before a lecture?    Y    N

24. Do you identify the main idea of a lecture?    Y    N

25. Do you know how teachers emphasize important information?    Y    N

26. Do you know how to take notes from a class lecture?    Y    N

27. Do you know how to use abbreviations when taking notes?    Y    N

28. Do you read and review your notes immediately following a lecture?    Y    N

29. Do you compare your notes with a friend's notes before studying for a test?    Y    N

30. Do you review your notes several times a week?    Y    N

### V. Recalling Information

31. Do you know the importance of overlearning material when preparing for a test?    Y    N

32. Do you know what the effect of spaced study is on learning material for tests?    Y    N

33. Do you know what types of information you need to remember for different subjects?    Y    N

34. Do you know tricks for remembering information on a test?    Y    N

35. Do you know what causes you to forget important information?    Y    N

### VI. Library and Research

36. Do you know your library's organizational system?    Y    N

37. Do you know how to use a periodical index?    Y    N

38. Do you know how to use a card catalog?    Y    N

39. Do you know how to read diagrams, tables, charts, and timelines?    Y    N

*(continued)*

**Secondary Study Habits Inventory (continued)**

40. Do you know how to read bar graphs, circle graphs, and line graphs?     Y     N

41. Do you know how to read maps?     Y     N

42. Do you know how to choose a topic for a research paper?     Y     N

43. Do you know how to quote or paraphrase information in a research report?     Y     N

44. Do you know how to put together information from a variety of sources to write a report?     Y     N

45. Do you know how to prepare a final draft of a research paper including a bibliography?     Y     N

If you answered "No" to questions 1–5, you need to improve your test-taking skills. If you answered "Yes" to these questions, this topic is one of your learning strengths.

Total "Yes" responses for Test Taking questions _____

If you answered "No" to questions 6–10, you need to improve your time management skills. If you answered "Yes" to these questions, this topic is one of your learning strengths.

Total "Yes" responses for Time Management questions _____

If you answered "No" to questions 11–20, you need to improve your textbook-reading skills. If you answered "Yes" to these questions, this topic is one of your learning strengths.

Total "Yes" responses for Textbook Reading questions _____

Divide by 2: _____

If you answered "No" to questions 21–30, you need to improve your skills in learning from lectures. If you answered "Yes" to these questions, this topic is one of your learning strengths.

Total "Yes" responses for Lecture Learning questions _____

Divide by 2: _____

If you answered "No" to questions 31–35, you need to improve your skills in recalling information. If you answered "Yes" to these questions, this topic is one of your learning strengths.

Total "Yes" responses for Recalling Information questions _____

If you answered "No" to questions 36–45, you need to improve your library and research skills. If you answered "Yes" to these questions, this topic is one of your learning strengths.

Total "Yes" responses for Library and Research questions _____

Divide by 2: _____

## Summary of Results

On the lines below, enter the totals from the interpretation of results. Then, calculate percentages by multiplying that number by 20. When totals were divided by 2, use the resulting quotient.

| TITLE | TOTAL | | PERCENTAGE |
|---|---|---|---|
| Test Taking | ———— | × 20 = | ———— |
| Time Management | ———— | × 20 = | ———— |
| Textbook Reading | ———— | × 20 = | ———— |
| Lecture Learning | ———— | × 20 = | ———— |
| Recalling Information | ———— | × 20 = | ———— |
| Library and Research | ———— | × 20 = | ———— |

If your percentages were 80 percent or above, then your skills are strong in these areas. If you scored below 80 percent, then you may need improvement in these areas.

# LISTENING HABITS INVENTORY

| ALWAYS (2) | SOMETIMES (1) | NEVER (0) | |
|---|---|---|---|
| _____ | _____ | _____ | 1. I am in my seat and ready to listen shortly after the bell rings. |
| _____ | _____ | _____ | 2. I avoid doing other things while the teacher is talking. |
| _____ | _____ | _____ | 3. I avoid talking with friends while the teacher is talking. |
| _____ | _____ | _____ | 4. I listen to directions carefully. |
| _____ | _____ | _____ | 5. I ask questions when I don't understand the directions or the information that the teacher presents. |
| _____ | _____ | _____ | 6. I take notes when a great deal of oral information is presented. |
| _____ | _____ | _____ | 7. I know when the teacher is making an important point. |
| _____ | _____ | _____ | 8. If I catch myself daydreaming, I try to get back into focus. |
| _____ | _____ | _____ | 9. I look at the teacher while he or she is talking. |
| _____ | _____ | _____ | 10. I try to remember what the teacher is saying. |
| _____ | _____ | _____ | 11. If someone is keeping me from listening, I ask that person to stop talking. If that doesn't work, I ask for the teacher to help or change my seat. |
| _____ | _____ | _____ | 12. I spend more time listening in class than talking in class. |

Total Each Column

_____     _____     _____

Total Number of Points = _____
- 20–24 points = Super Listener
- 16–19 points = Good Listener
- 12–15 points = Need to Sharpen Up
- 11 or below points = You Can Do Better—Listening is *important*.

Are you a good listener?

If not, how can you improve your listening skills?

# TEST-TAKING TIPS FOR STUDENTS

**How to Get Ready for Standardized Tests**

1. *Get real.* Standardized tests are important, but they are only one measure of your progress in school. It is important to do your best. But remember, your daily work and performance on class tests are much better indicators of your academic achievement.

2. *Get sleep.* A good night's rest is a must for top-notch performance.

3. *Get food.* You need a good breakfast to nourish yourself for the test-taking task.

4. *Get equipped.* Bring extra No. 2 pencils to school for the test. If you have a watch or small clock, bring it along so that you can budget your test-taking time. Wear comfortable clothes.

5. *Get to school.* If you come to school late on the day of the test, you may feel rushed and text anxiety can build rapidly.

**How to Take Standardized Tests**

1. *Take notice.* Pay particular attention to the oral directions that your teacher gives you. Also, notice the written directions in your test booklet. On standardized tests it is important to follow directions carefully.

2. *Take time.* Most standardized tests are timed tests. Plan your time by skimming through the whole test section.

3. *Take advantage.* Take advantage of what you know by doing all the easy items first. This will help you earn more points on a test than if you waste too much time on the hard items. After you do all the easy items, go back and spend more time on the items that are more difficult.

4. *Take a chance.* Unless there is a penalty for guessing, don't skip any questions. You will not do well on a standardized test if you simply fill in any blank throughout the whole test. But if you have really thought about a question and have eliminated the most obviously incorrect answers, take a chance, fill in the blank, and move on to the next item.

5. *Take care.* If your standardized test requires you to fill in "bubbles," be sure to fill in the bubbles fully. If you erase an answer, do so completely. From time to time, check that the number in your test booklet matches the number on your answer sheet.

6. *Take a break.* If you feel panic coming on, take a twenty- or thirty-second mini-break to relax and refocus on the test. Simply close your eyes, take a few deep breaths, and then start working again.

7. *Take a check.* Take some time at the end of the test to review your answers and check for careless mistakes.

# Contract

student _____

## READING CONTRACT

Today's Date: _____ Due Date: _____

I, _____, agree to read _____

STUDENT'S NAME

books. I agree to complete the books on time. I also agree to indicate how I will share what I read by doing the following:

_____

_____

_____

| | | |
|---|---|---|
| STUDENT'S SIGNATURE | TEACHER'S SIGNATURE | PARENT'S SIGNATURE |

# READ-ALOUD CONTRACT

Today's Date: _____ Due Date: _____

I, _____, agree to read _____
READER'S NAME

books out loud to _____. I agree to
LISTENER'S NAME

complete the books on time.

_____          _____
STUDENT'S                        TEACHER'S
SIGNATURE                        SIGNATURE

Today's Date: _____ Due Date: _____

I, _____, agree to listen to _____
LISTENER'S NAME

books that _____ will read out loud
READER'S NAME

to me. I agree to complete the books on time.

_____          _____
STUDENT'S                        TEACHER'S
SIGNATURE                        SIGNATURE

WRITING CONTRACT

# WRITING CONTRACT

Today's Date: _____ Due Date: _____

I, _____, agree to write _____
STUDENT'S NAME

_____. I agree to
TITLE OF WORK

complete the written assignment on time.

_____          _____          _____
STUDENT'S                     TEACHER'S                    PARENT'S
SIGNATURE                     SIGNATURE                    SIGNATURE

# STRATEGY FOR HELPING STUDENTS FIND THE "RIGHT" BOOK

Have you been to a bookstore lately? Bookstores in the 1990s are lively, colorful, exciting places that offer thousands of choices of what to read. But many people still say, "I don't read because it's boring." It may well be that such people just haven't found the RIGHT BOOK!!!!

How do you find the RIGHT BOOK? We're not talking about the RIGHT BOOK for a book report or the RIGHT BOOK to please your teacher. We're talking about the RIGHT BOOK to please *you*!

Start with your interests. Are you interested in rock music, antique cars, hairstyles, skiing?

No RIGHT BOOK? Then move on to your current needs. Maybe you need to learn how to play golf, redecorate your room, learn more about Colorado for your upcoming family vacation.

No RIGHT BOOK yet? Then think about your favorite TV show or movie. Think about the type of TV show or movie you like. Do you like comedies? mysteries? horror shows? science fiction? history? biographies? fantasies? others? Try to find a book that has a similar focus to that of your favorite programs and shows.

No RIGHT BOOK yet? Then start with magazines. Find a magazine article you *really* like, and then ask the librarian if he or she knows of book that is similar to the article you read.

Still no RIGHT BOOK? Then talk to your friends, an adult you respect or share common interests with, or even your librarian. They may have some leads.

Used with permission of J. S. Schumm and M. C. Radencich, *School Power—Strategies for Succeeding in School* (Minneapolis, MN: FreeSpirit Publishing, 1992).

# READ-ALOUD LISTS

We have compiled a listing of our favorite read-aloud books for primary, intermediate, and secondary students. For additional books, you can also refer to: *Kids' Favorite Books* (International Reading Association/Children's Book Council, 1991); *The New Read-Aloud Handbook* (Trelease, 1989); *Choosing Books for Kids* (Oppenheim, Brenner, and Boegehold, 1986); *Teens' Favorite Books* (International Reading Association, 1992); or *Adventuring with Books: A Booklist for Pre-K–Grade 6* (Monson, 1985).

## Primary Read-Aloud List

Allard, H. (1978). *Miss Nelson is missing.* New York: Scholastic.

Allard, H. (1974, 1977). *The Stupids step out.* Boston: Houghton Mifflin.

Allsburg, C. V. (1989). *The polar express.* Boston: Houghton Mifflin.

Bemelmans, L. (1939). *Madeline.* New York: Viking.

Bonne, R. (1987). *I know an old lady.* New York: Scholastic.

Brown, M. (1988). *The three billy goats gruff.* New York: Harcourt Brace Jovanovich.

Brown, M. (1989). *Once a mouse.* New York: Scribner.

Brown, M. W. (1984). *Goodnight moon.* New York: Harper.

Buffet, J., & Buffet, S. (1988). *The jolly mon.* New York: Crowell.

Carle, E. (1986). *The very hungry caterpillar.* New York: Putnam.

Cohen, M. (1977). *When will I read?* New York: Greenwillow.

Delacre, L. (1989). *Arroz con leche: Popular songs and rhymes from Latin America.* New York: Scholastic.

de Paola, T. (1978). *Pancakes for breakfast.* New York: Harcourt Brace Jovanovich.

Flournoy, V. (1985). *The patchwork quilt.* New York: Dial.

Gag, W. (1928, 1977). *Millions of cats.* New York: Coward, McCann.

Guy, R. (1980). *Mother crocodile.* New York: Delacorte.

Hamilton, V. (1985). *American black folktales.* New York: Knopf.

Keats, J. (1964). *Whistle for Willie.* New York: Viking.

McCloskey, R. (1976). *Make way for ducklings.* New York: Viking.

Martin, B. (1983). *Brown bear, brown bear, what do you see?* New York: Holt, Rinehart & Winston.

Parish, P. (1970). *Amelia Bedelia.* New York: Scholastic.

Prelutsky, J. (1983). *The Random House book of poetry.* New York: Random House.

Rey, H. A. (1973). *Curious George.* Boston: Houghton Mifflin.

Sendak, M. (1988). *Where the wild things are.* New York: Harper.

Seuling, B. (1975). *You can't eat peanuts in church and other little-known laws.* New York: Doubleday.

Seuss, D. (1989). *The 500 hats of Bartholomew Cubbins.* New York: Vanguard.

Sharmat, M. (1984). *Gregory the terrible eater.* New York: Four Winds.

Stevenson, R. L. (1989). *A child's garden of verses.* Chicago: Contemporary.

Stover, J. (1989). *If everybody did.* New York: David McKay.

Tudor, T. (1961). *Tasha Tudor's book of fairy tales.* New York: Putnam.

Viorst, J. (1972). *Alexander and the terrible, horrible, no good, very bad day.* New York: Atheneum.

Wood, A. (1984). *The napping house.* New York: Harcourt Brace Jovanovich.

Zemach, M. (1965). *The teeny tiny woman.* New York: Scholastic.

### Intermediate Read-Aloud List

Aliki. (1976). *Corn is maize—The gift of the Indians.* New York: Crowell.

Asimov, I. (1977). *How did we find out about outer space?* New York: Walker.

Blume, J. (1972). *Tales of a fourth grade nothing.* New York: Dutton.

Brink, C. R. (1935/1973). *Caddie Woodlawn.* New York: Macmillan.

Burnett. F. H. (1989). *The secret garden.* New York: Viking.

Burnford, S. (1977). *The incredible journey.* Boston: Little, Brown.

Cisneros, S. (1991). *House on Mango Street.* New York: Random House.

Collier, J. L., & Collier, C. (1987). *Jump ship to freedom.* New York: Dell.

Dahl, R. (1990). *James and the giant peach.* New York: Knopf.

Cleary, B. (1968). *Ramona the pest.* New York: Morrow.

Estes, E. (1944). *The hundred dresses.* New York: Harcourt Brace Jovanovich.

Farley, W. (1941). *The black stallion.* New York: Random House.

Fitzgerald, J. D. (1985). *The great brain.* New York: Dell.

Graham, A., & Graham, F. (1981). *The changing desert.* New York: Sierra Club/ Scribner.

Hunt, I. (1987). *Across five Aprils.* Chicago: Follett.

L'Engle, M. (1962). *A wrinkle in time.* New York: Farrar, Straus, & Giroux.

McCloskey, R. (1943). *Homer Price.* New York: Puffin.

Manes, S. (1987). *Be a perfect person in just three days!* New York: Bantam.

Montgomery, L. M. (1908). *Anne of Green Gables.* Cutchoque, NY: Buccaneer Books.

Newman, R. (1984). *The case of the Baker Street irregulars.* New York: Atheneum.

Norton, M. (1952). *The borrowers.* New York: Harcourt Brace Jovanovich.

Rockwell, T. (1973). *How to eat fried worms.* New York: Watts.

Silverstein, S. (1974). *Where the sidewalk ends.* New York: Harper.

Simon, S. (1980). *Strange mysteries from around the world.* New York: Four Winds.

Sobol, D. J. (1970). *Encyclopedia Brown saves the day.* Nashville, TN: Nelson.

Stevenson, R. L. (1947). *Treasure Island.* New York: Grosset & Dunlap.

Wagner, J. (1971). *J.T.* New York: Dell.

White, E. B. (1952). *Charlotte's web.* New York: Harper & Row.

Wilder, L. I. (1975). *Little house on the prairie.* New York: Harper & Row.

Yolen, J. (1986). *Favorite folktales from around the world.* New York: Pantheon.

### Secondary Read-Aloud List

Adams, R. (1974). *Watership down.* New York: Macmillan.

Allende, I. (1991). *Stories of Eva Luna.* New York: Macmillan.

Alvarez, J. (1991). *How the García girls lost their accents.* New York: Algonquin.

(continued)

### Read-Aloud Lists (continued)

Angelou, M. (1972). *I know why the caged bird sings.* New York: Random House.

Armstrong, W. H. (1989). *Sounder.* New York: Harper & Row.

Asimov, I. (Ed.). (1978). *100 great science fiction short stories.* New York: Doubleday.

Auel, J. M. (1984). *The clan of the cave bear.* New York: Crown.

Blume, J. (1981). *Tiger eyes.* New York: Dell.

Bradbury, R. (1973). *When elephants last in the dooryard bloomed.* New York: Knopf.

Cerf, B. (Ed.). (1955). *Great modern short stories.* New York: Random House.

Cohen, D. (1990). *The ghosts of war.* New York: Putnam.

Du Maurier, D. (1948). *Rebecca.* New York: Doubleday.

Frank, A. (1967). *Anne Frank: The diary of a young girl.* New York: Doubleday.

Gaines, E. (1982). *Autobiography of Miss Jane Pittman.* New York: Dial.

Greene, B. (1973). *Summer of my German soldier.* New York: Bantam.

Hamilton, E. (1942). *Mythology.* Boston: Little, Brown.

Harris, R. (Ed.). (1982). *Best selling chapters.* Providence, RI: Jamestown.

Herriot, J. (1974). *All things bright and beautiful.* Boston: St. Martin's.

Hinton, S. E. (1968). *The outsiders.* New York: Dell.

Hughes, L. (1990). *Selected poems of Langston Hughes.* New York: Random House.

Janeczko, P. B. (1990). *The place my words are looking for: What poets say about and through their work.* Scarsdale, NY: Bradbury.

Lee, H. (1988). *To kill a mockingbird.* New York: Warner.

O'Dell, S. (1990). *Island of the blue dolphins.* Boston: Houghton Mifflin.

Paterson, K. (1977). *Bridge to Terabithia.* New York: Crowell.

Peck, R. N. (1972). *A day no pigs would die.* New York: Knopf.

Rawls, W. (1974). *Where the red fern grows.* New York: Bantam.

Rooney, A. (1987). *A few minutes with Andy Rooney.* New York: Atheneum.

Tolkien, J. R. R. (1973). *The Hobbit.* Boston: Houghton Mifflin.

# PREDICTABLE LANGUAGE BOOKS

Levels refer to average kindergarten and less proficient first-grade children being able to remember most of the text as follows:

Level I—following one or two read-alouds

Level II—following two or three read-alouds

Level III—following three or four read-alouds

## Predictable Language Trade Books

*Level I*
Brown, R. (1981). *A dark dark tale.* New York: Dial Press.
Ginsburg, M. (1972). *The chick and the duckling.* New York: Macmillan.
Krauss, R. (1948). *Bears.* New York: Scholastic.
Langstaff, J. (1974). *Oh, a-hunting we will go.* New York: Atheneum.
Mack, S. (1974). *10 bears in my bed.* New York: Pantheon.
Martin, B. (1983). *Brown bear, brown bear, what do you see?* New York: Holt, Rinehart & Winston.
Peek, M. (1985). *Mary wore her red dress and Henry wore his green sneakers.* New York: Clarion.
Robart, R. (1986). *The cake that Mack ate.* Glenview, IL: Scott Foresman.

*Level II*
Becker, J. (1973). *Seven little rabbits.* New York: Scholastic.
Brown, M. W. (1952). *Where have you been?* New York: Scholastic.
Hutchins, P. (1972). *Goodnight owl.* New York: Macmillan.
Kalin, R. (1981). *Jump, frog, jump.* New York: Scholastic.
Quackenbush, R. (1973). *She'll be comin' 'round the mountain.* Philadelphia: Lippincott.
Westcott, N. B. (1987). *Peanut butter and jelly.* New York: Dutton.
Zolotow, C. (1969). *Some things go together.* New York: Crowell.

*Level III*
Aliki. (1974). *Go tell Aunt Rhody.* New York: Macmillan.
Galdone, P. (1984). *The teeny tiny woman.* Boston: Houghton Mifflin.
Guarino, D. (1989). *Is your mama a llama?* New York: Scholastic.
Langstaff, J. (1957). *Over in the meadow.* New York: Harcourt Brace Jovanovich.
Westcott, N. B. (1988). *The lady with the alligator purse.* Boston: Little, Brown.

## Predictable Language Books from Commercial Series (One Sample per Series)

*Level I*
Allen, R. V. (1985). *I love ladybugs.* Allen, TX: DLM. Predictable Storybooks, Set 1.

*(continued)*

### Predictable Language Books (continued)

Cairns, S. (1986). *Oh, no!*. Crystal Lake, IL: Rigby. More Traditional Tales and Contemporary Stories.

Cowley, J. (1980). *Mrs. Wishy-Washy*. San Diego: The Wright Group. The Story Box Read-Together.

Nellie Edge Big Books. (1988). *Teddy bear, Teddy bear*. Salem, OR: Resources for Creative Teaching. Nellie Edge Big Books.

Nelson, J. (1989). *There's a dragon in my wagon*. Cleveland: Modern Curriculum Press. Reading Friends.

Robinson, E. (1987). *If I had a dragon*. Allen, TX: DLM. Read-aloud Predictable Storybooks.

Skelly, A. (1989). *If you're happy*. Crystal Lake, IL: Rigby. Literacy 2000, Stage 4, Set A.

*Level II*

Allen, C. (1986). *Beautiful breezy blue and white day*. Allen, TX: DLM. Predictable Storybooks, Set 2.

Allen, R. V. (1987). *Eating peanuts*. Allen, TX: DLM. Read-Aloud Predictable Storybooks.

Blocksma, M. (1984). *Rub-a-dub-dub, What's in the tub?* Chicago: Children's Press. Just One More.

Greenes, C. (1989). *Rebecca's party*. Allen, TX: DLM. Math Predictable Storybooks.

Martin, B., & Archambault, J. (1987). *Here are my hands*. Allen, TX: DLM. Bobber Books.

Parkes, B. (1986). *Who's in the shed?* Melbourne: Rigby. Traditional Tales, Rhymes, and Contemporary Stories.

*Level III*

Lucky, S. (1989). *There's a moose and a goose in the caboose*. Allen, TX: DLM. The Bill Martin Jr. Library.

Robinson, E. (1987). *The dinosaur ball*. Allen, TX: DLM. Predictable Storybooks, Set 3.

Robinson, E. (1989). *The garden walked away*. Allen, TX: DLM. Science Predictable Storybooks.

*Source:* Adapted from M. C. Radencich & A. G. McKinney (in press). Brown Bear, Brown Bear, What Do You See?—Levels for Predictables: 1, 2, 3. *Florida Reading Quarterly*.

# MAGAZINES AND CONTESTS THAT ACCEPT YOUNG WRITERS' WORK

(Send self-addressed stamped envelope with each submission. Note that submissions may not be returned.)

## Magazines for Young Children through Age 12 or 13

*Boys' Life.* 1325 Walnut Hill Lane, Irving, TX 75038-3096. Short stories or articles for boys (around 15,000 words). Age 8–18.

*Child Life.* 1100 Waterway Boulevard, Indianapolis, IN 46206. Short stories (1,000 words) and poetry. Age 10–12.

*Children's Album.* EGW Publishing Company, Box 6080, Concord, CA 94524. Short stories (adventure, humorous, religious, romance, science fiction, fantasy, horror), 50–1,000 words. Fillers—short humor, crossword puzzles, sayings, cartoons. Age 8–14.

*Children's Digest.* P.O. Box 567, Indianapolis, IN 46206. Drawings and poems, jokes, and riddles.

*Clubhouse* (Focus on the family). Family Clubhouse Editor, Pomona, CA 91799. Poems (4–24 lines), cartoons, short stories (adventure, historical, humorous, but not science fiction, romance, or mystery), responses to editor's questions (like "What's the funniest thing that ever happened to you?"), and some drawings. Submissions should depict positive family values such as bravery, kindness, and the like.

*Cobblestone Magazine* (History magazine). 20 Grove Street, Peterborough, NH 03458. Drawings, letters, and projects to "Ebenezer" with name, age, and address. Ebenezer also asks questions and publishes student answers.

*Cricket.* Cricket League, P.O. Box 300, Peru, IL 61354. Poetry, story-writing and art contests. Submissions must be accompanied by a statement signed by a teacher or parent assuring originality and that no help was given.

*Highlights for Children.* Honesdale, PA 18431. Poems, stories, black-and-white drawings to "Our Own Pages" with name, age, address.

*Jack and Jill Magazine.* 1100 Waterway Boulevard, P.O. Box 547, Indianapolis, IN 76206. Drawings and poems with name, age, school, and address.

*Kids Magazine.* P.O. Box 3041, Grand Central Station, New York, NY 10017. Short stories, poetry, nonfiction, black-and-white art, puzzles, games—400-word limit. Small honorary payments for published work. Age 5–15.

*National Geographic World.* 17th and M Streets, N.W., Washington, DC 20036. Short writings about hobby or special collection for column "Focus on Collections."

*Ranger Rick.* 1412 16th Street, N.W., Washington, DC 20036. Fiction, nonfiction, puzzles on nature themes.

*Reflections.* Dean Harper, Editor, Box 368, Duncan Falls, OH 43734. Attractive poetry magazine published by Duncan Falls Junior High students. Accepts

(*continued*)

### Magazines and Contests That Accept Young Writers' Work (continued)

poems by students from nursery school to high school. Authors include name, age, school, address, and teacher's name in upper right-hand corner. Include statement signed by author and teacher or parent attesting to the originality of the poetry. Payment is a copy of *Reflections.*

*Shoe Tree: The Literary Magazine by and for Children.* 215 Valle Del Sol Drive, Santa Fe, NM 87501. A quarterly published by the National Association for Young Writers, "Helping Children Write to the Top." All stories, poems, and artwork are done by children. Holds annual competition for young writers in fiction, poetry, and nonfiction. Age 5–14.

*Skipping Stones.* P.O. Box 3939, Eugene, OR 97403. A multiethnic magazine that encourages an understanding of different cultures and languages, with an emphasis on ecology and human relationships. Artwork, writings, riddles, book reviews, news items, and a pen pal section. Work by children around the world. English and Spanish/English editions.

*Stone Soup.* P.O. Box 83, Santa Cruz, CA 95063. A literary magazine written by children. Published by the Children's Art Foundation, a nonprofit organization devoted to encouraging children's creativity. Stories of any length, poems, book reviews, art (in any size and any color), and photographs.

### Magazines That Publish Teenagers' Writings

*Boys' Life.* 1325 Walnut Hill Lane, Irving, TX 75038-3096. Short stories or articles (around 15,000 words) for boys. Ages 8–18.

*Clubhouse.* Family Clubhouse Editor, Pomona, CA 91799. Focus on the family. Poems (4–24 lines), cartoons, short stories (adventure, historical, humorous, but not science fiction, romance, or mystery), responses to editor's questions (like "What's the funniest thing that ever happened to you?"), and some drawings. Submissions should depict positive family values such as bravery, kindness, and so on.

*Co-Ed Magazine.* Your Space, Co-Ed Magazine, 50 West 44th Street, New York, NY 10036. Poetry page (poems require written statement from author as well as his or her English teacher attesting to its originality—teacher's statement on school stationery. Poets must include name, address, home phone number, age, grade, and school.

*Dark Starr.* Drawer 4127, Oceanside, CA 92054. Science fiction to 5,000 words, poetry 1–40 lines (must be horror, science fiction, mystery).

*English Journal.* 1111 Kenyon Road, Urbana, IL 61801. Annual Spring Poetry Festival.

*Kids Magazine.* P.O. Box 3041, Grand Central Station, New York, NY 10017. Short stories, poetry, nonfiction, black-and-white art, puzzles, games—400-word limit. Small honorary payments for published work. Age 5–15.

*Merlyn's Pen.* P.O. Box 1058, East Greenwich, RI 02818. Dedicated to student writing and drawing. Short stories, science fiction, reviews, essays, and scripts up to 2,500 words, and poems up to 100 lines. Submissions should include author's name, grade, age, school and home address and phone numbers, county, and name of supervising teacher. Typed work preferred, with two-inch margins and double-spaced.

*National Council of Teachers of English Promising Young Writers Program.*

NCTE, 1111 Kenyon Road, Urbana, IL 61801. Open to eighth-graders nominated by February. Write NCTE for applications.

*Penworks.* P.O. Box 452, Belvedere, NJ 07823. A literary magazine by and for teens.

*Purple Cow.* Suite 320, 3423 Piedmont Rd., N. E., Atlanta, GA 30305. General-interest articles 1,000 words maximum and cartoons.

*Read Magazine.* Xerox Education Publications, 245 Long Hill Road, Middletown, CT 06467. Once a year features a special student issue devoted to students' poetry, short stories, plays, and feature articles. Regularly includes students' jokes and poetry. Grades 7–9.

*Reflections.* Dean Harper, Editor, Box 368, Duncan Falls, OH 43734. Attractive poetry magazine published by Duncan Falls Junior High students. Accepts poems by students from nursery school to high school. Authors include name, age, school, address, and teacher's name in upper right-hand corner. Include statement signed by author and teacher or parent attesting to the originality of the poetry. Payment is a copy of *Reflections.*

*Scholastic Scope Magazine.* 50 West 44th Street, New York, NY 10036. Grades 7–12. Poems, plays, stories, "mini-mysteries." Entries should be typed or neatly printed and accompanied by a note certifying originality and signed by the student and teacher or parent. Send entries in care of "Student Writing" or "Mini-Mysteries." Written for adolescents who read at fourth through sixth grade level.

*Scholastic Voice Magazine.* 50 West 44th Street, New York, NY 10036. Poems and stories of under 500 words. Frequent writing contests on specific themes. Entries should be typed or neatly printed and accompanied by a note certifying originality and signed by the student and teacher or parent. Grades 7–12, especially grades 8–10.

*Scholastic Writing Awards Program.* 50 West 44th Street, New York, NY 10036. Junior Division contest features essays, poetry, short stories, and dramatic scripts. Entries must be accompanied by an official entry blank. Deadline is January. Cash awards. Grades 7–9.

*Seventeen Magazine.* 850 Third Avenue, New York, NY 10022. Fiction, nonfiction, and poetry and a "Free for All" column.

*Skipping Stones.* P.O. Box 3939, Eugene, OR 97403. A multiethnic magazine that encourages an understanding of different cultures and languages, with an emphasis on ecology and human relationships. Artwork, writings, riddles, book reviews, news items, and a pen pal section. Work by children around the world. English and Spanish/English editions.

*Writing!* General Learning Corporation, P.O. Box 310, Highwood, IL 60040. Writing magazine ordered through schools. Student writing and articles on tips for writers.

*Young American, America's Newspaper for Kids.* Box 12409, Portland, OR 97212. Short stories (adventure, fantasy, humorous, mystery, science fiction, suspense—no stories relating to drugs, religion, or sex) (500–1,000 words). Poetry (4 lines to 500 words). Fillers—facts and short humor (30–300 words). Articles—general interest, crafts, humor, interview/profile, and newsworthy kids (350 words maximum).

*Young Author's Magazine* (YAM). 3015 Woodsdale Boulevard, Lincoln, NE 68502. All writing done by students. Personal experience articles, 1,000–2,500 words. Short stories (adventure, fantasy, humorous, mystery,

(*continued*)

**Magazines and Contests That Accept Young Writers' Work (continued)**

or science fiction—preferred four-page maximum). Poetry (preferred 10 lines maximum).

*Young Miss Magazine.* "Through Your Eyes . . . ," 685 Third Avenue, New York, NY 10017. Poetry page. Authors accompany submissions with a statement attesting to originality. Also "Youth Beat," where readers speak their own minds.

For a more extensive list of markets for young writers, see *Market Guide for Young Writers* by Kathy Henderson. Check your library or write P.O. Box 228, Sandusky, MI 48471. In addition to its lists of more than 100 markets and contests, it has many helpful tips, and it profiles young published authors. Also, keep your eyes open for local and state writing contests sponsored by local newspapers, civic organizations, teachers' organizations, professional organizations, and the like.

# APPENDIX C

# Tools of the Trade

# ACTION PLAN

COMMITTEE _____

CHAIRPERSON _____

| WHAT NEEDS TO BE DONE? | WHAT STEPS NEED TO BE TAKEN? | WHEN WILL IT BE DONE? | WHO WILL DO IT? | COST | HOW WILL YOU KNOW YOU'VE REACHED YOUR GOAL? |
|---|---|---|---|---|---|
| | | | | | |

# SAMPLE YEAR-LONG SCHEDULES

Following are two examples of year-long elementary, middle school, and senior high school schedules.

**Year-Long Elementary Models**

Gloria Plaza wrote Plan 1 in her second year as an RRS. Edye Norniella wrote Plan 2 in her first year. At the time they were two of the five reading resource specialists at Douglass Elementary, a large inner-city primary school with an increasing Hispanic population in Miami, Florida.

*Plan 1: First Quarter*
1. Assist in placing students in appropriate programs.

2. Assist with the placement of students in reading groups.

3. Assess teacher needs with a survey.

4. Interview department heads, the administration, and counselors.

5. Help with minimal skills test preparation.
   —Parent workshop
   —Homework packets
   —Fifteen-minute telecasts on closed-circuit television to reinforce skills
   —Demonstration of techniques to facilitate skills acquisition

6. Administer readiness test to kindergarten students.

7. Plan inservice workshops according to teacher and student needs.

8. Publish newsletter. Include message from resource teacher, techniques, expectations, research, services, poetry, upcoming events, and bibliography.

9. Encourage teachers and the administration to attend conferences and to join local, state, and international reading associations.

10. Provide assistance with local curricula and with pacing in the basal reader.

11. Promote the Pizza Hut Book It! program and the Fund-A-Book incentive program (cosponsored by the *Miami Herald*).

12. Encourage teachers to display up-to-date students' work on the bulletin boards.

13. Promote reading and writing by decorating the office area with students' work.

14. Keep books and magazines for visitors to read while they wait in the office.

15. Create an awareness for the importance of reading.

16. Demonstrate strategies in the classroom.

17. Increase library circulation through weekly raffles for students who have checked out books during the week.

18. Hold a Decorate-A-Door contest with the class's favorite story to motivate teachers to read aloud to students every day.

19. Observe the teaching of reading and language arts in the classrooms.

(continued)

**Sample Year-Long Schedules (continued)**

20. Order materials for reading such as big books, classroom libraries, and cassettes.

21. Provide a professional library for the staff.

22. Make presentations at conferences and share conference information with the staff.

23. Meet regularly with other resource teachers at the school and with those across the county.

*Plan 1: Second Quarter*

1. Help implement and monitor a schoolwide Sustained Silent Reading program.

2. Continue publishing newsletters.

3. Continue doing demonstrations and observations in classrooms.

4. Invite guest readers to the school.

5. Begin Stanford Achievement Test preparation.
   —Published test preparation materials
   —Test-taking tips
   —Handouts on ways to improve reading and listening skills

6. Assist teachers with a skills management program.

7. Assist teachers with remediation of skills missed on minimal skills test.

8. Organize workshops on the writing process, including publishing of students' books.

9. Display student work in the library.

10. Organize a presentation for parents on ways to help children at home with reading.

11. Provide inservice on reading in the content areas.

12. Distribute instructional materials as needed.

13. Write a suggested list of books for winter recess reading.

14. Participate in writing the meritorious school proposal.

15. Work with beginning teachers to help in planning and implementing an appropriate instructional program.

16. Be a role model of good teaching by using positive reinforcement and classroom management techniques.

17. Organize a bulletin board contest to display students' reading and writing work.

18. Help plan Black History Month and American history activities.

19. Organize a Decorate-A-Tree (with a storybook or storybook character) event; make an ornament for the event.

20. Meet regularly with other resource teachers at the school and with those across the county.

21. Make presentations at conferences and share conference information with the staff.

*Plan 1: Third Quarter*
1. Continue with ongoing tasks.

2. Assist with science experiments for the Science Fair and with Youth Fair projects.

3. Organize an annual Reading Day. Teachers dress as storybook characters and teach all subjects (including music, physical education, and art) through reading. Teachers' favorite childhood books are displayed in the library.

4. Invite storytellers and actors to perform for students.

*Plan 1: Fourth Quarter*
1. Continue with ongoing tasks.

2. Complete minimal skills test remediation.

3. Check skills management charts for reading progress and mastery.

4. Assist with decisions on retention of students.

5. Help media specialist categorize and count books.

6. Assist with completion and checking of cumulative folders.

7. Volunteer spare time to prepare materials for teachers.

8. Prepare a suggested summer reading list.

9. Prepare booklets with end-of-the-year activities to review and reinforce skills learned throughout the year.

10. Make a reading fair in the library with a display of students' work, a teacher idea exchange, and a student parade through the library.

11. Write a report of the year's accomplishments.

*Plan 2: August–September*
1. Become familiar with school culture and school needs.

2. Prepare for minimal skills test—grade 3.
   a. Meet with grade 3 teachers.
   b. Create and air lessons over closed circuit television.
   c. Provide individual classroom instruction.
   d. Identify students in need of further instruction.
      (1) Give or arrange for pre- and posttests.
      (2) Help with instruction and monitoring through classroom profile charts.
   e. Help to prepare daily homework packets.
   f. Help coordinate after-school and Saturday classes.

3. Model Directed Reading Lesson.

4. Help with basal management system and pacing.

5. Encourage attendance at October state reading conference through bulletin board display and flyers in mailboxes.

6. Plan regularly with other resource teachers at the school.

*(continued)*

**Sample Year-Long Schedules (continued)**

7. Receive training for Reading Reentry (a modification of Reading Recovery) and test candidates for program.

8. Hold informational meeting for whole language year-long inservice plan.

*Plan 2: October*
1. Continue with August–September efforts 1–6.

2. Promote Fund-A-Book Reading Incentive Program.

3. Model lessons on integrating science and reading.

4. Promote parental involvement.
   a. Hold at the school a parent meeting cosponsored by local reading council; provide for read-alouds to children attending.
   b. Plan Reading Reentry parents' meeting.
   c. Send home minimal skills test notices.

5. Attend district networking meeting for resource teachers and share information learned with staff.

6. Tutor students in Reading Reentry.

7. Attend state reading conference and share information learned with staff.

*Plan 2: November–December*
1. Model Directed Reading-Thinking Activity and process writing.

2. Develop listening packet for local reading conference.

3. Continue with October efforts 3, 5, and 6.

4. Begin whole language pilot.
   a. Select teachers.
   b. Provide overview of pilot at faculty meeting.
   c. Hold first inservice session with two guest speakers.

5. Visit exemplary reading program at another school.

6. Help plan end of Fund-A-Book media event at the school together with the *Miami Herald* and *Ronald McDonald Children's Charities.*

*Plan 2: January*
1. Model vocabulary development lessons: webbing, clustering, semantic mapping.

2. Continue with October efforts 3, 5, and 6, and November–December effort 1.

3. Continue with whole language pilot
   a. Have basal publisher representative provide overview of their integrated program.
   b. Have presentation by guest speaker.
   c. Model lessons in classrooms.
   d. Monitor the process.

4. Help with Stanford Achievement Test preparation. Plan test-taking skills schedule.

5. Hold articulation meeting with resource teachers from feeder intermediate school.

6. Encourage attendance at local reading conference in February.

7. Present at the National Reading Resource Specialist Conference sponsored by the state reading association.

8. Help with grade 2 minimal skills test preparation.
   a. Provide inservice session on the October test results.
   b. Help develop whole language instructional packets and explain and model their use.
   c. Help to pretest students on the test's spelling words and model spelling lessons on the morning telecast.

9. Help implement and monitor a Sustained Silent Reading program.

*Plan 2: February*
1. Continue with October efforts 5 and 6, November–December effort 1, and January efforts 3d, 4, 8b, and 9.

2. Model creative writing lessons.

3. Provide book-making workshop.

4. Promote countywide writing contests.

5. Develop Black History Month reading activities packets for teachers.

6. Promote local February reading conference, make presentation at conference, and share information learned with staff.

*Plan 2: March*
1. Continue with October efforts 5 and 6, November–December effort 1, and January efforts 3d, 4, 8b, and 9.

2. Guide tours of educators visiting pilot whole language classes.

3. Model lessons on integrating math and reading (word problems).

4. Promote schoolwide writing contest.

5. Begin reading textbook adoption activities.
   a. Have articulation meeting with feeder intermediate school.
   b. Attend county workshops.
   c. Form and train school adoption committee.

*Plan 2: April*
1. Continue with October efforts 5 and 6, and January efforts 3d, 4, 8b, and 9.

2. Provide whole language and cooperative learning lessons for ESOL classes.

3. Model lessons on integrating social studies and reading.

4. Provide guest speaker on whole language.

5. Conduct final vote on basal adoption.

*Plan 2: May*
1. Continue with October efforts 5 and 6, January efforts 3d, 4, 8b, and 9, and April effort 3.

2. Provide writing process lessons for ESOL classes.

3. Assist with administration of the Stanford Achievement Test.

4. Provide guest speaker on cooperative learning.

*(continued)*

**Sample Year-Long Schedules (continued)**

*Plan 2: June–July*
1. Help plan reading program development for summer school.
2. Help with minimal skills test posttesting.
3. Plan minimal skills test strategies for summer school.

**Year-long Middle School Models**

Rose Meltzer from Campbell Drive Middle wrote Plan 1. Stephanie McCamley at Norland Middle wrote Plan 2. At the time, Campbell Drive had a predominantly Hispanic and varied socioeconomic mix of students. Norland is a lower socioeconomic school that has won the U.S. Presidential Award of Excellence.

*Plan 1: September–October*
1. Distribute materials.
2. Work with eighth-grade classes on minimal skills test preparation.
3. Start SSR recreational reading.
4. Test students without scores.
5. Observe teachers to see their knowledge of incorporating reading strategies.

*Plan 1: October–November*
1. Work with content area teachers to help them make their textbooks student compatible (''My Textbook, a Friend'').
2. Model lessons and work with teachers on: vocabulary strategies, advance organizers, SQ3R, Directed Reading Activity.

*Plan 1: November–January*
1. Model lessons and work with teachers on: study skills, cooperative learning, report writing (including note cards), graphic organizers, K-W-L, reference skills, and critical thinking.
2. Help with book authors luncheon.

*Plan 1: February–April*
1. Prepare students for Stanford Achievement Test.
2. Model lessons and work with teachers on: skimming and scanning, advance organizers, main idea, inference skills, drawing conclusions, author's purpose, reading and interpreting poetry, author's point of view.

*Plan 1: April–June*
1. Model lessons and work with teachers on writing strategies and editing strategies (peer editing).
2. Pretest students on minimal skills test.
3. Do dramatic readings.
4. Conduct needs assessment to ascertain deficiencies that still exist.
5. Meet with ESL teachers to see which students can be resourced out.
6. Reclaim distributed materials from teachers.

*Plan 1: Ongoing Activities*
1. Be on call for teachers or students with specific needs.

2. Provide reading inservice workshops.

3. Provide informal inservice sessions (articles in mailboxes, chats in the lounge).

4. Write grade 7 reading curriculum.

5. Participate in the critical thinking training team.

6. Work with a bank in the community that displays student writing.

7. Work with a journalist who helped students with their newspaper and "adopted" some students.

8. Evaluate students having problems and match students to teachers.

9. Bring resource speakers to the school.

10. Inform the newspaper of newsworthy events.

11. Work on the reading committee, discipline committee, or school-based management committee.

12. Work with the media specialist on report writing, author bios, book briefs, and moving-sign vocabulary program.

13. Coordinate Lotto Read (Lubell, 1991).

14. Coordinate the Sustained Silent Reading program.

*Plan 2: First Semester*
1. General faculty meeting—Explain job functions of RRS.

2. Attend interdisciplinary team meetings and develop schedule for demonstration lessons and interdisciplinary units.

3. Organize schoolwide motivational reading programs. Plan for inservice.

4. Assist in planning and implementing basic skills program relating to state minimal skills test.

5. Develop method to evaluate effectiveness of RRS workshops.

6. Develop method to log workshops and demonstration lessons provided to teachers.

7. Organize Sustained Silent Reading during advisement program.

8. Organize a magazine/book drive to support the SSR program.

9. Assist media specialist in ordering new books for the media center.

10. Meet with interdisciplinary teams to provide information relative to basic skills mastery and other reading-related criteria.

11. Provide budget management for basic skills program.

12. Review new text materials to determine readability and considerateness of text.

13. Locate appropriate instructional materials for content teachers.

*Plan 2: Second Semester*
1. Develop and organize minimal skills test preparation program.

2. Assist science department in preparing students to complete science fair

(*continued*)

### Sample Year-Long Schedules (continued)

projects (e.g., demonstration lessons on bibliographies and organization of the report).

3. Make minimal skills test and standardized test scores available.

4. Do a foil analysis on school's test results.

5. Prepare for articulation with elementary and senior high schools.

6. Supply interdisciplinary teams and scheduling personnel with data to assist in building a master schedule.

7. Continue with activities from the first semester as needed.

### Year-long Senior High School Models

Dawna Lubell, an experienced RRS at Miami Southridge Senior High School, wrote Plan 1. It is a structured plan that focuses only on demonstration lessons. The school has a balanced triethnic predominantly black lower-socioeconomic-status student body. Margaret Bettendorf, another experienced RRS, wrote Plan 2, which focuses on the overall role of the resource specialist in a somewhat less structured fashion. Margaret is from Miami Beach Senior High School, a primarily Hispanic average- to high-socioeconomic-status school.

*Plan 1*

| Content Area | Days | Description |
|---|---|---|
| Biology | 1 | Text preview and organization |
| Biology | 3 | K-W-L; main idea comprehension; conceptual mapping |
| Language Arts | 3 | DRTA: QAR |
| Biology | 3 | Mapping review; summary writing; reciprocal teaching |
| Language Arts | 3 | Mapping short story structure; three-level guides |
| Biology | 3 | Review QAR and apply to text; pattern guides |
| Language Arts | 3 | Character analysis; thesis/proof |
| Biology | 2 | Minimal skills test—review selected skills |
| Language Arts | 2 | Stanford Achievement Test—test-taking strategies |
| Biology | 3 | Organizational guides (compare/contrast, etc.); notetaking |
| Language Arts | 3 | Fallacious reasoning or propaganda |

*Plan 2: First Quarter*

1. Write newsletters (September, October).

2. Make presentation to department heads on reading resource responsibilities.

3. Survey teachers—needs assessment.

4. Give workshop for beginning teachers on: "What the reading resource specialist can do for you."

5. Set up and implement a Sustained Silent Reading program.

6. Give Metropolitan Achievement Test for:
   —placement of new students without stanines
   —placement of questionable compensatory education students

7. Offer workshop for language arts teachers for literacy test preparation.

8. Give pull-out remediation for seniors who will take the literacy test in October.

9. Set up and assign minimal skills test remediation files for language arts teachers.

10. Locate materials for minimal skills test remediation.

11. Instruct new teachers regarding minimal skills test remediation.

12. Conduct ongoing activities:
    —readability of materials and materials assessment
    —individual diagnostic testing and recommendations
    —collegial conferences regarding reading strategies
    —demonstration lessons as requested by individual teachers, administrators, or department heads.

*Plan 2: Second Quarter*
1. Write newsletters (November, January).

2. Set up Reading Committee and hold monthly meetings.

3. Do workshop—TAP (Teachers as Advisors Program) on study skills.

4. Do class visitations for ninth- through twelfth-graders on SAT and PSAT preparation.

5. Do workshop for ninth- and tenth-grade content area teachers on minimal skills test preparation across the curriculum.

6. Assist with planning and hosting library open house.

7. Conduct ongoing activities:
   —individual diagnostic testing and recommendations
   —collegial conferences regarding reading strategies
   —demonstration lessons as requested by individual teachers, administrators, or department heads
   —monitoring SSR program

*Plan 2: Third Quarter*
1. Write newsletters (February, March).

2. Conduct literacy test workshops for language arts teachers.

3. Do class visitations of grade 10 classes on minimal skills test preparation for March test.

4. Do class visitations of grades 9–11 classes on SAT test preparation on test-taking skills.

5. Monitor minimal skills test remediation progress (of teachers).

6. Distribute materials for minimal skills test preparation.

7. Assist in planning book fair.

8. Offer Teacher Education Center course credit for Reading in Content

(*continued*)

**Sample Year-Long Schedules (continued)**

Area workshop (to be held during administrative planning period or after school).

9. Conduct ongoing activities:
   —individual diagnostic testing and recommendations
   —collegial conferences regarding reading strategies
   —demonstration lessons as requested by individual teachers, administrators, or department heads
   —monitoring SSR program

*Plan 2: Fourth Quarter*
1. Write newsletters (April, May).

2. Conduct workshop for content area teachers on Stanford Achievement Test preparation.

3. Do class visitations of language arts classes on test-taking skills for the SAT.

4. Hold Book Fair.

5. Prepare and distribute year-end summary report.

6. Prepare summer reading list (language arts teachers).

7. Locate materials for teachers teaching the minimal skills test thirteenth-year program.

8. Posttest students previously given individual tests and recommend following year placement.

9. Ongoing activities:
   —individual diagnostic testing and recommendations
   —collegial conferences regarding reading strategies
   —demonstration lessons as requested by individual teachers, administrators, or department heads
   —monitoring SSR program

*Daily responsibilities*
1. Two instructional periods of developmental reading.

2. One instructional period—team-teach compensatory education class.

3. One administrative period

# COPYRIGHT OR COPY WRONG:
# RULES ON PHOTOCOPYING

by Janet R. Binkley

Photocopying—it's a way of life for educators at all levels. But is what you're doing unethical? Or even illegal? Recent court decisions on copyright law and photocopying in the United States may affect the way you copy material.

The best-known U.S. case is a suit by eight publishers against Kinko's Graphics Corporation, a national chain of photocopying stores often located near college campuses. Kinko's has been ordered to pay the publishers more than $500,000 in damages and is prohibited from selling photocopied collections of copyrighted materials without obtaining permissions and paying royalties.

The key word is "permissions." Many educators have felt that copying for educational purposes fell under the U.S. Copyright Law's "fair use" provisions. In addition, many state-supported universities believed that a technical defect in the law protected them from having to pay damages for improper copying. That defect was eliminated in November 1990 when President Bush signed the Copyright Remedy Clarification Bill into law.

Teachers have thus been warned that mass photocopying without written permission from the publisher may be a no-no. But the questions remain—when may you copy, how much may you copy, and how often may you copy?

Although there are few hard and fast rules in the U.S. governing what constitutes fair use, here are some basic things you may and may not do:

- You may make a single copy of almost anything for your personal use.

- You may make and use multiple classroom copies (one copy per student in the class), but you may use that item only once, and then only if no other teacher in your institution has already used it.

- You may *not*, without written permission from the publisher, repeat the use of copies of any item from term to term.

- You may *not* photocopy from a work by the same author more than once a term, or make copies more than three times a term from the same collective work or periodical.

- You may *not* make extra copies for other people.

- You may *not* make copies of various works in place of using an anthology for the class.

- You may *not* copy materials from publications that are "consumable," such as workbooks.

There are also restrictions on the length of copied material allowed: complete or partial poems only if less than 250 words and not longer than two pages; a story, article, or essay only if less than 2,500 words; an excerpt from a prose work only if the copied material is shorter than 1,000 words or 10 per cent of the work (whichever is less); and only one cartoon, chart, etc., per book or periodical. Otherwise you need permission from the copyright holder.

The U.S. copyright law sets forth clear rules about library use. You may put copies on reserve, although your library may ask you to provide the copies.

Happily, getting permission to make repeated multiple copies is becoming easy. In 21 countries, central agencies negotiate school licenses or make it possible to arrange permissions and pay fees at your local copy center.

For example, in the United States, clearance may be handled through the Copyright Clearance Center (CCC); in the United Kingdom, through the Copy-

*(continued)*

**Copyright or Copy Wrong: Rules on Photocopying (continued)**

right Licensing Agency; in Australia, through the Copyright Agency, Ltd; and in Denmark, through Copy-Dan.

In the United States, journals registered with the CCC place a code number on the first page of each article, along with the fee if there is one. Copy centers now check for permissions for their patrons and handle the fee transaction, if needed. This permits permissions to be handled within a few days. The same procedure applies for registered books.

To facilitate processing of the growing number of copy requests for its journals, the International Reading Association has registered all four journals with the CCC. Codes and fees will appear in the next new volume year of each journal and will be available at copy centers.

Please note that individual members of the Association are exempt from the stated fees for multiple copying of IRA journal articles. You can show copy center personnel your membership card and the notice at the front of the journal stating that the fee is waived for members.

Since the Association's books are not registered with the CCC, users should seek permission to copy directly from the Permissions Editor, IRA, 800 Barksdale Rd., PO Box 8139, Newark, DE 19714-8139, USA.

For further information about copyright law and the right to make copies, try the video program produced by the Association for Information Media and Equipment. Entitled *Copyright Law: What Every School, College, and Public Library Should Know,* the tape is available directly from AIME, PO Box 865, Elkader, IA 52043, USA; telephone: (319) 245-1361.

AIME also has established a toll-free Copyright Hot Line (1-800-444-4203) for questions about U.S. copyright law.

*Source: Reading Today,* August–September, 1991, p. 4.

# STRATEGY LOG

Teacher's Name: _____

Date          Subject or Period          Strategy

_____

_____

_____

_____

Teacher's Name: _____

Date          Subject or Period          Strategy

_____

_____

_____

_____

Teacher's Name: _____

Date          Subject or Period          Strategy

_____

_____

_____

_____

Teacher's Name: _____

Date          Subject or Period          Strategy

_____

_____

_____

_____

# TRANSPARENCY DO'S AND DONT'S

| DO | DON'T |
|---|---|
| Focus and position transparency before beginning presentation. | Focus and position transparency after beginning to speak. |
| Stand so the students can see. | Stand so as to block the screen. |
| Turn off the projector between transparencies. | Turn projector on and off so much that it is a distraction. |
| Use six lines or fewer per visual. | Use "busy" transparencies. |
| Use six words or fewer per line. | Use hard-to-read transparencies. |
| Make letters at least one-half inch in size—the larger the better. | Use typewritten material or lettering that is too small. |
| Use color if possible. | Use only black and white. |
| Put captions on top and use top two-thirds of visual for images. | Put images near bottom of screen. |
| Face and talk to the students. | Talk to projector or screen. |
| Uncover information as you discuss or describe it. | Show all information at once. |
| Use and write notes on frames. | Refer to many pages of notes. |
| Use a variety of colors and types. | Use only one color or type. |
| Keep lights on except those closest to screen. | Turn off lights in classroom. |
| Use charts and illustrations. | Use only words, with no pictures. |
| Use cartoons and humor. | Use dry material. |
| Use both upper and lower case letters. | Use only upper-case letters. |
| Position projector so image fills up as much of screen as possible. | Use too small a portion of the screen. |
| Use only clean transparencies. | Show dirty transparencies. |
| Point to items on transparency. | Point to screen. |

## SAMPLE TRANSPARENCY

**Behaviors That Enhance Questioning Effectiveness**

—**Provide for all kinds of questions.**

—**Provide the opportunity for all students to participate.**

—**Provide for "Wait Time."**

—**Provide students with the opportunity to respond to each other.**

—**Provide prompting clues.**

—**Provide the right answer, when appropriate.**

—**Provide students with the opportunity to experience success.**

—**Provide praise for the student.**

Jo S. Tanner
Jupiter Middle School
Palm Beach County, Florida

# GRANT WRITING

You may be interested in writing a grant to initiate a new instructional program, to fund a motivational reading effort, or perhaps to support a research project. Grants are available through federal, state, and local governments; businesses; philanthropic foundations; and professional organizations. In some cases university faculty members interested in educational research will coauthor grants with school-based personnel. Money for good ideas is available, but it does take some effort to secure grant funds. Here are some suggestions for writing grants:

1. Activate your grant radar! Start looking for funding sources at your public library. Call the research office at your local school district and your state department of education. You may have to dig to find the right funding source for your project.

2. After you find a call for proposals that seems to fit your needs, read the proposal carefully. If any aspect of the proposal seems unclear to you, call the funding source immediately.

3. Check with your school principal to let her or him know of your intention to write the grant and to enlist support. Also ask the school principal if other district personnel need to be informed of the proposed project.

4. Make a list of all the components necessary to complete a grant proposal, and set a timeline for completion of each component.

5. If letters of support (e.g., from parent groups or your school principal) are necessary, request them early.

6. Format your proposal according to the structure suggested in the call for proposals. Reviewers may deduct points if you organize your proposal in a different way or if the proposal does not conform to length requirements.

7. To make your proposal easy to read, use an outline format where possible and appropriate.

8. Make certain that the proposal contains all components requested in the call for proposals. Incomplete proposals are often automatically rejected, particularly if the response rate for the call from proposals is high.

9. If an abstract or project summary is required, spend a great deal of time to polish this piece. This may be your best opportunity to ''sell'' your projects to hurried reviewers.

10. Include explicit statements explaining how your project's objectives are consistent with those delineated by the funding agency. For example, if the agency is seeking literacy projects that are replicable and sustainable, then explain in detail how your project plans to meet those objectives.

11. Include a resume that is up to date and complete. Provide a biographical sketch that highlights your training and experiences that relate to the management of the proposed project.

12. Enlist the help of colleagues to serve as inside reviewers of your proposal. It's a good idea to have several people give you suggestions for revising and editing.

13. Enlist the help of a colleague to double-check your budget calculations.

14. Allocate sufficient time to put together a polished final draft. Laser printing and graphics help. Think about what you know about "considerate" or "friendly" text—use plenty of headings and subheadings, highlight key ideas in boldfaced type, and so on.

15. Before mailing, do a thorough final check for each of the proposal elements.

16. Funding agencies often have stringent deadlines for proposals. Keep a post office receipt to verify that you mailed the proposal on time.

17. Keep trying. Proposals, even those written by experienced grant writers, are often not funded on the first submission. Use reviewers' comments to revise your proposal and try with another agency or with the same agency's next competition.

For further information, see L. F. Locke, W. W. Spirduso, & S. J. Silverman, *Proposals That Work*, 2nd ed. (Newbury Park, CA: Sage Publications, 1987).

# PUBLISHERS

Agency for Instructional Technology
1111 West 17th Street
Bloomington, IN 47401

Aldus
411 First Ave.
Seattle, WA 98104-2871

Allyn & Bacon
160 Gould Street
Needham Heights, MA 02194

American School Publishers
A Macmillan/McGraw-Hill Company
11 West 19th Street
New York, NY 10011

Amsco School Publications, Inc.
315 Hudson Street
New York, NY 10013

Barnell Loft, Ltd.
958 Church Street
Baldwin, NY 11510

Berrent Publications, Inc.
1025 Northern Boulevard
Roslyn, NY 11576

Broderbund Software-Direct
P.O. Box 12947
San Rafael, CA 94913-2947

William C. Brown Publishers
2460 Kerper Boulevard
Dubuque, IA 52001

Carson-Dellosa Publishing Company,
 Inc.
4321 Piedmont Parkway
P.O. Box 35665
Greensboro, NC 27425

Childrens Press
5440 North Cumberland Avenue
Chicago, IL 60656

Claris Corp.
5201 Patrick Henry Drive
Santa Clara, CA 95052

Christopher-Gordon Publishers, Inc.
480 Washington Street
Norwood, MA 02062

The Continental Press, Inc.
520 East Bainbridge
Elizabethtown, PA 17022

CTB
Macmillan/McGraw-Hill
2500 Garden Road
Monterey, CA 93940

Curriculum Associates, Inc.
5 Esquire Road
North Billerica, MA 01862

DLM Teaching Resources
One DLM Park
Box 4000
Allen, TX 75002

DRP Services, TASA, Inc.,
P.O. Box 382
Brewster, NY 10509

EDL (Educational Development
 Laboratories)
P.O. Box 21076
Columbia, SC 29221

Educational Testing Service/"BOOK-
 WHIZ"
Library and Reference Services
Princeton, NJ 08541

Educators Publishing Service
75 Moulton Street
Cambridge, MA 02138

Encyclopedia Britannica Educational
 Corporation
310 South Michigan Avenue
Chicago, IL 60604

Fearon Teacher Aids
1204 Buchanan Street
Carthage, IL 62321

Free Spirit Publishing, Inc.
123 North Third Street
Minneapolis, MN 55401

Globe Book Company
190 Sylvan Avenue
Englewood Cliffs, NJ 07632

Good Apple
1204 Buchanan Street
Carthage, IL 62321

Harcourt Brace Jovanovich School
  Division
6277 Sea Harbor Drive
Orlando, FL 32887

DC Heath and Company
125 Spring Street
Lexington, MA 02173

Heinemann Educational Books, Inc.
70 Court Street
Portsmouth, NH 03801

Highlights for Children
2300 West Fifth Avenue
P.O. Box 269
Columbus, OH 43216-0269

Holt, Rinehart and Winston College
  Publishing
301 Commerce Street
Fort Worth, TX 76102

Houghton Mifflin Company
One Beacon Street
Boston, MA 02108

IBM Corporation
360 Hamilton Avenue
White Plains, NY 10601

Ideal School Supply
11000 South Lavergne
Oak Lawn, IL 60453

Jamestown Publishers, Inc.
P.O. Box 9168
Providence, RI 02940

Judy/Instructo
4325 Hiawatha Avenue South
Minneapolis, MN 55406

Kendall/Hunt Publishing Company
2460 Kerper Boulevard
Dubuque, IA 52001

Learning Links Inc.
2300 Marcus Avenue
New Hyde Park, NY 11042

Macmillan/McGraw-Hill School
  Publishing Company
866 Third Avenue
New York, NY 10022

Midwest Publications
P.O. Box 448
Pacific Grove, CA 93950-0448

Modern Curriculum Press, Inc.
13900 Prospect Road
Cleveland, OH 44136

Newsweek
610 Oakland Hills Drive
Arnold, MD 21012

Open Court Publishing Company
315 Fifth Street
P.O. Box 599
Peru, IL 61354

Richard C. Owen Publishers, Inc.
135 Katonah Avenue
Katonah, NY 10536

Perfection Form Company
1000 North 2nd Avenue
Logan, IA 51546

Power Op
2929 Campus Drive #400
San Mateo, CA 94403

Prentice-Hall School Division
Route 9W
Englewood Cliffs, NJ 07632

The Psychological Corporation
555 Academic Court
San Antonio, TX 78204

Random House, Inc.
201 East 50th Street
New York, NY 10022

Reading Is Fundamental, Inc.
600 Maryland Ave., S.W., Suite 500
Washington, DC 20024

Rigby Education
P.O. Box 797
Crystal Lake, IL 60014

(continued)

**Publishers (continued)**

The Riverside Publishing Company
8420 Bryn Mawr Avenue
Chicago, IL 60631

Frank Schaffer Publications, Inc.
23740 Hawthorne Boulevard
Torrance, CA 90505

Scholastic Inc.
730 Broadway
New York, NY 10003

Science Research Associates, Inc.
155 N. Wacker Drive
Chicago, IL 60606

Scott, Foresman and Company
1900 East Lake Avenue
Glenview, IL 60025

Silver Burdett & Ginn
250 James
Morristown, NJ 07962

Society for Visual Education
1345 F Diversey Parkway
Chicago, IL 60614-1299

Spinnaker
Springboard Publishing
338 Commerce Drive
Fairfield, CT 06430

Steck-Vaughn Company
P.O. Box 26015
Austin, TX 78755

Sunburst Communications
101 Castleton Street
Pleasantville, NY 10570

Sundance Publishers and Distributors
P.O. Box 1326
Newton Road
Littleton, MA 01460

Tapestry Learning Corporation
2023 Aspen Glade
Kingswood, TX 77339

Teacher Support Software, Inc.
1035 N.W. 57th Street
Gainesville, FL 32605

Teachers College Press
1234 Amsterdam Avenue
New York, NY 10027

The Learning Co. (TLC)
6493 Kaiser Drive
Fremont, CA 94555

Unison World
1321 Harbor Bay Parkway
Alameda, CA 94501

USA Today
1901 Montreal Road
Tucker, GA 30084

Weekly Reader Corporation
245 Longhill Road
Middletown, CT 06457

Word Perfect Corp.
288 West Center Street
Orem, UT 84052

The Wright Group
10949 Technology Place
San Diego, CA 92127

Zaner-Bloser, Inc.
1459 King Avenue
P.O. Box 16764
Columbus, OH 43216-6764

# SUGGESTED READINGS*

**A Core Professional Library for the Reading Resource Specialist**

E = Elementary

S = Secondary (Middle and Senior High)

B = Both

Atwell, N. (1987). *In the middle.* Portsmouth, NH: Heinemann. (S)

Bos, C. S., & Vaughn, S. (1991). *Strategies for teaching students with learning and behavior problems,* 2nd ed. Boston: Allyn and Bacon. (B)

Calkins, L. (1986). *The art of teaching writing.* Portsmouth, NH: Heinemann. (E)

Calkins, L., & Harwayne, S. (1991). *Living between the lines.* Portsmouth, NH: Heinemann. (E)

Cunningham, P. M. (1991). *Phonics they use: Words for reading and writing.* New York: HarperCollins. (E)

Duffy, G. G. (Ed.). (1991). *Reading in the middle school.* Newark, DE: International Reading Association. (S)

Fry, E. B., Polk, J. K., & Fountoukidis, D. (1984). *The Reading Teacher's Book of Lists.* Englewood Cliffs, NJ: Prentice-Hall, (B)

Goodman, K. S., Bird, L. B., & Goodman, Y. M. (1991). *The whole language catalog.* Santa Rosa, CA: American School Publishers. (B)

Graves, D. (1983). *Writing: Teachers and children at work.* Portsmouth, NH: Heinemann. (B)

Gunderson, L. (1991). *ESL literacy instruction: A guidebook to theory and practice.* Englewood Cliffs, NJ: Prentice Hall Regents. (B)

Harris, A. J., & Sipay, E. R. (1990). *How to increase reading ability: A guide to developmental and remedial methods,* 9th ed. New York: Longman. (B)

Heald-Taylor, G. (1989). *The administrator's guide to whole language.* Katonah, NY: Owen. (E)

Irwin, J. W., & Baker, I. (1990). *Promoting active reading comprehension strategies.* Englewood Cliffs, NJ: Prentice-Hall. (B)

Monahan, J. N., & Hinson, B. (1988). *New directions in reading instruction.* Newark, DE: International Reading Association.(B)

Readence, J. E., Bean, T. W., & Baldwin, R. S. (1992). *Content area reading: An integrated approach,* 4th ed. Dubuque, IA: Kendall/Hunt. (S)

Taylor, S. E., Frackenpohl, H., & White, C. E. (1979). *EDL core vocabularies in reading, mathematics, science, and social studies.* New York, NY: McGraw-Hill. (B)

Tierney, R. J., Readence, J. E., & Dishner, E. K. (1990). *Reading strategies and practices: A compendium,* 3rd ed. Boston: Allyn and Bacon. (B)

Vacca, R., & Vacca, J. (1989). *Content area reading,* 3rd ed. Glenview, IL: Scott, Foresman. (S)

Wilson, R. M., & Gambrell, L. B. (1988). *Reading comprehension in the elementary school: A teacher's practical guide.* Boston: Allyn and Bacon. (E)

* See also the section on Professional Organizations (p. 36).

(*continued*)

## Suggested Readings (continued)

### Resources for Parents

*Books*

Barron, M. (1990). *I learn to read and write the way I learn to talk.* Katonah, NJ: Owen.

Binkley, M. R. (1988). *Becoming a nation of readers: What parents can do.* Washington, DC: U.S. Department of Education.

Butler, D., & Clay, M. (1987). *Reading begins at home.* Portsmouth, NH: Heinemann.

Graves, R. (Ed.). (1987). *The RIF guide to encouraging young readers.* New York: Doubleday.

Hartmann, D., & Stump, A. (1980). *Your child can read better: A handbook for parents.* Holmes Beach, FL: Learning Publications.

Kimmel, M. M., & Segel, E. (1988). *For reading out loud! A guide to sharing books with children.* New York: Delacorte.

Lamme, L. L. (1985). *Highlights for children growing up reading.* Washington, DC: Acropolis Books.

Larrick, N. (1983). *A parent's guide to better reading.* Philadelphia: Westminster.

Lipson, E. R. (1988). *Parent's guide to children's reading.* Garden City, NY: Doubleday.

Oppenheim, J., Brenner, B., & Boegehold, B. D. (1986). *Choosing books for kids.* New York: Ballantine.

Radencich, M. C., & Schumm, J. S. (1988). *How to help your child with homework.* Minneapolis, MN: Free Spirit Publishing.

Russell, W. (1984). *Classics to read aloud to your children.* Knob Noster, MO: Crown.

Taylor, D. (1986). *Family storybook reading.* Portsmouth, NH: Heinemann.

Trelease, J. (1989). *The new read-aloud handbook.* New York: Penguin.

### Resources from International Reading Association

*International Reading Association,* 800 Barksdale Road, P.O. Box 8139, Newark, DE 19714.

Baghban, M. *How can I help my child learn to read English as a Second Language?* (This publication has also been translated into Spanish by R. L. Garcia and R. M. Deyoe.)

Baghban, M. *You can help your young child with writing.*

Beverstock, C. *Your child's vision is important.*

Chan, J. *Why read aloud to children?*

Eberly, D. W. *How does my child's vision affect his reading?*

Glazer, S. M. *Creating readers and writers.*

Glazer, S. M. *How can I help my child build positive attitudes toward reading?*

Grinnel, P. C. *How can I prepare my young child for reading?*

Idaho Literacy Project. *Read to me* (a videotape for parents).

Myers, J. *You can encourage your high school student to read.*

Ransbury, M. K. *How you can encourage your primary grade child to read.*

Reed, A. *Comics to classics: A parent's guide to books for teens and preteens.*

Roser, N. L. *Helping your child become a reader.*

Shefelbine, J. *Encouraging your junior high student to read.*

Silvern, S. B., & Silvern, L. R. *Beginning literacy and your child.*
Winebrenner, R. *How can I get my teenager to read?*

*Note:* IRA also offers single copies of brochures for parents at no charge. When requesting copies, please enclose a self-addressed, stamped envelope:

- "Good Books Make Reading Fun for Your Child"

- "Summer Reading Is Important"

- "You Can Encourage Your Child to Read"

- "Your Home Is Your Child's First School"

American Library Association, 50 E. Huron Street, Chicago, IL 60611.

The ALA develops book lists for a variety of age groups.

National Council of Teachers of English, 1111 Kenyon Road, Urbana, IL 61801.

The NCTE offers brochures for parents:

- "How to Help Your Child Become a Better Writer"

- "How to Help Your Child Become a Better Reader"

Reading Is Fundamental, Inc. (RIF), 600 Maryland Avenue, S.W., Washington, DC 20024.

RIF offers brochures for parents:

- "Children Who Can Read, But Don't"

- "Choosing Good Books for Children"

- "TV and Reading"

- "Upbeat and Offbeat Activities to Encourage Reading"

# APPENDIX D

# Evaluation/
# Assessment Tools

# TEACHER LESSON EVALUATION

Reading Resource Specialist _____

Date of Service _____

Type of Service _____

Please rate the following checklist using this scale:

3 — Strongly agree      1 — Disagree

2 — Agree            N/A — Not applicable

## Goals and Objectives

_____ There was a definite goal or purpose for the lesson.

_____ The goal was evident to the students.

## Procedure

_____ The lesson was planned and systematic.

_____ The lesson was flexible to the dynamics of the classroom situation.

_____ There was rapport between students and resource specialist.

*Comments*
Was the strategy useful to you? Will you integrate it into your lessons? If so, how?

_____

_____

_____


What comments did your students make regarding the lesson?

_____

_____

_____


Would you be willing to invite the RRS to work on future projects with you?

_____

# INTEREST AND ATTITUDE INVENTORY

Everybody is SUM/BODY—a total of many things. Please help me know the SUM that is YOU by filling out this form.

Name _____

Age _____ Date _____ Grade _____

1. My favorite television show is _____ .

2. My favorite kind of music is _____ .

3. My favorite sport is _____ .

4. My favorite song is _____ .

5. My favorite person is _____ .

6. I like to read about _____ .

7. My favorite magazine is _____ .

8. When I am asked to read aloud in school, I feel _____
   _____ .

9. The part of the newspaper I read first is _____
   _____ .

10. My three favorite books are:

    a. _____

    b. _____

    c. _____

11. I like to collect _____ .

12. The best storyteller I know is _____ .

13. When I get a book for a present I feel _____
    _____ .

14. The person who can do the best job reading a story to me is
    _____ .

15. My favorite kind of story is _____ .

16. I like to collect _____ .

17. When I have free time I _____ .

18. I first got a public library card when I was _____ years old.

19. I go to the public library about _____ times a month.

20. I like to write stories about _____ .

(*continued*)

**Interest and Attitude Inventory (continued)**

21. I like to write letters to _____ .

22. My favorite subject in school is _____ .

23. My hardest subject in school is _____ .

24. I'm really good at _____ .

25. My favorite person to talk with is _____ .

26. The most fun I ever had was _____
_____ .

27. Places I'd like to visit are _____
_____ .

28. When I finish school I plan to _____
_____ .

29. Overall, I think that as a reader I am _____
_____ .

30. Overall, I think that as a writer I am _____
_____ .

# CONTENT SELF-EVALUATION

FREQUENTLY   OCCASIONALLY   NEVER

Do I

- Keep a log of my daily activities?

- Prepare/monitor schoolwide reading assessment data?

- Prepare and then model lessons regularly?

- Plan, act, follow up, and evaluate?

- Promote and coordinate schoolwide recreational reading programs?

- Maintain an active role in local and state reading organizations?

- Highlight articles and share them with my colleagues?

- Keep current by reading professional journals and attending conferences?

- Involve parents?

- Volunteer to do unpopular tasks that need to be done?

- Produce or contribute to a newsletter?

- Share my school's accomplishments with the district and the media?

- Work with school committees?

- Encourage the use of newspaper in education activities?

- Carry out a Sustained Silent Reading program?

- Enlist the aid of community resources?

- Make sure that students are exposed to a variety of both narrative and expository genres?

- Coordinate or help with textbook selection?

# PROCESS SELF-EVALUATION

FREQUENTLY    OCCASIONALLY    NEVER

Do I

- Have focused long- and short-term goals that stem from faculty requests as well as from my own perceptions of need?

- Regularly work on these goals?

- Show flexibility?

- Encourage others to attend conferences?

- Talk enthusiastically about what I learn with my colleagues in informal settings?

- Read and talk about trade books?

- Make every effort to be accessible?

- Accept people with views different from mine?

- Serve as an advocate for teachers in my dealings with administrators?

- Help teachers by using a development rather than a deficit model?

- Provide several alternatives rather than one "right" solution?

- Find ways to use the strengths and motivations of others for the good of the cause?

- Share leadership?

- Use good planning rather than devote time to "putting out fires" that could have been prevented by better planning?

- Give feedback that is specific and well timed?

- Work with a time budget?

FREQUENTLY   OCCASIONALLY   NEVER

Do I

- Organize my materials for easy retrieval?
- Promptly follow through on requests?
- Take initiative in program improvement?
- Radiate self-confidence?
- Help to create a positive climate?
- Show decisiveness?
- Show a proper degree of assertiveness?
- Make every effort to be fair?
- Concentrate as much on listening as I do on talking?
- Avoid gossip?
- Help each faculty member feel important and needed?
- Find ways to enlist the support of potential dissenters?
- Show high expectations?
- Show persistence?
- Make sure that teachers experience success with any innovation that I encourage?
- Work hard?

# LETTER TO HIGHLIGHT ACCOMPLISHMENTS

Dear _____:

As we approach the end of the school year, I would like to recap some of the reading programs and projects held at the school this year.

- School goals were supported by . . .
- A total of _____ teachers have participated in _____ (list for each project, inservice session, etc.).
- The total number of teachers/students/classes I served was . . .
- I modeled _____ (#) lessons in classes as follows:
- Strategies that appeared to be most popular were:
- The events I actively participated in were (list dates and events) . . .
- I helped with instructional materials selection by . . .
- The library/media specialist and I . . .
- Contacts I made outside the school included . . .
- Parent education was enhanced by . . .
- Test preparation was improved by . . .
- Visitors to our school included . . .
- Materials that I disseminated included . . .
- Goals for next year include . . .

My sincerest thanks go out to all of you who took part in this year's program. I hope that, with your help, the program will be even more successful next year.

# PROGRAM REVIEW

REVIEWER _____ DATE _____

| INDICATORS | STATUS (check one) 1  2  3 | COMMENTS/ RECOMMENDATIONS |
|---|---|---|
| I. Program organization: | | |
| A. Grade/department/ team leadership facilitates achievement of goals. | | |
| B. Each teacher has relevant district and state materials. | | |
| C. There is evidence of appropriate pacing. | | |
| D. Lesson plans, grade books, and classroom activities correlate with each other and reflect instructional objectives that correlate to students' assessed needs. | | |
| E. Appropriate texts and support materials are available. | | |
| F. All teachers are properly certified in their field. | | |
| II. General program delivery strategies: | | |
| A. Students are aware of specific course objectives and expectations. | | |
| B. Both direct instruction and flexible group activities (e.g., cooperative learning, buddy reading, peer editing) are used. | | |

1 = Appropriate          2 = Needs Improvement          3 = Not Applicable

(*continued*)

209

**Program Review (continued)**

| INDICATORS | STATUS (check one) 1 2 3 | COMMENTS/ RECOMMENDATIONS |
|---|---|---|
| C. Teachers use strategies to meet different learning styles. | | |
| D. Support materials (i.e., books, audiovisual) and/or personnel are used in a planned way to meet individual needs. | | |
| E. Homework is varied, correlates with course objectives, and is checked promptly. | | |
| F. Students are engaged. | | |
| G. The climate is conducive to interaction (student–teacher, student–student). | | |
| H. Parent/community support is active. | | |
| III. Specific language arts strategies: | | |
| A. Teaching of reading/ writing strategies extends across the curriculum. | | |
| B. Compositions give evidence that students are engaged in the writing process. | | |
| C. Opportunities are provided for writing in several modes and for authentic audiences. | | |
| D. A continuous program for the improvement of spelling, punctuation, and standard American | | |

1 = Appropriate    2 = Needs Improvement    3 = Not Applicable

| INDICATORS | STATUS (check one) 1  2  3 | COMMENTS/ RECOMMENDATIONS |
|---|---|---|
| usage is integrated into the total language arts program. | | |
| E. Recently dated student writing is readily visible. This writing includes individual work, not just "carbon copies," for all students. | | |
| F. Students are encouraged to see the language arts as parts of an integrated whole. | | |
| G. Techniques, materials, and the like that have been recommended in workshops, program reviews, and elsewhere are in use (if applicable). | | |
| H. Strategic instruction includes teaching *what* is to be learned, *why* it is to be learned, and *when* to use it. | | |
| I. The study of literature is planned to provide for students' growth. | | |
| J. The use of the library and reference resources is taught in relation to needs. | | |
| K. Media specialists support overall program (e.g., organizing materials by themes, supporting ongoing schoolwide motivational reading programs). | | |

1 = Appropriate       2 = Needs Improvement       3 = Not Applicable

(*continued*)

**Program Review (continued)**

| INDICATORS | STATUS (check one) 1 2 3 | COMMENTS/ RECOMMENDATIONS |
|---|---|---|
| L. Students are encouraged in a variety of ways to do voluntary reading and report their individual reading experiences. | | |
| M. Instruction in listening, speaking, and viewing is an integral part of the program. | | |
| N. Student-directed problem solving is evident in discussions, projects, and written work. | | |
| O. Study skills instruction is ongoing within each subject area. | | |
| P. Class activities place emphasis on the growth of each child toward higher cognitive levels. | | |
| Q. Learning centers, including library corners, are attractive and well stocked with varied and appropriate materials. | | |
| IV. Student records: | | |
| A. Records adhere to school policies. | | |
| B. Student folders contain work in creative and expository composition, all major tests and/or assessment items, and only representative samples of practice exercises of grammar, vocabulary, and spelling. | | |

1 = Appropriate        2 = Needs Improvement        3 = Not Applicable

| INDICATORS | STATUS (check one) 1 2 3 | COMMENTS/ RECOMMENDATIONS |
|---|---|---|
| C. Portfolios are kept. These can include reading logs, informal assessment, writing samples from different stages of the writing process, ''can do'' lists, and the like. | | |
| D. A variety of formal and informal evaluative techniques is used (e.g., objective and essay tests, self- and peer evaluations, projects). | | |
| V. Professional growth: | | |
| A. Schoolwide professional activities are available. | | |
| B. Teachers participate in professional growth activities (attending professional meetings, reading journals). | | |
| VI. Program articulation: | | |
| A. Program continuity is maintained through communication within grade levels/ teams/departments, and among all teachers and administrators. | | |
| B. Program continuity exists for all students, including those in special programs. | | |
| C. Program continuity is maintained through communication among feeder elementary and secondary schools. | | |

*(continued)*

213

**Program Review (continued)**

| INDICATORS | STATUS (check one) 1 2 3 | COMMENTS/ RECOMMENDATIONS |
|---|---|---|
| VII. Facilities | | |
| A. Instructional equipment is adequate and in good working order. | | |
| B. Storage facilities for instructional materials are adequate. | | |

Adapted with permission from Program Review forms used by Dade County (Miami, Florida) Public Schools.

# APPENDIX E

# Supervising Reading Resource Specialists

## Ways to Encourage Networking

The job of a reading resource specialist (RRS) can be a lonely one. Although RRSs will build many solid collegial relationships at their respective schools, they will have a critical need for networking with others in job roles like their own. Some networking will occur at one level through the reading of ideas shared in the literature by colleagues, but a person-to-person network is, of course, irreplaceable. The district supervisor/director can do much to facilitate the interchanges that will create person-to-person networking.

The section on staff development has pointers that will apply to networking meetings of RRSs. Following are some more ideas.

## TIPS · NETWORKING

- Call sessions anything but "meetings." *Sharing* (or *networking*) *sessions,*  *institutes,* or *seminars* can spark more interest.

- Consider grouping middle and secondary RRSs together but providing separate sessions for those at the elementary level.

- Schedule sessions at a time that is most convenient to RRSs. Teacher planning days might be a good choice because some RRSs will have class responsibilities part of the day and would otherwise need substitute coverage. Using planning days, however, shouldn't be overdone—they are also good times for the RRS to be in the building and working with teachers. Another alternative is occasional weekend breakfasts. The crowd is not as big as during the work week, but the gatherings are nice social affairs as well as being informative. If possible, set up a schedule for the year so that RRSs can plan ahead.

- Provide RRSs with a list of their colleagues and their work phone numbers. Encourage RRSs to visit each other for renewed perspectives. Let principals know you are encouraging this. Point new RRSs to colleagues who will be especially valuable to them.

- Encourage RRSs to network at local council meetings and at professional conferences. Special interest groups of the International Reading Association (IRA) such as the Secondary Special Interest Group can be invaluable.

## Share and Tell

A sure-fire way to motivate the RRS to attend meetings is to provide "share and tell" time at the meetings. Talk ahead of time to participants who are doing something even a little bit special. Invite them to prepare a short presentation; this gets the ball rolling. Sharing can be dull if it goes on for too long, but otherwise it is beneficial to speakers and listeners alike. The RRS may be more willing to undertake extra efforts if he or she knows that a pat on the back will be forthcoming. Listeners can always pick up a pointer or two from the twists their colleagues may give to old ideas. "Share and tell" is also a way of keeping the interest of both old-timers and neophytes. These sharing sessions can blossom into presentations or articles that RRSs can contribute (together with the supervisor/director if necessary) to local, state, and national professional organizations.

## Role-Play Scenarios

Once the RRSs are comfortable with their leader and with each other, they can be asked to role-play touchy scenarios during meetings. This is guaranteed to produce nervous mannerisms or giggles as familiar situations are enacted. There's nothing like a role-play situation for learning the role of an RRS. Following are some ideas. They are not meant to imply that all experiences will be this difficult, but we all run into some of these!

1. Try to convince a group of secondary department heads at a meeting that Sustained Silent Reading is worth teachers' time. Teachers feel that it would take away too much time from their teaching.

2. Try to persuade a teacher to change a questionable method. Phonics as a sole means of dealing with decoding? Oral drills in teaching limited English proficient students? Directions to just read the chapter and answer the questions? Round-robin reading? Make the task a little harder by pretending that you've already worked with this teacher on this topic.

3. Try to convince a principal in a low-scoring school that isolated skills work is not an appropriate curriculum.

4. Try to convince your principal to let you be an RRS. The principal wants you to have a lab.

5. Try to work with a teacher whose performance has been found to be unsatisfactory. You've been asked to help this teacher, who is older than you are and who does not want your help. One of the teacher's problems is teaching vocabulary only by asking students to "look up words in the dictionary and write a sentence" for each.

6. Begin your first inservice session on content area reading. The attitude of the teachers is that they "don't have time for reading."

7. Try to convince the media specialist to have some exciting events to get students to increase library use. The media specialist's hidden agenda is that he or she does not want the library used more because this will create extra work for him or her.

8. Try to convince teachers at an elementary grade-level meeting that they should try alternatives to ability grouping. The school is adopting an integrated reading/language arts basal series with which it is virtually impossible to fit three ability groups into the school's ninety-minute reading/language arts block.

9. Picture yourself at your first meeting with a middle school team. Set a tempo for peer collaboration rather than assuming the role of instructional authority figure.

## Roundtable Discussions

Roundtable discussions are fail-proof ways of getting RRSs involved at networking sessions. Presenters are less intimidated when sitting around a table with a small group of colleagues than they would be if standing in front of a group. With several roundtables to choose from, RRSs can go to those that best suit their needs. And, of course, the smaller roundtable setting results in greater participation. RRSs can be asked ahead of time to lead specific roundtables, perhaps on cooperative grouping or on newsletter writing or on building classroom libraries. Optimum length will vary depending on the topic and the group; thirty minutes often works well.

## Formal Presentations

Inviting exciting presenters to talk to a group of RRSs can result in a real shot in the arm! If this is expensive, costs can be shared with another district. Local professional organizations might be able to help. Also, textbook publishers often will sponsor speakers. Another resource is the best faculty members in local colleges or universities. And district supervisors/directors shouldn't forget their RRSs and other stars in their own back yard!

## Study Groups

Prior to a session, a group of RRSs can be sent literature to read on a topic of interest. The group can then discuss this material in light of their collective experience. Suggestions might be teacher as researcher columns in IRA's *Reading Today* newspaper, or Neilsen's (1991) delightful article on the woes of RRSs.

A supervisor/director who builds a cadre of strong RRSs will find enhanced programs throughout each school. Carefully planned meetings and other forms of networking as described here can make it happen!

# References

Allington, R. (1977). If they don't read much, how they ever gonna get good? *Journal of Reading, 21,* 57–61.

Allington, R. (1985). The congruence of classroom and remedial reading instruction. *Elementary School Journal, 85,* 465–477.

Alvermann, D. E., & Moore, D. (1991). Secondary school reading. In R. Barr, M. L. Kamil, P. Mosenthal, & P. D. Pearson (Eds.), *Handbook of reading research,* Vol. II (pp. 951–983). White Plains, NY: Longman.

Alvermann, D. E., Moore, D. W., & Conley, M. W. (Eds). (1987). *Research within reach: Secondary school reading.* Newark, DE: IRA.

Alvermann, D. E., & Swafford, J. (1989). Do content area reading strategies have a research base? *Journal of Reading, 32,* 388–394.

Anders, P. L. (1985). Dream of a secondary reading program? People are the key. In W. J. Harker (Ed.). *Classroom strategies for secondary reading,* 2nd ed. Newark, DE: International Reading Association.

Anders, P. L., & Levine, N. S. (1990). Accomplishing change in reading programs. In G. G. Duffy (Ed.), *Reading in the middle school* (pp. 157–170). Newark, DE: International Reading Association.

Anderson, R. C., Hiebert, E. H., Scott, J. A., & Wilkinson, I. A. G. (1985). *Becoming a nation of readers: A report of the Commission on Reading.* Washington, DC: National Institute of Education.

Arhar, J. M., Johnston, J. H., & Markle, G. C. (1988, July). The effects of teaming and other collaborative arrangements. *Middle School Journal,* 22–25.

Atwell, N. (1987). *In the middle.* Portsmouth, NH: Heinemann.

Au, K. H. (Ed.). (1991). Organizing for instruction. [Guest edited issue]. *The Reading Teacher, 44*(8).

Au, K. H., Scheu, J. A., Kawakami, A. J., & Herman, P. A. (1990). Assessment and accountability in a whole literary curriculum. *The Reading Teacher, 43,* 574–578.

Bailey, G. (1988, March). Guidelines for improving the textbook/material selections process. *NASSP Bulletin,* pp. 87–92.

Balbi, P. F. (1986). Teaching through a language experience approach in a multilingual setting. *Reading Improvement, 23,* 182–190.

Baldwin, R. S. (1985). Children's literature and the reading program. In L. W. Searfoss & J. E. Readence (Eds.), *Helping children learn to read* (pp. 393–408). Englewood Cliffs, NJ: Prentice-Hall.

Baldwin, R. S., & Leavell, A. G. (1991). When was the last time you bought a textbook just for kicks? In E. K. Dishner, T. W. Dishner, T. W. Bean, J. E. Readence, & D. W. Moore (Eds.), *Reading in the content areas: Improving classroom instruction* (pp. 106–111). Dubuque, IA: Kendall/Hunt.

Barnard, D. P., & Hetzel, R. W. (1986). *Principal's handbook to improve reading instruction,* 2nd ed. Lexington, MA: Ginn.

Barr, R. (1989). The social organization of literacy instruction. In S. McCormick &

J. Zutell (Eds.), *Cognitive and social perspectives for literacy research and instruction*. Thirty-eighth Yearbook of the National Reading Conference (pp. 19–33). Chicago: National Reading Conference.

Barron, M. (1990). *I learn to read and write the way I learn to talk*. Katonah, NJ: Owen.

Baumann, J. F., & Johnson, D. D. (Eds.). (1991). *Writing for publication in reading and language arts*. Newark, DE: International Reading Association.

Baumann, J. F., & Stevenson, J. A. (1982). Using scores from standardized tests. *The Reading Teacher, 35,* 528–532.

Bean, R. M. (1989). Effective reading program development. In S. B. Wepner, J. T. Feeley, & D. S. Strickland (Eds.), *The administration and supervision of reading programs* (pp. 3–21). New York: Teachers College Press.

Bean, R. M., & Wilson, R. M. (1981). *Effecting change in school reading programs: The resource role*. Newark, DE: International Reading Association.

Beers, P. (1986a). Accelerated reading for high school students. *Journal of Reading, 29,* 311–315.

Beers, P. (1986b). Using newsletters for reading resource success. *Florida Reading Quarterly, 22,* 31–32.

Bergeron, B. S. (1990). What does the term whole language mean? Constructing a definition from the literature. *Journal of Reading Behavior, 22,* 301–329.

Bos, C. S., & Vaughn, S. S. (1991). *Strategies for teaching students with learning and behavior problems,* 2nd ed. Boston: Allyn and Bacon.

Bragstadt, B. J., & Stumpf, S. M. (1982). *A guidebook for teaching study skills and motivation*. Boston: Allyn and Bacon.

Brandt, R. (Ed.). (1990). Learning styles and the brain [Special issue]. *Educational Leadership, 48.*

Brandt, R. (Ed.). (1991). The reflective educator [Special issue]. *Educational Leadership, 48.*

Brown, R. (1989). Testing and thoughtfulness. *Educational Leadership, 46,* 31–33.

Brozo, W. G. (1990). Hiding out in secondary content classrooms: Coping strategies of unsuccessful readers. *Journal of Reading, 33,* 324–328.

Burgett, R. E. (1976). Increasing the effectiveness of the reading specialist. *Journal of Reading, 29,* 6–8.

Caine, R. N., & Caine, G. (1991). *Making connections*. Alexandria, VA: Association for Supervision and Curriculum Development.

Calfee, R., & Hiebert, E. (1991). Classroom assessment of reading. In R. Barr, M. L. Kamil, P. Mosenthal, & P. D. Pearson (Eds.), *Handbook of reading research* Vol. II, pp. 281–309). White Plains, NY: Longman.

Calkins, L., & Harwayne, S. (1991). *Living between the lines*. Portsmouth, NH: Heinemann.

Carbo, M. (1983). *The Reading Style Inventory*. Roslyn Heights, NY: Learning Research Associates.

Cardarelli, A. F. (1992). Teachers under cover: Promoting the personal reading of teachers. *The Reading Teacher, 45,* 664–668.

Carlson, R. O. (1964). Environmental constraints and organizational consequences: The public school and its clients. In *National Society for Secondary Education Yearbook*. Chicago: University of Chicago Press.

Carter, B., & Abrahamson, R. F. (1991). Nonfiction in a read-aloud program. *Journal of Reading, 34,* 638–642.

Carnine, D. (1988). How to overcome barriers to student achievement. In S. J. Samuels & P. D. Pearson (Eds.), *Changing school reading programs* (pp. 59–91). Newark, DE: International Reading Association.

# REFERENCES

Center for the Study of Reading. (1990). *A guide to selecting basal reading programs.* Urbana-Champaign: University of Illinois.

Cheyney, A. (1992). *Teaching reading skills through the newspaper*, 3rd ed. Newark, DE: International Reading Association.

Cocchiarella, J. F. (1985). Vocabulary word of the day at Satellite High. *Florida Reading Quarterly, 21*, 26–27.

Cohen, P. A., Kulik, J. A., & Kulik, C. C. (1982). Educational outcomes of tutoring: A meta-analysis of findings. *American Educational Research Association, 19*, 237–248.

Condon, M. W. F., & Hoffman, J. V. (1990). The influence of classroom management. In G. G. Duffy (Ed.), *Reading in the middle school* (pp. 41–59). Newark, DE: International Reading Association.

Conley, M. W. (1989). Middle school and junior high reading programs. In S. B. Wepner, J. T. Feeley, & D. S. Strickland (Eds.), *The administration and surpervision of reading programs* (pp. 76–105). New York: Teachers College Press.

Conn, S. (1988). Textbooks: Defining the new criteria. *Media and Methods, 24*, 30–31, 64.

Coons, P. (1989, March 12). Educators say those who learn together learn better. *Boston Globe.*

Cotton, E. G., Casem, C. B., Kroll, M. A., Langas, E. U., Rhodes, A. W., & Sisson, J. R. (1988). Using a skill trace to solve the basal reader adoption dilemma. *The Reading Teacher, 41*, 550–554.

Cowart, D., & Fabre, A. (1986, March). *LEAP for success.* Paper presented at the meeting of the National Association of Laboratory Schools, New Orleans.

Crandall, D. P. (1982). *Models of the school improvement process: Factors contributing to success.* Andover, MA: Network of Innovative Schools.

Cunningham, P. M. (1991a). *Phonics they use: Words for reading and writing.* New York: HarperCollins.

Cunningham, P. M. (1991b). Research directions: Multimethod, multilevel literacy instruction in first grade. *Language Arts, 68*, 578–584.

Cunningham, P. M., & Hall, D. P. (1991). Non-ability-grouped, multilevel instruction: A year in a first-grade classroom. *The Reading Teacher, 44*, 566–571.

Darquea, D. (1988). *Sound expressions.* Bakersfield, CA: D & D Productions.

Degrees of Reading Power. (1984). Brewster, NY: The College Entrance Examination Board.

Duffy, G. G. (Ed.). (1991). *Reading in the middle school.* Newark, DE: International Reading Association.

Duffy, G. G., & Roehler, L. R. (1989). *Improving classroom reading instruction: A decision-making approach.* New York: Random House.

Dunn, R., Dunn, K., & Price, G. E. (1985). *Learning Style Inventory.* Lawrence, KS: Price Systems.

Durkin, D. (1981). Reading comprehension instruction in five basal reader series. *Reading Research Quarterly, 16*, 515–544.

Edwards, P. A. (1990). *Parents as partners in reading.* Chicago: Children's Press.

Ehly, S., & Larsen, S. C. (1984). Peer tutoring in the regular classroom. In A. J. Harris & E. R. Sipay (Eds.), *Readings on reading instruction*, 3rd ed. (pp. 187–189). New York: Longman.

Ericson, D. P., & Ellett, F. J. (1990). Taking student responsibility seriously. *Educational Researcher, 19*, 3–10.

Evertson, C., & Emmer, E. (1982). Preventive classroom management. In D. Duke

(Ed.), *Helping teachers manage classrooms*. Alexandria, VA: Association for Supervision and Curriculum Development.

Fast, J. (1979). *Body language*. New York: M. Evans.

Fielding, L. G., Wilson, P. T., & Anderson, R. C. (1986). The new focus on free reading: The role of tradebooks in reading instruction. In T. E. Raphael (Ed.), *The contexts of school-based literacy* (pp. 149–160). New York: Random House.

Flood, J., & Lapp, D. (1989). Reporting reading progress: A comparison portfolio for parents. *The Reading Teacher, 42,* 508–512.

Floyd, C. (1954). Meeting children's reading needs in the middle grades: A preliminary report. *Elementary School Journal, 55,* 99–103.

Forgan, H. W., & Mangrum, C. T. (1989). *Teaching content area reading skills,* 4th ed. Columbus, OH: Merrill.

Fraatz, J. M. B. (1987). *The politics of reading*. New York: Teachers College Press.

Fry, E. (1977). Fry's readability graph: Clarifications, validity, and extension to level 17. *Journal of Reading, 21,* 242–252.

Gallagher, M. C., Goudvis, A., & Pearson, P. D. (1988). Principles of organizational change. In S. J. Samuels & P. D. Pearson (Eds.), *Changing school reading programs* (pp. 11–39). Newark, DE: International Reading Association.

Gilbert, T. F. (1978). *Human competence*. New York: McGraw-Hill.

Gillet, J. W., & Temple, C. (1982). *Understanding reading problems: Assessment and instruction*. Boston: Little, Brown.

Ginott, H. (1969). *Between parent and child*. New York: Avon.

Goleman, D. (1986, April 8). Studies point to power of nonverbal signals. *New York Times*, p. 17.

Good, T. (1981). Teacher expectations and student perceptions: A decade of research. *Educational Leadership*, 415–422.

Goodlad, J. (1984). *A place called school*. New York: McGraw-Hill.

Goodman, K. S., Bird, L. B., & Goodman, Y. M. (1991). *The whole language catalog*. Santa Rosa, CA: American School Publishers.

Gordon, C. (1985). Modeling inference awareness across the curriculum. *Journal of Reading, 28,* 444–447.

Graham, C. (1978). *Jazz chants*. New York: Oxford University Press.

Grant, B. M., & Hennings, D. G. (1971). *The teacher moves: An analysis of nonverbal activity*. New York: Teachers College Press.

Graves, D. (1983). *Writing: Teachers and children at work*. Portsmouth, NH: Heinemann.

Green, J. L. (1987). Course materials, The Ohio State University.

Gunderson, L. (1991). *ESL literacy instruction: A guidebook to theory and practice*. Englewood Cliffs, NJ: Prentice Hall Regents.

Gutmann, A. (1987). *Democratic education*. Princeton, NJ: Princeton University Press.

Gwynne, F. (1970a). *A chocolate moose for dinner*. Englewood Cliffs, NJ: Messner.

Gwynne, F. (1970b). *The king who rained*. Englewood Cliffs, NJ: Messner.

Hansen, J. (1992). The language of challenge: Readers and writers speak their minds. *Language Arts, 69,* 100–105.

Harp, B. (Ed.). (1991). *Assessment and evaluation in whole language programs*. Norwood, MA: Christopher-Gordon.

Harris, A. J., & Sipay, E. R. (1990). *How to increase reading ability: A guide to developmental and remedial methods,* 9th ed. New York: Longman.

Harste, J. (1990). Forward. In M. W. Olson (Ed.), *Opening the door to classroom research* (pp. v–viii). Newark, DE: International Reading Association.

# REFERENCES

Heald-Taylor, G. (1989). *The administrator's guide to whole language.* Katonah, NH: Owen.

Henk, W. A. (1985). Assessing children's reading abilities. In L. W. Searfoss & J. E. Readence (Eds.), *Helping children learn to read* (pp. 280–320). Englewood Cliffs, NJ: Prentice-Hall.

Herber, H. L. (1978). *Teaching reading in the content areas.* Englewood Cliffs, NJ: Prentice-Hall.

Hiebert, E. F. (1983). An examination of ability grouping for reading instruction. *Reading Research Quarterly, 18,* 231–255.

Hinchman, K. (1987). The textbook and three content-area teachers. *Reading Research and Instruction, 26,* 247–263.

Hinson, B., & Radencich, M. C.(1990, January). *Accountability and assessment.* Paper presented at the First National Reading Resource Specialist Conference, Miami, FL.

Idaho Literacy Project. (1992). *Read to me.* Newark, DE: International Reading Association.

International Reading Association. (1989). *Secondary school reading.* Newark, DE: International Reading Association.

International Reading Association. (1981). *Misuse of grade equivalents.* Newark, DE: International Reading Association.

International Reading Association/Children's Book Council. (1991). *Kids' favorite books.* Newark, DE: Author.

International Reading Association. (1992). *Teens' favorite books.* Newark, DE: International Reading Association.

Iowa tests of basic skills. (1990). Chicago: Riverside.

Irwin, J. W., & Baker, I. (1990). *Promoting active reading comprehension strategies.* Englewood Cliffs, NJ: Prentice-Hall.

Irwin, J. W., & Davis, C. J. (1980). Assessing readability: The checklist approach. *Journal of Reading, 24,* 124–130.

Jachym, N. K., Allington, R. L., & Broikou, K. A. (1989). Estimating the cost of seatwork. *The Reading Teacher, 43,* 30–35.

Johnson, D. E., Meiller, L. R., Miller, L. C., & Summers, G. F. (1987). *Needs assessment: Theory and methods.* Ames: Iowa State University Press.

Johnson, D. W., & Johnson, R. T. (1989). *Cooperative learning.* An Association for Supervision and Curriculum Development National Curriculum Study Institute. Orlando, FL.

Johnson, D. W., & Johnson, R. T. (1992). *What to say to advocates of the gifted. Educational Leadership, 50*(2), 44–47.

Johnson, D. W., Johnson, R. T., & Holubec, E. (1990). *Circles of learning: Cooperation in the classroom* (3rd ed.). Edina, MN: Interaction Book Company.

Johnson, R. E., & Vardain, E. B. (1975). Reading, readability, and social studies. *The Reading Teacher, 26,* 483–488.

Johnston, P. H. (1984). Assessment in reading. In P. D. Pearson, R. Barr, M. L. Kamil, & P. Mosenthal (Eds.), *Handbook of reading research* (Vol. I, pp. 147–182). White Plains, NY: Longman.

Joyce, B., Hersh, R., & McKibbon, M. (1983). *The structure of school improvement.* New York: Longman.

Joyce, B., & Showers, B. (1982). The coaching of teaching. *Educational Leadership, 40,* 4–10.

Juel, C. (1991). Cross-age tutoring between student athletes and at-risk children. *The Reading Teacher, 45,* 178–186.

Kanter, R. M. (1989). Paper presented at the Association for Supervision and Curriculum Development Annual Conference, Orlando, FL.

Kast, S. E., & Rosenzweig, J. E. (1974). *Organization: A systems approach,* 2nd ed. New York: McGraw-Hill.

Katz, M. (1982). Critical literacy: A conception of education as a moral right and social ideal. In *The public school monopoly.* Cambridge, MA: Ballinger.

Keating, P., & Oakes, J. (1988). *Access to knowledge: Breaking down school barriers to learning.* Denver, CO: Education Commission of the States.

Kelly, P. R., & Farnan, N. (1990). Practicing what we teach in reading education programs. *Journal of Reading, 33,* 264–269.

Kindsvatter, R., Wilen, W., & Ishler, M. (1988). *Dynamics of teaching.* New York: Longman.

Knapp, M. L. (1974). *Nonverbal communication in human interaction.* New York: Holt, Rinehart & Winston.

Kohn, A. (1987, October). It's hard to get left out of a pair. *Psychology Today,* 53–57.

Kohn, A. (1991, February). Group grade grubbing versus cooperative learning. *Educational Leadership, 48,* 83–87.

Korinek, L., Schmid, R., & McAdams, M. (1985). Inservice types and best practices. *Journal of Research and Development in Education, 18,* 33–38.

Kutz, E. (1992). Teacher research: Myths and realities. *Language Arts, 69,* 193–197.

Labbo, K. D., & Teale, W. H. (1990). Cross-age reading: A strategy for helping poor readers. *The Reading Teacher, 43,* 362–369.

Lakein, A. (1973). *How to get control of your time and your life.* New York: P. H. Wyden.

Lamme, L. L., & Hysmith, C. (1991). One school's adventure into portfolio assessment. *Language Arts, 68,* 629–640.

Littky, D., & Fried, R. (1988). The challenge to make good schools great. *National Education Association,* pp. 4–8.

Lubell, D. (1991). Spartan Lotto-Read. *Phi Delta Kappan, 73*(3), 257–258.

Martin, B. (1967). *Brown bear, brown bear.* New York: Holt.

Martin, M. (1991, May). *Grade-level instruction with flexible heterogeneous groups—The San Diego story.* Paper presented at the annual conference of the International Reading Association, Las Vegas.

Marzano, R. (1987, Fall). Staff development for teaching thinking: A matter of restructuring. *Journal of Staff Development,* 6–10.

Matthews, J. (1992). Gifted students talk about cooperative learning. *Educational Leadership, 50*(2), 48–50.

McCauley, J. K., & McCauley, D. S. (1992). Using choral reading to promote language learning for ESL students. *The Reading Teacher, 45,* 526–533.

McDonnell, G., Frey, J., & Smith, T. (Eds.). (1991). *Teaching and researching.* Falls Church, VA: IRA Special Interest Group's Newsletter.

McTighe, J., & Lyman, F. T. (1988, April). Cueing thinking in the classroom: The promise of theory-embedded tools. *Educational Leadership,* 18–24.

Medley, D. M. (1977). *Teacher competence and teacher effectiveness: A review of process-product research.* Washington, DC: American Association of Colleges for Teacher Education.

Meyer, J. W., Scott, W. R., & Deal, T. E. (1979). *Institutional and technical sources of organizational structure explaining the structure of educational organizations.* Paper prepared for a conference on human service organizations, Center for Advanced Study in the Behavior Sciences, Stanford, CA.

Miller, P. (1988). *Nonverbal communication.* Westhaven, CT: National Education Association.

# REFERENCES

Miller, S. D., & Yochum, N. (1991). Asking students about the nature of their reading difficulties. *Journal of Reading Behavior, 23,* 465–485.

Minkoff, D. (1984). Game activities for practicing English as a second language. *Journal of Reading, 28,* 40–42.

Monahan, J. N., & Hinson, B. (1988). *New directions in reading instruction.* Newark, DE: International Reading Association.

Monson, D. L. (Ed.). (1985). *Adventuring with books: A booklist for Pre-K–Grade 6.* Urbana, IL: National Council of Teachers of English.

Moore, D. W., & Readence, J. E. (1983). Approaches to content area reading instruction. *Journal of Reading, 26,* 397–402.

Morrice, C., & Simmons, M. (1991). Beyond reading buddies: A whole language cross-age program. *The Reading Teacher, 44,* 572–577.

Morrow, L. M., & Strickland, D. S. (Eds). (1989). *Emerging literacy: Young children learn to read and write.* Newark, DE: International Reading Association.

Moustafa, M., & Penrose, J. (1985). Comprehensible input plus the language experience approach: Reading instruction for limited English speaking students. *The Reading Teacher, 38,* 640–647.

Muther, C. (1985a, January). How to evaluate a basal textbook: The skills trace. *Educational Leadership,* 79–80.

Muther, C. (1985b, February). Reviewing research when choosing materials. *Educational Leadership,* 86–87.

Muther, C. (1985c, April). What every textbook evaluator should know. *Educational Leadership, 42,* 4–8.

Muther, C. (1987, October). Evaulating reading textbooks with the story-sort comparison. *Educational Leadership,* 87–90.

Muther, C. (1988). *Textbook adoption: A process for decision-making.* Manchester, CT: Textbook Adoption Advisory Services.

Neal, J. C., & Langer, M. A. (1992). A framework of teaching options for content area instruction: Mediated instruction of text. *Journal of Reading, 36,* 227–230.

Neilsen, L. (1991). Professional conversations: How to open the staffroom door. *The Reading Teacher, 44,* 676–678.

Newman, J. M., & Church, S. M. (1991). Myths of whole language. *The Reading Teacher, 44,* 20–26.

Nurss, J. R., & Hough, R. A. (1992). Reading and the ESL student. In S. J. Samuels & A. E. Farstrup (Eds.), *What research has to say about reading instruction* (pp. 277–313). Newark, DE: International Reading Association.

Oakes, J. (1986, September). Keeping track: Part 1. The policy and practice of curriculum inequality. *Phi Delta Kappan,* 15–20.

O'Brien, D. G. (1988). Secondary preservice teachers' resistance to content reading instruction: A proposal for a broader rationale. In J. E. Readence & R. S. Baldwin (Eds.), *Dialogues in literacy research,* Thirty-seventh Yearbook of the National Reading Conference (pp. 237–244). Chicago: National Reading Conference.

O'Brien, D. G., & Stewart, R. A. (1990). Preservice teachers' perspectives on why every teacher is not a teacher of reading. *Journal of Reading Behavior, 22,* 101–129.

Ogle, D. (1986, February). K-W-L: A teaching model that develops active reading of expository text. *The Reading Teacher, 39,* 364–370.

Olson, M. W. (1990). The teacher as researcher: A historical perspective. In M. W. Olson (Ed.), *Opening the door to classroom research* (pp. 1–20). Newark, DE: International Reading Association.

Onore, C., & Lester, N. B. (1985). Immersion and distancing: The ins and outs of inservice education. *English Education, 17,* 7–13.

Oppenheim, J., Brenner, B., & Boegehold, B. D. (1986). *Choosing books for kids.* New York: Ballantine.

Osborn, J. (1984). Purposes, uses, and content of workbooks. In R. C. Anderson, J. Osborn, & R. J. Tierney (Eds). *Learning to read in American schools: Basal readers and content texts* (pp. 110–111). Hillsdale, NJ: Erlbaum.

Paratore, J. (1991). Flexible grouping: Why and how. *The Leadership Letters-Issues and Trends in Reading and Language Arts.* Columbus, OH: Silver Burdett & Ginn.

Paris, S. G., Calfee, R. C., Filby, N., Hiebert, E. H., Pearson, P. D., Valencia, S. W., & Wolf, K. P. (1992a). A framework for authentic literacy assessment. *The Reading Teacher, 46,* 88–98.

Paris, S. G., Lawton, T. A., & Turner, J. C. (1992b). Reforming achievement testing to promote students' learning. In C. Collins & J. N. Mangieri (Eds.), *Teaching thinking: An agenda for the twenty-first century.* Hillsdale, NJ: Erlbaum.

Paris, S. G., Wasik, B. A., & Turner, J. C. (1991). The development of strategic readers. In R. Barr, M. L. Kamil, P. Mosenthal, & P. D. Pearson (Eds.), *Handbook of reading research* (Vol. II, pp. 609–640). New York, Longman.

Parish, P. (1986). *Amelia Bedelia.* New York: Harper & Row.

Pauk, W. (1983). *How to study in college.* Boston: Houghton Mifflin.

Pearson, P. D. (1992, May). *Effective literacy assessment: Practices and possibilities.* Chair of Preconvention Institute of the 37th Annual Convention of the International Reading Association, Orlando, FL.

Peters, C. W. (1990). Content knowledge in reading: Creating a new framework. In G. G. Duffy (Ed.), *Reading in the middle school* (pp. 62–80). Newark, DE: International Reading Association.

Peters, C. W. (1991). You can't have authentic assessment without authentic content. *The Reading Teacher, 44,* 590–591.

Pincus, J. (1974). Incentives for innovation in the public schools. *Review of Educational Research,* 113–144.

Pinnell, G. S., DeFord, D. E., & Lyons, C. A. (1988). *Reading Recovery: Early intervention for at-risk first graders.* Arlington, VA: Educational Research Service.

Pinnell, G. S., & Matlin, M. L. (Eds.). (1989). *Teachers and research: Language learning in the classroom.* Newark, DE: International Reading Association.

Power, J. (1988). What is your body language telling your students? *NEA Today, 6*(8), 5.

Radencich, M. C. (1991). Publishing computer software. In J. F. Baumann & D. D. Johnson (Eds.). *Writing for publication in reading and language arts* (pp. 169–191). Newark, DE: International Reading Association.

Radencich, M. C., Flash, R., Miller, D., Minges, N., & Starrett, M. (1992). *Yes, but how do we start? Ways of beginning portfolio assessment.* Manuscript submitted for publication.

Radencich, M. C., & McKay, L. (Eds.). (1992). *Grouping in the elementary grades.* Manuscript submitted for publication.

Radencich, M. C., McKay, L., Paratore, J. R., Nelms, P., Moore, P., Plaza, Gloria L., & Lustgarten, K. (1992). Keeping flexible groups flexible—Grouping options and grouping models. In M. C. Radencich & L. McKay (Eds.), *Grouping in the elementary grades.* Manuscript submitted for publication.

Radencich, M. C., & McKinney, A. G. (in press). Brown Bear, Brown Bear, What do you see?—Levels for predictables: 1, 2, 3. *Florida Reading Quarterly.*

Ratekin, N., Simpson, M. L., Alvermann, D. E., & Dishner, E. K. (1985). Why teachers resist content reading instruction. *Journal of Reading, 28,* 432–437.

# REFERENCES

Raygor, A. (1977). The Raygor readability estimate: A quick and easy way to determine difficulty. In P. D. Pearson (Ed.), *Reading: Theory, research and practice*. Twenty-sixth Yearbook of the National Reading Conference (pp. 259–263). Clemson, SC: National Reading Conference.

Readence, J., Baldwin, R. S., & Dishner, E. K. (1980). Establishing content reading programs in secondary schools. *Journal of Reading, 23*, 522–526.

Readence, J. E., Bean, T. W., & Baldwin, R. S. (1992). *Content area reading: An integrated approach*, 4th ed. Dubuque, IA: Kendall/Hunt.

Roe, B. D., Stoodt, B. D., & Burns, P. C. (1978). *Reading instruction in the secondary school*. Chicago: Rand-McNally.

Roehler, L. R., Foley, K. U., Lud, M. T., & Power, C. A. (1990). Developing integrated programs. In G. Duffy (Ed.), *Reading in the middle school*, 2nd ed. (pp. 184–199). Newark, DE: International Reading Association.

Rosenshine, B. V. (1979). *Content, time, and direct instruction. In P. L. Peterson & H. J. Walberg (Eds.), Research on teaching: Concepts, findings, and implications*. Berkeley, CA: McCutchan.

Rothlein, L., & Meinbach, A. M. (1991). *The literature connection: Using children's books in the classroom*. Glenview, IL: Scott, Foresman.

Rowan, B. (1977). Bureaucratization in the institutional environment: The case of California Public Schools, 1930–1970. In M. R. Davis, T. E. Deal, J. W. Merey, B. Rowan, W. R. Scott, & E. A. Stackhouse (Eds.), *The structure of educational systems: Explorations in the theory of loosely coupled organization*. Stanford, CA: Stanford Center for Research and Development in Teaching.

Ryder, R. J., Graves, B. B., & Graves, M. F. (1989). *Easy reading: Book series and periodicals for less able readers*, 2nd ed. Newark, DE: International Reading Association.

Samuels, S. J. (1979). The method of repeated readings. *The Reading Teacher, 32*, 403–408.

Samuels, S. J. (1981). Characteristics of exemplary reading programs. In J. T. Guthrie (Ed.), *Comprehension and teaching: Research reviews* (pp. 255–273). Newark, DE: International Reading Association.

Samuels, S. J., & Edwall, G. (1976). An overview of the research literature on educational innovation. In J. T. Guthrie (Ed.), *A study of the locus and nature of reading problems in elementary schools*. Washington, DC: National Institute of Education.

Samuels, S. J., & Pearson, P. D. (1988). *Changing school reading programs*. Newark, DE: International Reading Association.

Santa, C., Isaacson, L., & Manning, G. (1987). Changing content instruction through action research. *The Reading Teacher, 40*, 434–438.

Schumm, J. S. (1988, February). *A strategy for planning comprehensive secondary reading programs*. Paper presented at the International Reading Association Southwest Regional Reading Conference, Oklahoma City, OK.

Schumm, J. S., & Doucette, M. (1991). Improving the effectiveness and efficiency of textbook selection procedures: A smorgasbord of suggestions and strategies. *Reading Horizons, 31*, 272–285.

Schumm, J. S., Konopak, J. P., Readence, J. E., & Baldwin, R. S. (1989). Considerate text: Do we practice what we preach? In S. McCormick & J. Zutell (Eds.). *Cognitive and social perspectives for literacy research and instruction*, Thirty-eighth Yearbook of the National Reading Conference (pp. 205–211). Chicago: National Reading Conference.

Schumm, J. S., & Mangrum, C. T. (1991). FLIP: A framework for fostering textbook thinking. *Journal of Reading, 35*, 120–125.

Schumm, J. S., & Radencich, M. C. (1991). *A decision-making framework for structuring secondary reading programs.* Manuscript submitted for publication.

Schumm, J. S., & Strickler, K. (1991). Guidelines for adapting content area textbooks: Keeping teachers and students content. *Intervention, 27,* 79–84.

Schumm, J. S., & Vaughn, S. (1991). Making adaptations for mainstreamed students: General classroom teachers' perceptions. *RASE—Remedial and Special Education, 12*(4), 18–27.

Schumm, J. S., & Vaughn, S. (1992). Planning for mainstreamed special education students: Perceptions of general classroom teachers. *Exceptionality, 3,* 81–98.

Schumm, J. S., Vaughn, S., & Saumell, L. (1992). *Assisting students with difficult textbooks: Teacher perceptions, planning, and practices.* Paper presented at American Educational Research Association Conference, San Francisco, CA.

Schumm, J. S., Vaughn, S., & Saumell, L. (1992). What teachers do when the textbook is tough: Students speak out. *Journal of Reading Behavior, 24,* 481–503.

*Secondary reading: A new direction for the future.* (1990). Grand Rapids: Michigan Reading Association.

Shannon, P. (1987). Commercial reading materials: A technological ideology, and the de-skilling of teachers. *Elementary School Journal, 87,* 311–313.

Showers, B., Joyce, B., & Bennett, B. (1987). Synthesis of research on staff development: A framework for future study and state of the art analysis. *Educational Leadership, 45*(3), 77–88.

Simmons-Wolpow, R., Farrell, D. P., & Tonjes, M. J. (1991). Implementing a secondary reading/study skills program across disciplines. *Journal of Reading, 34,* 590–594.

Singer, H. (1986). Friendly texts: Description and criteria. In E. K. Dishner, T. W. Bean, J. E. Readence, & D. W. Moore (Eds.), *Reading in the content areas: Improving classroom instruction* (pp. 112–118). Dubuque, IA: Kendall/Hunt.

Slavin, R. E. (1987a, Summer). Ability grouping and its alternatives: Must we track? *American Educator,* pp. 32–36, 47–48.

Slavin, R. E. (1987b). Ability grouping and student achievement in elementary schools: A best-evidence synthesis. *Review of Educational Research, 57,* 293–336.

Slavin, R. E. (1990, April). Success for all shows large reading gains. *CDS.* Baltimore, MD: Center for Research on Effective Schooling for Disadvantaged Students, pp. 5–7.

Smith, F. R., & Feathers, K. M. (1983). Teacher and student perceptions of content area reading. *Journal of Reading, 26,* 348–354.

Smith, N. B. (1986). *American reading instruction.* Newark, DE: International Reading Association.

Sparks-Langer, G. M., & Colton, A. B. (1991). Synthesis of research on teachers' reflective thinking. *Educational Leadership, 48*(6), 37–44.

Stallings, J. (1975). Implementation and child effects of teaching practices in follow through classrooms. *Monographs of the Society for Research in Child Development, 40,* (Serial No. 163).

Stanchfield, J. (1988). *Ways to develop enthusiasm within yourself.* Gold Coast, Australia: International Reading Association World Congress.

Stanford Achievement Test, 8th ed. (1989). San Antonio, TX: Psychological Corporation.

Stern, P., & Shavelson, R. J. (1983). Reading teachers' judgments, plans, and decision making. *The Reading Teacher, 35,* 884–889.

Stoll, D. E. (1989). *Magazines for children.* Newark, DE: International Reading Association.

# REFERENCES

Stoodt, I. (1981). *Reading instruction*. Boston: Houghton Mifflin.

Strickland, D. S. (1988). The teacher as researcher: Toward the extended professional. *Language Arts, 65,* 754–764.

Sulzby, E., & Teale, W. (1991). Emergent literacy. In R. Barr, M. L. Kamil, O. Mosenthal, & P. D. Pearson (Eds.). *Handbook of reading research, Vol. II* (pp. 727–757). New York: Longman.

Swafford, J. (1990). A comparison of the effectiveness of content area reading strategies at the elementary, secondary, and postsecondary levels, In N. D. Padak, T. V. Rasinski, & J. Logan (Eds.), *Challenges in reading*. Twelfth Yearbook of the College Reading Association (pp. 111–126). Provo, UT: College Reading Association.

Swafford, J., & Alvermann, D. E. (1989). Postsecondary research base for content reading strategies. *Journal of Reading, 33,* 164–169.

Taylor, B., Harris, L. A., & Pearson, P. D. (1988). *Reading difficulties: Instruction and assessment*. New York: Random House.

*Teachers on the cutting edge: Textbook adoption*. (1990). Orlando: Florida Reading Association.

Teale, W. H. (1987). Emergent literacy: Reading and writing development in early childhood. In J. E. Readence & R. S. Baldwin (Eds.), *Research in literacy: Merging perspectives*. Thirty-sixth Yearbook of the National Reading Conference. Rochester, NY: National Reading Conference.

Teale, W. H., Hiebert, E. F., & Chittendon, E. A. (1987). Assessing young children's literacy development. *The Reading Teacher, 40,* 772–777.

Tierney, R. J., Carter, M. A., & Desai, L. E. (1991). *Portfolio assessment in the reading-writing classroom*. Norwood, MA: Christopher-Gordon.

Tierney, R. J., Readence, J. E., & Dishner, E. K. (1990). *Reading strategies and practices: A compendium,* 3rd ed. Boston: Allyn and Bacon.

Topping, K. (1989). Peer tutoring and paired reading: Combining two powerful techniques. *The Reading Teacher, 42,* 488–494.

Trelease, J. (1989). *The new read-aloud handbook*. New York: Penguin.

Vacca, R. T. (1989). High school reading programs: Out of the past and into the future. In S. B. Wepner, J. T. Feeley, & D. S. Strickland (Eds.), *The administration and supervision of reading programs*. New York: Teachers College Press.

Vacca, R. T., & Vacca, J. L. (1989). *Content area reading,* 3rd ed. Glenview, IL: Scott Foresman.

Valencia, S. W., McGinley, W., & Pearson, P. D. (1990). Assessing reading and writing. In G. G. Duffy (Ed.), *Reading in the middle school* (pp. 124–153). Newark, DE: International Reading Association.

Valencia, S. W., & Pearson, P. D. (1987). Reading assessment: Time for a change. *The Reading Teacher, 40,* 726–732.

Vaughn, S., Schumm, J. S., Niarhos, F., & Gordon, J. (in press). Students' perceptions of two hypothetical teachers' instructional adaptations for low achievers. *Elementary School Journal*.

Weaver, C. (1990). *Understanding whole language: From principles to practice*. Portsmouth, NH: Heinemann.

Wepner, S. B., Feeley, J. T., & Strickland, D. S. (1989). *The administration and supervision of reading programs*. New York: Teachers College Press.

Whimbey, A. (1983). *Analytic reading and reasoning*. Stamford, CT: Innovative Sciences.

Wilkinson, L. C., & Calculator, S. (1982). Requests and responses in peer-directed reading groups. *American Educational Research Journal, 19,* 107–120.

Wilson, R. M., & Gambrell, L. B. (1988). *Reading comprehension in the elementary school: A teacher's practical guide*. Boston: Allyn and Bacon.

Winograd, P., Paris, S. G., & Bridge, C. (1991). Improving the assessment of literacy. *The Reading Teacher, 45,* 108–116.

Wolf, D. P. (1989). Portfolio assessment: Sampling student work. *Educational Leadership, 46,* 35–39.

Wollman-Bonilla, J. E. (1991, February). Shouting from the tops of buildings: Teachers as learners and change in schools. *Language Arts, 68,* 114–120.

Wood, K. D., & Muth, K. D. (1991). The case for improved instruction in the middle grades. *Journal of Reading, 35,* 84–91.

Woods, A. R., & Topping, M. H. (1986). The reading resource specialist: A model. *Journal of Reading, 29,* 733–738.

Young, M. J., & Riegeluth, C. (1988). *Improving the textbook selection process.* Bloomington, IN: Phi Delta Kappa Educational Foundation.

Ysseldyke, J. E., & Christenson, S. L. (1987). *TIES—The Instructional Environment Scale.* Austin, TX: PRO-ED.

# Index